Palgrave Studies in Economic History

Series Editor
Kent Deng, London School of Economics, London, UK

AF795503

Palgrave Studies in Economic History is designed to illuminate and enrich our understanding of economies and economic phenomena of the past. The series covers a vast range of topics including financial history, labour history, development economics, commercialisation, urbanisation, industrialisation, modernisation, globalisation, and changes in world economic orders.

Eoin O'Malley

Ireland's Long Economic Boom

The Celtic Tiger Economy, 1986–2007

palgrave
macmillan

Eoin O'Malley
Dublin, Ireland

ISSN 2662-6497 ISSN 2662-6500 (electronic)
Palgrave Studies in Economic History
ISBN 978-3-031-53072-2 ISBN 978-3-031-53070-8 (eBook)
https://doi.org/10.1007/978-3-031-53070-8

© The Editor(s) (if applicable) and The Author(s) 2024. This book is an open access publication.

Open Access This book is licensed under the terms of the Creative Commons Attribution 4.0 International License (http://creativecommons.org/licenses/by/4.0/), which permits use, sharing, adaptation, distribution and reproduction in any medium or format, as long as you give appropriate credit to the original author(s) and the source, provide a link to the Creative Commons license and indicate if changes were made.
The images or other third party material in this book are included in the book's Creative Commons license, unless indicated otherwise in a credit line to the material. If material is not included in the book's Creative Commons license and your intended use is not permitted by statutory regulation or exceeds the permitted use, you will need to obtain permission directly from the copyright holder.
The use of general descriptive names, registered names, trademarks, service marks, etc. in this publication does not imply, even in the absence of a specific statement, that such names are exempt from the relevant protective laws and regulations and therefore free for general use.
The publisher, the authors, and the editors are safe to assume that the advice and information in this book are believed to be true and accurate at the date of publication. Neither the publisher nor the authors or the editors give a warranty, expressed or implied, with respect to the material contained herein or for any errors or omissions that may have been made. The publisher remains neutral with regard to jurisdictional claims in published maps and institutional affiliations.

Cover illustration: Tuul & Bruno Morandi

This Palgrave Macmillan imprint is published by the registered company Springer Nature Switzerland AG
The registered company address is: Gewerbestrasse 11, 6330 Cham, Switzerland

Paper in this product is recyclable.

Acknowledgements

I have benefited a great deal from working with others on various subjects that are covered in this book. I also received helpful comments from others on earlier drafts of parts of the book. I am grateful to Frank Barry, Paula Clancy, Nola Hewitt-Dundas, David Jacobson, Kieran Kennedy, Alan Matthews, Dermot O'Doherty, Rory O'Donnell, Colm O'Gorman, Stephen Roper, Sue Scott, Paul Sweeney and Chris Van Egeraat, as well as two anonymous referees.

Contents

1 Introduction 1

1.1 Dimensions of the Boom 2

1.2 The Approach and Structure of This Book 11

References 14

2 Before the Boom: The Historical Background 17

2.1 Employment, Emigration and Incomes: Long-Term Trends 17

2.2 Industrial Development 21

Independence and Protection 22

Outward-Looking Policies and Industrial Growth 24

Irish Indigenous Industry 26

Foreign-Owned Industry 31

Industrial Policy Developments in the 1980s 34

2.3 Macroeconomic Trends 1960s–1980s 37

2.4 Conclusion 44

References 45

3 A Review of Explanations for the Boom 49

3.1 Explanations for the Boom 50

Fiscal Stabilisation 50

Tax Cuts, Smaller Government 51

Delayed or Belated Convergence 52

Strong Demand Growth in Export Markets 54

Supply of Labour 54
Education, Human Capital 54
The Single European Market 56
EU Structural Funds 57
Social Partnership, Wage Moderation 58
Foreign Direct Investment 60
A Small Open Economy—Like a Region 62
Irish Indigenous Industry 63
Other Explanations 64
3.2 Assessment of the Explanations 65
Necessary But Normal Conditions 66
Delayed or Belated Convergence 67
Tax Cuts 71
Minor Explanations 74
3.3 Conclusion 75
References 76

4 Sectoral Growth and Export Earnings 83
4.1 Sectoral Growth 84
Gross Value Added (GVA) 84
"Retained GVA" 86
Employment 89
Summary 91
4.2 Sectoral Export Earnings 92
The Importance of Exports 92
Sectoral Export Earnings During the Boom 95
4.3 Conclusion 113
Appendix: Estimation of Profit Outflows, Retained GVA and Net Foreign Earnings 115
Profit Outflows and Retained GVA 115
Net Foreign Earnings 118
Profit Outflows for 1985 120
References 121

5 Irish Indigenous Companies 123
5.1 Growth and Development of Indigenous Manufacturing 123
Employment Trends 124
Output Trends 131
Exports and Net Foreign Earnings 134

R&D and Innovation 143
Company Size 151
5.2 *Growth and Development of Indigenous Market Services* 154
Output, Exports and Net Foreign Earnings 154
The Irish Indigenous Software Industry 162
5.3 *The Indigenous Contribution to the Boom* 170
5.4 *The Role of Industrial Policy* 173
5.5 *Conclusion* 177
Appendix: Data and Estimates for This Chapter 179
Table 5.1 179
Figure 5.1 179
Table 5.2 180
Dairy Products Exports in 1986–1990 180
Net Foreign Earnings 182
References 184

6 **Foreign-Owned Companies** 189
6.1 *Growth and Composition of Foreign-Owned Companies* 190
6.2 *The Nature and Characteristics of FDI in Ireland* 193
Purchasing Linkages 195
R&D 197
Decision-Making Autonomy 199
Pay Levels 200
Sector Studies 201
Conclusion 203
6.3 *Motivations for Investing in Ireland* 203
The Increase in FDI During the Boom 205
The Increase in Services FDI 210
Conclusion 212
6.4 *Secondary Effects of FDI on the Irish Economy* 213
Balance of Payments 213
Potential Adverse Effects on Indigenous Companies 214
Purchasing Linkages 216
Effects on Indigenous Technology and Productivity 219
Development of Clusters or Groups of Related Industries 220
Conclusion 223
6.5 *Conclusion* 223
References 225

7 The End of the Boom 229
7.1 The End of the Boom 229
A Loss of Competitiveness? 232
The Housing Boom 234
7.2 Conclusion 243
References 244

8 Conclusion 247
8.1 Causes of the Boom 247
8.2 Other Conclusions 254
References 257

Index 259

About the Author

Eoin O'Malley is a graduate of University College Dublin and the Institute of Development Studies at the University of Sussex, where he took his doctorate in Development Studies.

He was a researcher in the Economic and Social Research Institute, Dublin, for twenty-five years. He has been a consultant to various public bodies in Ireland and to six Directorates-General of the European Commission. He was also a Research Associate at the Institute of International Integration Studies, Trinity College Dublin.

His work has been published by, among others, Cambridge University Press, Edward Elgar, the EU, Macmillan, Oxford University Press, Routledge, *Cambridge Journal of Economics, European Economy, European Planning Studies* and (in Ireland) the Economic and Social Research Institute, Gill and Macmillan, Irish Management Institute, National Economic and Social Council and *Economic and Social Review.*

List of Figures

Fig. 1.1	Average annual growth rates in Ireland, USA and EU-15	3
Fig. 1.2	GDP or GNP per head of population relative to average level in the EU (EU-15 GDP per head = 100)	4
Fig. 1.3	Employment Index, Ireland, USA and EU-15 (1986 = 100)	6
Fig. 1.4	Unemployment rate, Ireland, USA and EU-15 (%)	7
Fig. 1.5	Net migration, Ireland (thousands)	8
Fig. 2.1	Total number at work, 1926–1986 (thousands)	18
Fig. 3.1	Tax as a percentage of GNP and GDP, 1982–2007	73
Fig. 3.2	Irish labour market tax wedge, 1982–2007	74
Fig. 4.1	Sectoral shares of gross value added (%)	85
Fig. 4.2	Sectoral shares of employment (%)	90
Fig. 4.3	Merchandise and services shares of total exports, 1986–2007 (%)	96
Fig. 4.4	Composition of Total Exports, 1985–2005 (%)	101
Fig. 4.5	Exports, net exports and net foreign earnings, by Sector, 2000 (€ million)	104
Fig. 4.6	Increase in the value of exports and net foreign earnings, selected sectors, 1985–2000, million Euros	108
Fig. 4.7	Increase in the value of exports and net foreign earnings, selected sectors, 2000–2005, million Euros	109
Fig. 5.1	Manufacturing employment index (1988 = 100), Ireland total, Irish indigenous, EU-15 and USA, 1988–2007	126

List of Tables

Table 1.1	Annual percentage change in Ireland's GDP and GNP	2
Table 2.1	Annual percentage change in output, employment and income per head	37
Table 4.1	Sectoral shares of gross value added (%)	84
Table 4.2	GVA adjusted to remove profit outflows, 2000	86
Table 4.3	Sectoral shares of employment (%)	89
Table 4.4	Composition of merchandise exports, 1986–2007 (%)	97
Table 4.5	Composition of services exports, 1998–2007 (%)	98
Table 4.6	Composition of total exports, 1985–2005 (%)	100
Table 4.7	Exports, net exports and net foreign earnings, by sector, 2000 (€ million)	103
Table 4.8	Net foreign earnings, 1985–2005, million Euros, current values	107
Table 4.9	Growth rates of exports, net foreign earnings and GNP (% p.a.), current values	111
Table 5.1	Employment in Irish indigenous and foreign-owned manufacturing, 1980–2006	125
Table 5.2	Employment growth by sector in Irish indigenous manufacturing, 1991–2006	127
Table 5.3	Irish indigenous industry's share of EU-15 manufacturing employment, by sector, 1991–2006 (%)	130
Table 5.4	Irish indigenous industry's share of EU-15 manufacturing gross output, by sector, 1991–2006 (%)	133
Table 5.5	Irish indigenous industry's share of EU-13 manufacturing exports, by sector, 1991–2000 (%)	136

Table 5.6	Estimated net foreign earnings as a percentage of exports, Irish indigenous and foreign-owned by sector, 2005	140
Table 5.7	Percentage distribution of exports and estimated net foreign earnings, Irish indigenous and foreign-owned, 1985, 2000 and 2007	142
Table 5.8	BERD intensity (BERD as % of gross output), by nationality of ownership and manufacturing sector, compared to the OECD, 1997	146
Table 5.9	Average annual percentage employment change in Irish indigenous manufacturing, by size class of establishments, 1973–2001	152
Table 5.10	Average annual percentage employment change in Irish indigenous manufacturing, by size class of enterprises, 2001–2007	153
Table 5.11	Irish indigenous services exports by sector, 2008–2012	160
Table 6.1	Employment in foreign-owned and Irish indigenous manufacturing, 2000	191

CHAPTER 1

Introduction

For a period of about twenty years, starting in the late 1980s, the rate of economic growth in Ireland was exceptionally high compared with most other countries. Incomes rose from little more than 60% of the average level in the EU to well above the average level. The number of people in employment almost doubled, the unemployment rate declined from 17% to 4%, and the traditional flow of emigration from a country where jobs had usually been scarce was transformed into a substantial flow of immigration.

This episode, or part of it, is commonly called the Celtic Tiger boom. Of course, there is no strictly precise definition of that term, and its usage varies. The phrase "Celtic Tiger" was originally coined in 1994. It referred to the fact that by that time Ireland's growth had been relatively fast for seven or eight years when compared to wider international experience. During the remainder of the 1990s, "Celtic Tiger" was generally understood to refer to the period since about 1986 or 1987. However, by about 2000, some people were arguing that the real Celtic Tiger boom was the period of about seven years around 1993–2000 when the rate of growth was even higher than previously, regularly exceeding 8% per year. For many people nowadays, the phrase "Celtic Tiger" mainly recalls the four or five years leading up to 2007, when there was a massive construction boom and an ultimately destructive property price bubble leading to financial collapse.

© The Author(s) 2024

E. O'Malley, *Ireland's Long Economic Boom*, Palgrave Studies in Economic History, https://doi.org/10.1007/978-3-031-53070-8_1

This book is concerned with the whole two decades or so when Ireland's economic growth was relatively fast compared with most other countries, encompassing all the years that were ever described as the Celtic Tiger boom. It examines the nature of that growth and it aims to explain why the long boom occurred. The focus of the book is primarily on economic events, economic causes and economic policies, rather than the social or political aspects of the boom. Before examining matters in more detail in later chapters, this introductory chapter first sets out some of the principal facts and figures relating to the boom, and then outlines the approach and structure of the book.

1.1 Dimensions of the Boom

Before the boom began, the Irish economy had experienced a long period of slow growth or recession in 1980–1986 when GDP grew by just 1.5% per year and GNP did not grow at all (Table 1.1). The economy then recovered and grew by 3.9% per year in terms of GDP and 3.4% per year in terms of GNP in 1986–1993. Although these may not seem like particularly impressive growth rates, this was in fact a strong performance by international standards in a period that included an international recession. It can be seen in Fig. 1.1 that Ireland's growth had been slow compared with the EU and USA in 1980–1986, particularly when measured in terms of GNP, whereas Ireland's growth was relatively fast compared with these other countries in 1986–1993.

When the growth rate of the international economy increased in 1993–2000, Ireland's growth accelerated to an even greater degree, resulting in remarkably high absolute growth rates as well as continuing fast growth in relative terms (Table 1.1 and Fig. 1.1). During the international slowdown of 2000–2002, Ireland's growth slowed too, particularly when

Table 1.1 Annual percentage change in Ireland's GDP and GNP

	1980–1986	*1986–1993*	*1993–2000*	*2000–2002*	*2002–2007*
GDP	1.5	3.9	9.6	5.5	5.0
GNP	0.0	3.4	8.8	2.6	5.0

Source Central Statistics Office (CSO), *National Income and Expenditure*. Creative Commons Attribution BY 4.0

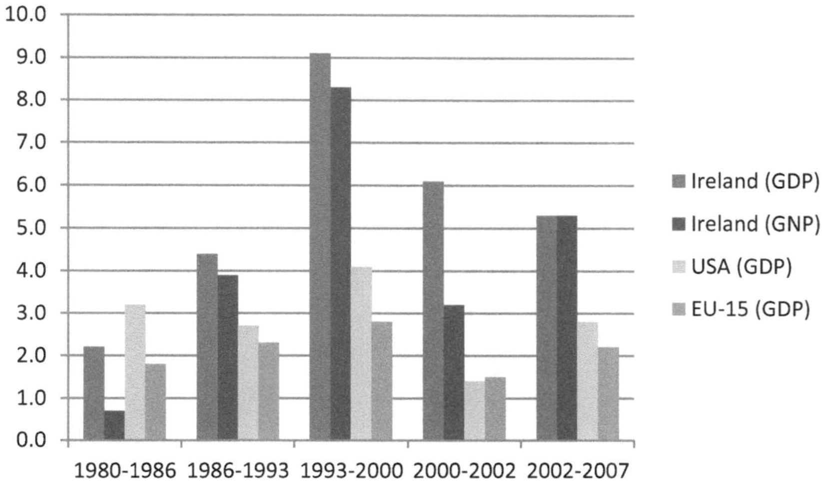

Fig. 1.1 Average annual growth rates in Ireland, USA and EU-15 (*Notes* Since GNP data are not available from this source, the figures for Ireland's GNP in this chart are estimates based on the GDP data together with Irish *National Income and Expenditure* data on GDP/GNP differentials. EU-15 includes the 15 countries that were already members of the EU prior to May 2004. They are Austria, Belgium, Denmark, Finland, France, Germany, Greece, Ireland, Italy, Luxembourg, Netherlands, Portugal, Spain, Sweden and UK. *Source*: *European Economy*, Spring 2010, Statistical Annex, for GDP data. Creative Commons Attribution BY 4.0)

measured in terms of GNP, but it remained relatively fast. Then in 2002–2007, Ireland's growth rate increased again to around 5% per year and this continued to be relatively fast growth by international standards.

During the two decades from 1986 to 2007, Ireland's average income per head of population grew faster than the average in the EU or the USA in almost every year (Fig. 1.2). GNP per head rose from 62% of the average EU level in 1986 to 72% in 1993, 97% in 2000 and 114% in 2007. GDP per head rose from 69% of the average EU level in 1986 to 81% in 1993, 114% in 2000 and 133% in 2007. By 2007, GDP per head in Ireland had almost reached the level of the USA, which generally ranged between 132 and 140% of the average EU level.

GDP is conventionally used as the principal measure of the size of a country's economy, and the change in GDP is normally used as the basic

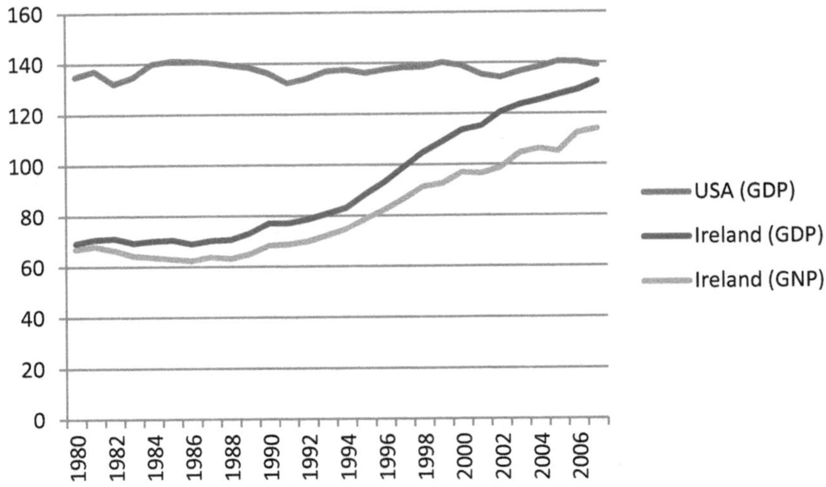

Fig. 1.2 GDP or GNP per head of population relative to average level in the EU (EU-15 GDP per head = 100) (*Note* All figures in this chart are in terms of purchasing power parities. *Source*: *European Economy*, Spring 2010, Statistical Annex, for relative GDP per head; together with Irish *National Income and Expenditure* data to derive relative GNP per head for Ireland. Creative Commons Attribution BY 4.0)

measure of its economic growth. In many countries, GDP and GNP are almost equal so that it makes little difference which of these two indicators is used. In Ireland, however, there was a substantial and usually growing difference between the two throughout the boom period. GNP amounted to just 90.6% of GDP in 1986 and, since it usually grew more slowly than GDP, it amounted to only 85.9% of GDP by 2007. The main reason for this was because GDP included large and growing amounts of profits of foreign-owned multinational companies (MNCs), which were mostly withdrawn from the country rather than accruing to anyone in Ireland. GNP did not include such profits of foreign MNCs that were withdrawn from the country.

In view of this situation, it has often been argued that GDP gave a misleading and exaggerated impression of the size of the national income that was available to Irish residents, and the growth of GDP exceeded the growth of the national income whenever the activities of foreign MNCs were growing relatively fast. Consequently, GNP was often preferred to GDP as an indicator of trends in the national income that were relevant for Irish residents. As can be seen in Figs. 1.1 and 1.2, Ireland's economic boom looks somewhat less remarkable when measured in terms of GNP than it does in terms of GDP, but it is nevertheless clear from the GNP trends that an exceptional boom did occur.

The issue concerning the best way to measure Ireland's economic growth became a good deal more complicated in the years after the end of the boom in 2007. FitzGerald (2015) discussed several important causes of such complications, including the "patent cliff" for pharmaceutical products, the effects of "redomiciled plcs", and changes in national accounting rules for aircraft leasing and for goods and services produced offshore for companies resident in Ireland. Although such issues had important effects on national accounts later on, they were of little or no significance in the period up to 2007, which is the focus of this book. For our purposes here, the trend in GNP can be regarded as a meaningful indicator.[1]

The trend in employment provides further evidence that the boom was very real and substantial. Total employment in Ireland rose by 89% between 1986 and 2007, which amounted to an average growth rate of 3.1% per year. As shown in Fig. 1.3, the growth in employment was a little slow to take off at first in the late 1980s and early 1990s, but the slowly rising trend at that time was a marked improvement from the declining trend that had prevailed earlier in the 1980s. From about 1993 onwards, there was very strong growth in employment and it is clear from Fig. 1.3 that employment growth in Ireland was unusually fast by international standards.

Employment as a percentage of the population had been very low at 31% in 1986, but the strength of employment growth over the following two decades made it possible for that figure to rise to 49% by 2007.[2] That change on its own, if nothing else had changed, would have been sufficient to raise Ireland's GNP per head of population from 62% of

[1] FitzGerald (2018) discussed further developments of relevance to this issue.

[2] Data derived from Department of Finance, *Budgetary and Economic Statistics*, October 2012. In addition to the impact of rapid employment growth, there was also a declining fertility rate in the 1980s and early 1990s which tended to reduce the youth dependency rate, and this also contributed something to the rise in employment as a percentage of the population (see Bloom and Canning 2003).

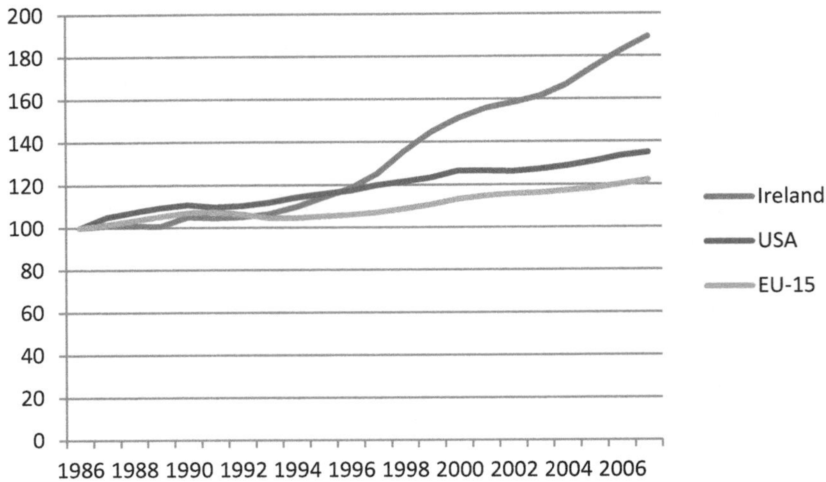

Fig. 1.3 Employment Index, Ireland, USA and EU-15 (1986 = 100) (*Source* Derived from *European Economy*, Spring 2010, Statistical Annex. Creative Commons Attribution BY 4.0)

the average EU level to 98%. Considering that the actual increase that occurred was a rise in Ireland's GNP per head of population from 62% of the EU level in 1986 to 114% by 2007, it is clear that rapid employment growth was a highly influential factor underlying the rise in average incomes.

As regards labour productivity growth during the boom years, GDP per person employed rose by 2.9% per year in 1986–2007 while GNP per person employed increased by 2.2% per year.[3] For comparison, the average annual growth rate of GDP per person employed was 1.7% in the EU-15 and 1.6% in the USA in the same period.[4] Thus Ireland's productivity growth was somewhat faster than in these other countries but it was not really outstanding. Seen from the viewpoint of Ireland's own longer-term experience, productivity growth during the boom was not particularly impressive since it was actually a little slower in 1986–2007

[3] Data derived from Department of Finance, *Budgetary and Economic Statistics*, October 2012.

[4] Derived from *European Economy*, Spring 2010, Statistical Annex.

than in 1970–1986. Rather, it was the strong trend in employment that was the impressive new feature compared to Ireland's previous experience.

The rapid growth of employment was accompanied by a number of related changes, namely a fall in unemployment, a decline in net emigration followed by a rise in net immigration, and a rise in the participation of women in the labour force.

The fall in the rate of unemployment is illustrated in Fig. 1.4. The unemployment rate declined from 17% in 1986 to 4% by 2001 and then it stabilised at a level well below the average in the EU and a little below the USA. During the early years of this long-term decline in unemployment, the trend was interrupted and reversed temporarily in 1990–1993, which was primarily a result of an international recession that also raised the unemployment rates in the EU and USA at that time (see Fig. 1.4).

Although the Irish economy had been growing relatively fast by international standards since 1986, there probably was not a popular perception of an economic boom until well into the 1990s because of the trends in employment and unemployment in 1986–1993. Although economic growth was relatively fast in 1986–1993, it was actually not a great deal faster than labour productivity growth, which meant that

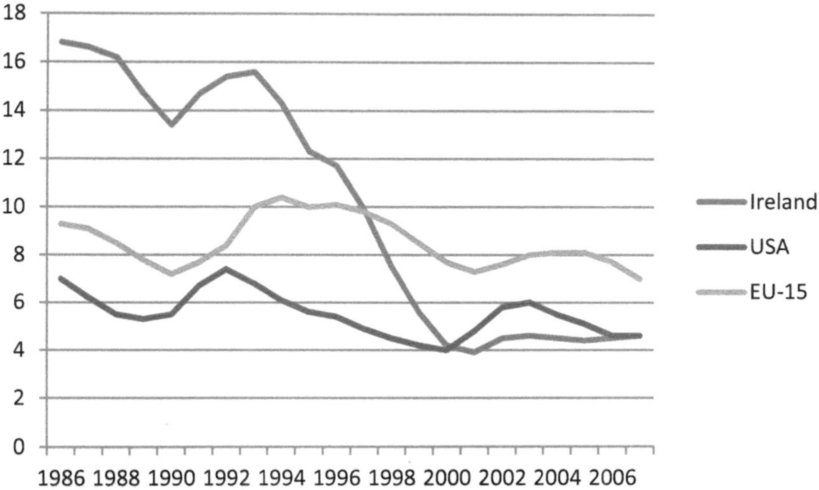

Fig. 1.4 Unemployment rate, Ireland, USA and EU-15 (%) (*Source*: *European Economy*, Spring 2010, Statistical Annex. Creative Commons Attribution BY 4.0)

employment growth was fairly slow in those years. Then the unemployment rate had scarcely begun to decline in 1986–1990, and it was still at a very high level, when it was pushed back up again temporarily in 1990–1993 by the international recession.

The trend in net migration is shown in Fig. 1.5. Net emigration of over 40,000 per year in the late 1980s was transformed into net immigration of about 70,000 per year by 2006 and 2007. Net emigration was equivalent to about 1.2% of the population per year in the late 1980s, whereas net immigration amounted to about 1.6% of the population per year in 2006 and 2007.

As regards female participation in the labour force, while the increase in male employment was substantial at 49% in 1986–2006, female employment rose by as much as 135% in the same period. Women accounted for just 32% of all those at work in 1986, but this figure rose to 43% by 2006. Or to look at this another way, in 1986 just 28% of females aged 15 years and over were at work compared with 60% of males. By 2006, the figure for females rose to 48% compared with 66% for males.[5]

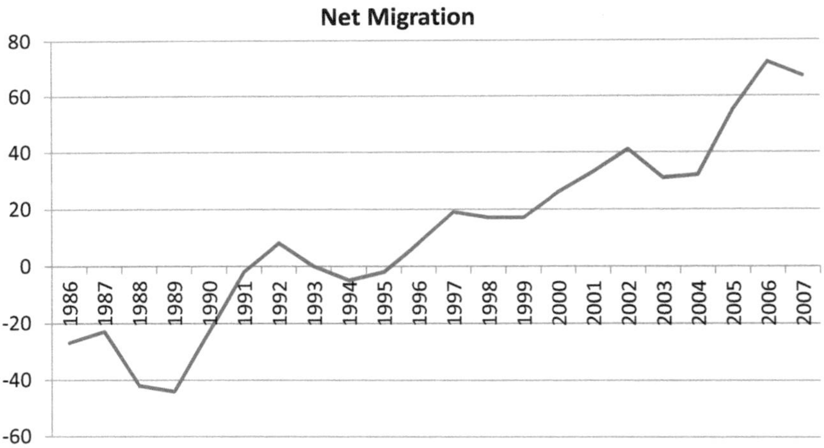

Fig. 1.5 Net migration, Ireland (thousands) (*Source* Department of Finance, *Budgetary and Economic Statistics*, October 2012)

[5] Census of Population data.

The Irish government had been struggling with a serious financial crisis for a number of years before the boom but that problem was brought under control quite rapidly from 1987 onwards. The current budget deficit dropped from more than 7% of GNP in 1985 and 1986 to little more than 1% of GNP throughout 1988–1995 and then turned into a surplus every year until 2007. The total exchequer balance, including the current and capital account, followed a similar trend. Thus, the total exchequer deficit was over 11% of GNP in 1984–1986, falling to just 1–3% of GNP in 1988–1996, and then turning into a small surplus most years until 2007. Consequently, the national debt as a percentage of GNP declined every year from a peak of 118% in 1987 to just 23% by 2007.[6]

There had also been a major crisis with the balance of payments earlier in the 1980s but that issue ceased to be a problem during the boom, at least until its closing years. The deficit on the current account of the balance of payments had amounted to at least 7% of GNP each year in the period 1978–1984. However, it then dropped sharply and throughout 1987–2004 any deficits that occurred were never more than 1 or 2% of GNP, while surpluses were just as common and were mostly somewhat larger than the deficits. However, a significant current account deficit opened up again in the last few years of the boom, amounting to 4% of GNP in 2005 and 2006 and 6% in 2007.[7]

There was generally no serious problem with price inflation during the boom, with the important exception of property prices which clearly did become a major issue relatively late in the boom period. The rate of increase in the consumer price index (which does not include property prices) had generally been in the range 10–20% per year for a decade up to 1983, but it then dropped substantially in the mid-1980s. In 1987–1999, it mostly ranged between 1.5 and 3.3%, rising somewhat to a range of 2.2–5.0% in 2000–2007.

The boom did not have a substantial overall impact on income distribution in Ireland. Various summary measures of income inequality remained rather stable from the late 1980s until the mid-2000s. Nolan (2009) also found that "Ireland's position relative to other EU and OECD countries has also been broadly stable over the past quarter-century, insofar as comparative data allow that to be reliably assessed". Some factors such

[6] Department of Finance, *Budgetary and Economic Statistics*, October 2012.

[7] Department of Finance, *Budgetary and Economic Statistics*, October 2012.

as rising profits tended to increase inequality, but they were counteracted by other factors with the opposite effect such as falling unemployment (Nolan 2009). However, as Nolan (2009) observed, if everyone experiences the same proportional increase in their incomes, which would leave measures of income distribution and inequality unchanged, there would be widening absolute gaps in incomes. Such widening absolute gaps could be particularly striking when incomes are rising as rapidly as they did during the boom.

In the mid-2000s, the degree of inequality in Ireland's income distribution was above average among developed economies, although it was not unique or exceptional. According to a number of summary measures of income inequality, Ireland ranked 10–12th within the EU-15, 17–18th within the EU-27 and 18–22nd within the OECD. Income inequality in Ireland was similar to the UK, Spain, Italy, Australia and Canada, for example (Nolan 2009).

It is well known that part of the Celtic Tiger boom was an extraordinary construction boom, which involved soaring property prices and excessive construction output relative to actual market requirements, financed by imprudent lending by banks which were able to source large amounts of funding from abroad. This naturally raises the question to what extent was the Celtic Tiger boom real and sustainable economic growth, as opposed to being an artificial product of a debt-financed property and construction boom. This issue will be considered in more detail in Chapter 7, but it may be useful to make a few brief points about it at this stage to put it in some perspective.

In particular, it is clear that abnormal or excessive growth of construction played no part in about the first two-thirds of the twenty-year boom. In the 1960s–1980s, employment in construction had generally been in a range of 6–9% of total employment, and that continued to be the case throughout the 1990s. However, construction employment increased to 10% of total employment in 2000 and it rose further to 13% by 2007.[8] Construction output also grew faster than the total economy in this period.

Property-related lending and construction activity probably started to become excessive and unsustainable sometime during 2001–2004. However, in those years this was still very largely financed by Ireland's

[8] Department of Finance, *Budgetary and Economic Statistics*, October 2012.

own domestic savings rather than by additional injections of funding sourced from abroad. This was reflected in the fact that balance of payments current account deficits were small in that period, averaging just 0.7% of GNP. In that sense, the overall rate of economic growth was not too high to be sustainable. The economy could have had much the same growth rate even if there had been no property and construction boom, if the investments that went into that sector had been spent in more usual ways.

Then in 2005–2007, borrowing abroad by banks for property-related lending increased rapidly and this was reflected in a rise in the current balance of payments deficit to 4.1% of GNP in 2005 and 2006 and 6.2% in 2007. Thus, in those final few years of the boom, it was the case that a large inflow of finance from abroad for property-related lending was making it possible for the economy to grow at a rate that was unsustainable and that would not have been attained otherwise.

1.2 The Approach and Structure of This Book

The remainder of this book examines the nature of Ireland's economic growth in more detail, and it aims to explain what caused the long boom.

The general approach of the book is to treat Ireland as a relative latecomer to economic development. Such latecomers face certain significant difficulties.[9]

For example, since economies of scale are common in many industries, the consequent presence of large established firms in a range of important industries in advanced industrial countries, presents a substantial barrier to the development of those industries by new or small firms in a relatively late-developing country that trades freely with advanced countries. For they generally lack the resources that would be required to enter into competition on a competitive scale of production, or to survive a period of initial loss-making while building up to an adequate market share to support a competitive scale of production.

There are also other significant types of barriers to entry for new or small firms arising from the strength of established competitors in other industries. For example, it can be very difficult for new or small firms

[9] The difficulties faced by latecomers are outlined briefly here, and they are discussed in somewhat greater detail in Sect. 2.2 in Chapter 2. They have also been discussed previously in, for example, O'Malley (1989) and O'Malley (1998).

to match the technological capabilities already developed by established companies in sectors where technology is of key importance. Similarly, if strong marketing is a key requirement for an industry, the established marketing strength of existing firms presents an important entry barrier for new or small firms.

In addition, the advantages of external economies, which are enjoyed by firms in existing industrial centres or districts, can represent a further obstacle to the development of newcomers in late-industrialising countries. Such external economies consist mainly of the advantages of close contact with related firms, specialist suppliers and services, pools of specialised labour skills, supportive institutions and perhaps a large local market. These types of advantages, in some form, are commonly reflected in the existence of large and often specialised industrial towns and geographically concentrated clusters of related industries. If advantages of external economies are important in an industry, it may be relatively easy for many new firms to emerge and grow within existing locations of that industry while, at the same time, this is a good deal less likely to happen in late-industrialising countries that do not have strong industrial centres or districts and would have to compete with the existing industries.

Given this understanding of the context faced by a relatively late developer such as Ireland, important issues to be considered in this book are whether, and how, did Irish indigenous companies make progress when faced with such barriers, and whether the alternative strategy of attracting foreign direct investment (FDI) proved to be an adequate substitute.

As regards the structure of the book, Chapter 2 outlines the historical experience of the economy before the boom. This chapter is relevant for the purpose of the book since it aims to explain how the economy came to be in the difficult situation that it was in before the start of the boom, with very low growth, low-income levels, high unemployment and emigration rates, and a high level of government debt. Thus, the chapter serves to illuminate the obstacles and problems that had to be overcome in order for stronger growth to be attained. It also shows how the difficulties confronting late developers had shaped the experience of the Irish economy before the boom, and it outlines the limitations of previous strategies for growth that had been attempted before the boom.

Chapter 3 contains a survey of the literature that has aimed to explain what caused the boom. It briefly presents the various explanations that have been put forward in the quite extensive literature on this topic. In addition, it includes some assessment of the suggested explanations, concluding that a number of them are not convincing or not very important whereas the others will merit further consideration and assessment in later chapters in this book.

Chapter 4 analyses the contribution made by different sectors to economic growth during the boom. In doing this, it pays attention to the very large outflows of profits from foreign-owned multinational companies, noting that the profit outflows came disproportionately from certain sectors. Since this naturally raises the question whether those sectors were really as important for the Irish economy as they appeared to be, this chapter aims to clarify this issue. It focuses particularly on the contribution of sectors to exports because, in a small and very open economy, export growth makes an essential contribution that drives the rest of the economy. As an essential part of this, it estimates how much net foreign earnings remained in the Irish economy after deducting the profit outflows and payments for imported inputs that were associated with each sector's exports.

Chapter 5 examines the role of Irish indigenous companies in the boom. As noted above, a key issue to be considered in this book is whether, and how, did Irish indigenous companies make progress when faced with the barriers to late development. The role of foreign-owned MNCs has generally had a higher profile but some have argued that Irish-owned companies also played an important part. In this context, we again pay particular attention to exports and net foreign earnings. This chapter also examines matters such as the changing sectoral composition and size structure of indigenous industry, trends in R&D and innovation, and the impact of industrial policy in assisting the development of indigenous companies. The chapter looks at the record of manufacturing and services in two separate sections.

Chapter 6 is concerned with the role of foreign-owned MNCs in the boom since it is well known that foreign MNCs were an important part of the story. This chapter again pays particular attention to exports and net foreign earnings. It also examines aspects of foreign MNCs such as their purchasing linkages in Ireland, R&D, pay levels, their motivation for investing in Ireland, and secondary effects on the economy including the balance of payments and their effects on indigenous companies. An important issue here is the extent of industrial upgrading in terms of skills and technology, and the extent to which foreign establishments may have become more embedded or integrated in the Irish economy. Such issues are relevant to the question whether attracting FDI could be an adequate alternative to indigenous development.

Chapter 7 deals with the final phase of the boom and its end. Although export growth slowed down after 2000, this chapter argues that fast economic growth continued to be sustainable until 2005 because there continued to be strong growth in net foreign earnings due to the changing sectoral composition of exports. It was only in its last two years or so, from about 2005 until its end in 2007, that the boom came to be largely driven by a debt-fuelled housing boom which ultimately had disastrous consequences.

Finally, Chapter 8 presents the conclusions. The first part of this chapter aims to explain the causes of Ireland's long boom. It draws from material in the survey of literature discussed in Chapter 3 and from the findings of Chapters 4–7. The second part of the chapter discusses some other conclusions from Ireland's experience in the boom.

References

Bloom, David E., and David Canning. 2003. Contraception and the Celtic Tiger. *Economic and Social Review* 34 (3): 229–247.

FitzGerald, John. 2015. *Problems Interpreting National Accounts in a Globalised Economy—Ireland*. Quarterly Economic Commentary Special Article. Dublin: Economic and Social Research Institute.

FitzGerald, John. 2018. *National Accounts for a Global Economy: The Case of Ireland*. Quarterly Economic Commentary Special Article. Dublin: Economic and Social Research Institute.

Nolan, Brian. 2009. Income Inequality and Public Policy. *Economic and Social Review* 40 (4): 489–510.

O'Malley, Eoin. 1989. *Industry and Economic Development: The Challenge for the Latecomer*. Dublin: Gill and Macmillan.

O'Malley, Eoin. 1998. Industrial Policy in Ireland and the Problem of Late Development In *Latecomers in the Global Economy*, ed. Michael Storper, Stavros B. Thomadakis and Lena J. Tsipouri. London and New York: Routledge.

Open Access This chapter is licensed under the terms of the Creative Commons Attribution 4.0 International License (http://creativecommons.org/licenses/by/4.0/), which permits use, sharing, adaptation, distribution and reproduction in any medium or format, as long as you give appropriate credit to the original author(s) and the source, provide a link to the Creative Commons license and indicate if changes were made.

The images or other third party material in this chapter are included in the chapter's Creative Commons license, unless indicated otherwise in a credit line to the material. If material is not included in the chapter's Creative Commons license and your intended use is not permitted by statutory regulation or exceeds the permitted use, you will need to obtain permission directly from the copyright holder.

CHAPTER 2

Before the Boom: The Historical Background

The Celtic Tiger boom was a major departure from earlier experience since the Irish economy had a previous history of relative weakness compared with many other European countries. In particular, for a long time before the boom the Irish economy had a problem with insufficient generation of employment which commonly resulted in substantial emigration. It also had relatively low-income levels compared with most of Western Europe.

2.1 Employment, Emigration and Incomes: Long-Term Trends

Mass emigration resulted in a steep population decline from 5.1 million in 1851 just after the Great Famine to 3.0 million in 1926. This represents a decline from 25% of the size of Great Britain's population in 1851 to just 7% in 1926.[1] The number of people at work in 1926 was 1,223,000 and throughout the next 60 years, 1926–1986, the number at work either remained approximately stable in some periods or declined in other

[1] The whole island of Ireland was part of the UK of Great Britain and Ireland until 1922. The Irish population figures here refer to the area that became an independent state in 1922, leaving out the area that became Northern Ireland and remained within the UK.

© The Author(s) 2024

E. O'Malley, *Ireland's Long Economic Boom*, Palgrave Studies in Economic History, https://doi.org/10.1007/978-3-031-53070-8_2

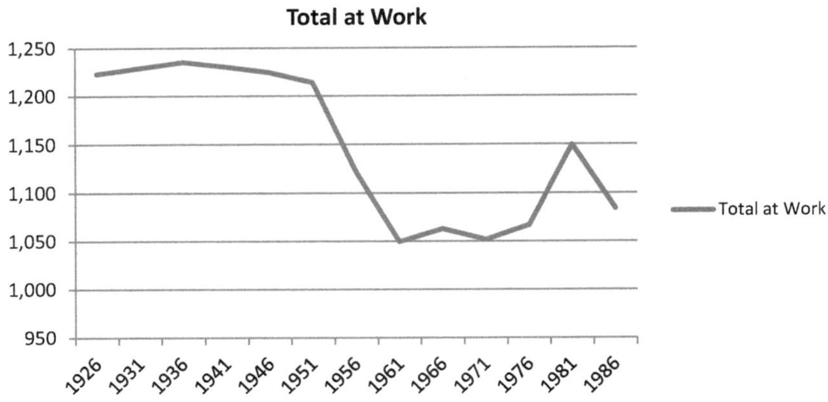

Fig. 2.1 Total number at work, 1926–1986 (thousands) (*Source* CSO StatBank and ESRI Databank. Creative Commons Attribution BY 4.0)

periods, except for the 1970s when there was growth in employment (see Fig. 2.1). By 1986 the number at work was down to 1,091,000.

Even in periods of employment stability, there was usually significant emigration because employment would have needed to grow to provide job opportunities for all of a potential labour force that was naturally tending to increase. For example, between 1961 and 1971—one of the better periods for the Irish economy in most respects—the total at work scarcely changed and net emigration amounted to about 13,400 per year. This rate of net emigration was equivalent to about one-quarter of the number reaching the age of sixteen each year.

As regards incomes and wages, Irish average income per head of population was 61% of the UK level in 1913 and was also a little over 60% in the mid-1980s (Barry 1999).[2] There were some fluctuations between those dates but Ireland's average income per head did not rise much above 60–65% of the UK level before the late 1980s. A number of studies made the further point that, as average income growth was slower in the UK than in most of Europe, income per head was growing more slowly in Ireland than in most of Europe (e.g. Kennedy et al. 1988; Ó Gráda and O'Rourke 1996).

[2] Average income per head of population is measured by net output per head in 1913 and GDP per head in the 1980s.

Wages in Ireland were about 100% of the UK level by 1913 and about the same in the 1980s, although Irish wages fell well below that level at the time of the Second World War and then took a few decades to regain approximate parity with the UK (Barry 1999). Thus, over the period from 1913 to the late 1980s there was little evidence of convergence in Irish average income per head of population towards the level of higher-income countries, whereas wages were apparently drawn quite close to the UK level for much of the time.

This tendency regarding wages can be seen as essentially a consequence of the fact that there was generally free movement of labour between Ireland and the UK, although the freedom of movement was in practice hindered at times by recessions and unemployment while there were also other factors that had an influence on relative wage levels in Ireland and the UK.

There were two main reasons why the average income per head of population remained far lower in Ireland than in the UK despite the recurring tendency towards approximate parity in wage levels. First, compared with the UK a high proportion of people in the Irish labour force were not wage-earners but self-employed farmers, mostly small farmers with relatively low incomes. Agriculture accounted for 53% of the total at work in 1926 falling to 15% by 1986. This 1986 figure was still high compared with a figure of just 2.5% for the UK, but clearly the influence of Ireland's low-income agriculture on the relative income levels of the two countries was diminishing over time.

The other main reason why the average income per head of population was much lower in Ireland than in the UK was because a smaller proportion of the population was at work in Ireland compared with the UK. The influence of this factor was increasing over time since employment as a percentage of the population in Ireland declined in each decade from 41% in 1951 to 37% in 1961, 35% in 1971, 33% in 1981 and 31% in 1986. For comparison, the figure for the UK was 47% in 1986.[3] The difference between these figures for the two countries in 1986 would have resulted in Ireland's average income per head of population being at just 66% of the UK level, other things being equal. Thus, this factor explains

[3] O'Leary (2015, Chapter 2) shows that the Irish figure for employment as a percentage of the population in the 1980s was also very low compared with the EU 15, the USA and the Asian "tiger" economies.

the bulk of the difference in the two countries' incomes per head at that time.

Ireland had a relatively low proportion of its population at work mainly because there was usually insufficient growth of non-agricultural employment to compensate for the secular decline in the numbers engaged in agriculture, and to cater for the natural potential growth of the total labour force. This usually resulted in significant emigration of people of working-age as outlined above, as well as unemployment. As Ó Gráda and O'Rourke (1996) put it, the proportion of the population in employment "is not just a function of birth rates, death rates and attitudes towards female labour force participation. It is significantly affected by emigration, which is in turn produced by the same problem as leads to unemployment: a failure by the economy to create sufficient employment".

When discussing the long-term record of economic growth in Ireland, a distinction is sometimes made between "intensive" growth and "extensive" growth. Intensive growth means the growth of average income or output per head of population, whereas extensive growth means the growth of the absolute size of the economy. In much of the nineteenth century and the early years of the twentieth century, Ireland was able to have quite strong intensive growth, despite the fact that extensive growth was weak as the labour force and population fell. Heavy emigration and a declining population meant that there was an increasing area of agricultural land per head of the remaining population and—in a largely agricultural economy—this helped substantially to boost the intensive growth rate of the whole economy.

However, as the relative importance of agriculture diminished during the twentieth century, this effect became less significant. Instead, the more influential effect of weak employment trends and continuing emigration was the effect that they had in leaving a low proportion of the population in employment. Consequently, it became a good deal more difficult than it had been for Ireland to have a strong trend in intensive growth without also having a strong trend in employment and in extensive growth.

2.2 Industrial Development

A fundamental difference between Ireland and other European countries that developed more successfully was the fact that Ireland did not have a strong process of industrialisation. This was the basic reason why Ireland usually had insufficient growth of non-agricultural employment.[4] Ireland did experience the beginning of an industrial revolution in the late eighteenth century, and by the early nineteenth century it had a fairly substantial industrial sector by the standards of many countries at that time. In the Belfast area in the north-east, in what is now Northern Ireland, industrial growth continued into the twentieth century in a manner similar to that of large industrial centres in Great Britain. In the rest of Ireland, however, early industrial growth turned into industrial decline during much of the nineteenth century.

A number of different explanations have been suggested for the decline of industry in most of Ireland, but the most convincing type of explanation focuses on Ireland's position as a relatively late starter in industrialisation compared with Great Britain, which was the leading industrial country in the world at that time. As part of the UK, Ireland had to compete in a free trade relationship with Great Britain.

In most of the important nineteenth-century industries, it was generally important for producers to develop relatively large-scale, specialised and centralised production in the quite early stages of mechanisation, while proximity to large markets could also be important. Unprotected industries found it difficult to grow successfully from relatively small beginnings into large-scale producers after competitors had already made substantial progress in mechanisation and large-scale development elsewhere. Rather, those regional centres of an industry that began the process relatively early tended to gain increasing advantages from scale, specialisation and geographical centralisation, disposing of lesser competitors as they did so. Within the UK in the nineteenth century, this process generally favoured a number of growing urban areas in Great Britain,

[4] The growth of the other main sectors, services and construction, was very largely determined by domestic demand with little competition from imports or potential for exports, at least until the scope for internationally traded services increased in the last two or three decades of the twentieth century. The growth of services and construction in Ireland was not very different from much of European experience.

as well as the Belfast area in Ireland, while relatively small and late-developing industries in other regions of the UK, including most of Ireland, were gradually eliminated by competition.[5]

Independence and Protection

When it became independent in 1922, the new Irish state had a very small industrial sector that employed only about 5–9% of the labour force.[6] Almost half of industrial employment was in the food and drink industry. The government's economic policy in the 1920s was predominantly orthodox, relying on free trade and free market forces, although a small number of protective tariffs were introduced in order to support the growth of certain selected industries.

From 1932 onwards, a much stronger and more wide-ranging policy of protection against imports was introduced and rapid growth of industrial employment followed for two decades, apart from during the Second World War when it was difficult to import necessary inputs. Manufacturing employment increased by 4.2% per year between 1931 and 1951 (*Census of Industrial Production*). Ireland's experience of considerable industrial growth beginning during the international depression of the 1930s corresponds quite well with the experience of some of the less-developed countries (e.g., Argentina, Brazil, Chile and Mexico) that were independent at the time and resorted to protection during the depression.

Labour productivity growth in Irish industry tended to be sluggish as the volume of output per worker increased by only 1.4% p.a. in 1931–1951. If this labour productivity trend suggests that the protected industries were inefficient, this impression is strengthened by the fact that sales were concentrated on the small protected domestic market, and few industries were able to compete effectively in export markets. Food, drink & tobacco had been the only substantial export industries in the

[5] For more on this interpretation of the historical experience of Irish industry, see O'Malley (1981) or O'Malley (1989, Chapter 3). O'Malley (1981) also includes a brief review of a range of other explanations for Ireland's industrial weakness. Ó Gráda (1994, Chapter 13, Sect. 13.6) includes a review of the concepts of "economies of scale, external economies and path-dependence" in explaining Ireland's industrial history, which is relevant to the interpretation outlined above.

[6] In 1926 the figure was 9% according to the *Census of Population*, but less than 5% according to the *Census of Industrial Production*, which would have left out self-employed craftsmen and very small enterprises with only a few employees.

1920s, and they exported 25% of their output in 1951, but the rest of manufacturing exported only 6% of its output in 1951.

The Committee on Industrial Organisation (1965) reported further evidence of industrial inefficiency in the early 1960s. They noted that companies commonly had high production costs because of old equipment, small scale, short production runs and wide ranges of products (resulting from the prevailing orientation towards the small protected domestic market).

Although many former imports had been substituted by domestic production in protected industries, there continued to be other imports that had not been replaced by domestic production, including many of the capital goods, materials, fuels and components required to sustain production. These imports had to grow whenever the economy was growing. As the economy grew over time, the cost of imports of goods that had not been substituted by domestic production eventually grew to exceed the cost of all imports before the process of import-substitution began. The failure to achieve much growth of exports then became critically important, because the result was a chronic balance of payments crisis that emerged in the 1950s. The deflationary measures taken to reduce imports resulted in prolonged recession, rapid decline in employment and large-scale emigration during most of the 1950s.[7]

The industrial structure generated by protection was rather inefficient and largely unable to export, thus ultimately causing further growth to be constrained by a lack of foreign exchange. This does not mean, however, that the introduction of protection was the original cause of industrial and economic stagnation. Seen in a longer-term perspective it is evident that there had already been industrial decline or stagnation, in a context of free trade and reliance on free markets, for a century or so before the introduction of protection. Protection, for a time, probably generated considerably more industrial growth than would have occurred under a continuation of the former policies.

Ireland's experience in the 1950s was a fairly typical conclusion to a process of import-substituting industrialisation, in which wide-ranging protection was the main policy used. Other late-developing countries with the same type of policy commonly experienced a similar problem eventually with a balance of payments constraint on further growth. However,

[7] For more on the 1930s–1950s period, and for further references, see O'Malley (1989, Chapter 4) and O'Malley (1999).

many of them went through these difficulties later than Ireland did, because they acquired the independence necessary to adopt protection later than Ireland.

Outward-Looking Policies and Industrial Growth

In view of the difficulties experienced in Ireland in the 1950s a number of major changes in industrial policy were introduced. The new approach that evolved in the 1950s and 1960s was much more open or outward-looking in three important respects. First, the emphasis shifted to developing exports, and new tax concessions and grants were introduced to encourage and assist firms to produce for export markets. Second, measures were introduced to attract foreign industrial firms to produce in Ireland for export markets. The potential for attracting such investment was still a newly emerging opportunity at that time since export-oriented foreign direct investment (FDI) in industry was only starting to become a significant phenomenon in the international economy in the 1950s.[8] Third, the protectionist measures against imports were gradually dismantled, opening the home market to foreign competition.

The reorientation of industrial policy towards a more outward-looking approach was an evolutionary process that took some time.[9] Steps to attract export-oriented FDI began in the early 1950s, and grants intended primarily to assist export-oriented firms were introduced during the 1950s. Major tax incentives for exporters were introduced in 1956 and 1958. As a result, no corporation tax was charged on profits arising from increases in export sales above the 1956 level. This meant there was no tax on all profits arising from the exports of firms that started up after 1956, including new foreign-owned establishments.

The main elements of the policy package to promote exports, and to encourage FDI for that purpose, were in place by the end of the 1950s, although further additions and refinements to the same general approach were made over the next 25 years. Such later changes included

[8] Of course, FDI in primary sectors such as mining, oil or plantation agriculture, or in industrial production for *local* (often protected) markets, was quite a common feature of the international economy much earlier.

[9] Further details on the changes in policy measures, and further references, can be found in O'Malley (1989, Chapter 5) and O'Malley (1999).

the introduction of grants to support R&D and training. Also, beginning in the 1970s, companies engaged in specified internationally traded services became eligible to benefit from industrial policy supports. The tax relief on export profits remained in place during the 1960s and 1970s. However, beginning in 1981, it was replaced by a new low rate of corporation tax of just 10% for all of the manufacturing industry's profits (not just for profits relating to exports), and also for profits of specified internationally traded services.

In the 1970s and early 1980s, a number of observers concluded that the Irish package of tax and grant incentives for industry, and particularly for exports, was one of the most attractive in Europe. They also concluded that the efforts to market Ireland as a location for export-oriented foreign industries were among the most effective (O'Malley 1989, Chapter 5).

The process of dismantling protection and returning to free trade began in 1963 and 1964 with small reductions in all tariffs. This was followed in 1965 by the Anglo-Irish Free Trade Area Agreement, which required Ireland to remove protection against imports of British manufactured products by ten annual reductions of 10% each. When Ireland, the UK and Denmark joined the EEC (now the EU) in 1973, Ireland agreed to remove protection against other EEC manufactured products by five annual tariff reductions of 20% each.

Under the new outward-looking strategy, industrial production grew significantly faster in the 1960s and 1970s compared with the 1950s. Manufacturing output had grown by just 1.7% p.a. in 1951–1958, and the growth rate then increased to 6.7% p.a. in 1958–1973 and 5.1% p.a. in 1973–1979. Manufacturing employment had grown by just 0.2% p.a. in 1951–1958 and it then grew by 2.4% p.a. in 1958–1973 and 0.8% p.a. in 1973–1979 (*Census of Industrial Production*). This period of growth was characterised by particularly rapid export growth. The percentage of manufacturing output going for export had increased only slightly from 16% in 1951 to 19% in 1960, but this figure rose to 41% in 1978 and further to 55% by 1986. This trend helped to ease the balance of payments difficulties that had been a feature of the 1950s, and thus it facilitated growth of the economy.

In the 1980s, however, the trends became more worrying. Manufacturing employment declined by one-fifth between 1979 and 1987. A decline in manufacturing employment of such a magnitude and duration had not happened before during Ireland's time as an independent state. On the other hand, during most of the period 1979–1987 industrial output continued to grow quite rapidly. The roots of these apparently paradoxical developments lie in the major structural changes that had been occurring within Irish industry, and in the differing experience and performance of Irish indigenous companies and foreign-owned multinational companies.

Irish Indigenous Industry

Even in the 1960s and 1970s, Ireland's industrial growth had an important weakness.[10] While new investment by highly export-oriented foreign-owned companies was largely responsible for the improved performance of industrial employment, output and especially exports, native Irish-owned or indigenous industry did not fare so well. Most of indigenous industry was apparently not able to increase its export-orientation significantly, while at the same time it was losing market share to competing imports in the home market as the protectionist measures were dismantled.[11]

Thus, leaving aside new foreign-owned companies, the exports of other industrial companies amounted to 0.26% of manufactured exports of all developed market economies in 1966, and the same percentage in 1976. The exports of these companies grew, but only in line with the market and without any improvement in market share. Meanwhile the rising domestic market share taken by competing imports cost these companies about 15% of the home market between 1966 and 1979, which was equivalent to about 15% of their total sales.[12] Consequently, leaving aside new foreign-owned companies, the rest of the industry in Ireland was a significant net loser of market share during the transition to free trade. Competing imports continued to take a rapidly rising share of the domestic market in 1980–1988 (*Employment Through Enterprise*, 1993, Appendix 3), while there was little or no increase in the export-orientation of Irish indigenous industry until about 1986 (O'Malley 1998a).

[10] Parts of the following pages are adapted from O'Malley (1998b).

[11] See O'Malley (1989, Chapter 6) for more details on developments outlined in this section.

[12] "Competing" imports include imports of only the types of products that were produced in Ireland. The classification of imports as competing with domestic producers was done by the Department of Industry and Commerce in consultation with business interests, and official data on such competing imports used to be published regularly.

In this context, indigenous industrial employment did not grow between the mid-1960s and the end of the 1970s, and it then fell by 27% in just seven years in the 1980s. Indigenous industry had just about maintained its overall employment level while domestic demand was growing sufficiently strongly in the late 1960s and 1970s to compensate for the loss of domestic market share. But when domestic demand weakened considerably in the 1980s, its employment slumped.

Within indigenous industry, however, some sectors fared relatively well. These were mostly engaged in either basic processing of local primary products such as food, or else in sheltered or non-traded activities which have a significant degree of natural protection against distant competitors and do not have much involvement with international trade. Some non-traded activities can be sheltered in the local market by high transport costs for products with a low value-weight ratio (e.g., building materials, packaging materials, soft drinks). Others can be sheltered because of a need for local knowledge, close contact with customers, or a significant element of on-site installation or servicing (e.g., general printing, newspapers, structural wood and metal products). While indigenous firms in these types of activities grew and increased in relative importance, other internationally traded activities declined.

A second structural change within indigenous industry was a particularly rapid decline among larger companies in internationally traded activities, while the number of small companies grew. This point was acknowledged by Mac Sharry and White (2000, p. 305) who observed "The casualty rate among Irish industry in this progression towards free trade was horrendous ... in the bigger companies with over 500 employees, the losses were even more devastating ... the stars of the traditional Irish industrial firmament were grievously, if not mortally, damaged".

The larger companies were generally engaged in activities in which there are significant economies of scale—hence their relatively large size by Irish standards. But they were generally not large enough to match larger foreign competitors under free trade, so that they were at a competitive disadvantage which hastened their decline. Thus, the National Economic and Social Council (1989, Chapter 6) noted that it is usually expected that introducing more free trade will induce an increased concentration of industry because of the existence of economies of scale. But they found that this did not hold true in Ireland's case, observing that "even the larger Irish producers, instead of eliminating the tail of smaller higher cost local producers, were themselves a part of the tail of smaller producers in a British and Irish, or European Market".

At the same time as many larger firms were declining, smaller firms, which would generally have been engaged in activities in which economies of scale are not important, increased in numbers. Even during the slump in indigenous industrial employment in the 1980s when there were many closures of existing firms, there was quite a high start-up rate of new small firms so that the total number of indigenous manufacturing firms scarcely changed.

By the mid-1980s, Irish indigenous industry was relatively lacking in large-scale enterprises, and there was relatively little indigenous activity in the sectors where economies of scale were most important and which were dominated by large firms in advanced economies. For example, there were seven sectors where large firms employing over 500 people accounted for over 70% of the sector's employment in West Germany, France, the UK and Italy in the mid-1980s.[13] About 40% of manufacturing employment in the European Community was in these seven sectors, but only 12% of Irish indigenous manufacturing employment was in the same sectors in 1987.

The existence of significant economies of scale, and the consequent presence of large established firms in many important industries in advanced economies, can be seen as a substantial barrier to the development of these industries by indigenous firms in a late-developing country that trades with advanced countries. For the indigenous firms generally would not have the resources needed to enter into competition on a competitive scale, or to survive a period of losses while trying to gain an adequate market share to be competitive. Protection was supposed to make it possible for Irish industries to get established by shutting out overwhelming competition from stronger firms already existing elsewhere. This succeeded to some extent but the Irish firms, in their small home market, often did not attain a scale of operation that was adequate to match foreign competitors under free trade.

Apart from economies of scale, there are also other significant types of barriers to entry for new or small firms arising from the strength of

[13] The seven sectors concerned were motor vehicles, other means of transport, chemicals, man-made fibres, production and preliminary processing of metals, office & data processing machinery and electrical engineering. The source of data on industry size structures is Eurostat, *Structure and Activity of Industry: Data by Size of Enterprises—1984.*

established competitors.[14] For example, new or small firms may not be able to match the technological capabilities already developed by established companies in sectors where technology is of key importance. Also, if strong marketing is an important requirement for an industry, the marketing strength of existing firms is a real entry barrier for new or small firms.

In addition, the advantages of external economies in existing industrial centres or districts can be a further obstacle to the development of newcomers in late-industrialising countries. Such external economies consist of the benefits of close contact with related firms, specialist suppliers and services, specialised labour skills, supportive institutions and perhaps a large local market. These types of advantages are commonly reflected in the existence of large and often specialised industrial towns and "clusters" of related industries. If external economies are important for an industry, it may be relatively easy for new firms to grow in existing locations of that industry, but this is a good deal less likely to happen in late-industrialising countries that do not have such strong industrial locations if they have to compete with the existing industries.

It is likely that such barriers to the development of latecomers are a major part of the explanation for the relatively poor development of Irish indigenous industry until the late 1980s. Many other potential explanations are not convincing. For example, the record of quite a high rate of start-ups of new small firms (see O'Farrell and Crouchley 1984) indicates that a spirit of entrepreneurial initiative was not lacking. Rather, the problem was that new start-ups were mostly restricted to small-scale activities, while large firms were declining. Also, many foreign MNCs found the Irish economic environment quite attractive (see Chapter 6), and they operated successfully in it. This shows that there must have been reasonably acceptable conditions in areas such as the quality of the labour force, transport and communications, the tax system or the political and administrative system.

It may be that the quality of native management skills had room for improvement, but it seems clear, nevertheless, that there was a certain amount of good quality management talent available. Thus, most of the foreign-owned MNCs in Ireland were willing to recruit their local management from within the country. Also, many of the larger Irish firms,

[14] Porter (1980, Chapter 1) includes a useful review of the principal types of barriers to entry that can occur in different industries.

including those in non-traded types of business, showed that they had the competence to engage successfully in international markets by taking over foreign firms in their own type of industry and becoming MNCs.

It has been argued that part of the problem of Irish indigenous industry in the 1980s was excessive wage increases, driven in particular by the presence of foreign-owned companies, which had higher and faster-growing productivity, and could therefore afford to pay wage increases that were excessive for indigenous companies with slower productivity growth. Barry (1996) argued along these lines, distinguishing between a group of "modern" predominantly foreign-owned sectors and a group of "traditional" predominantly Irish-owned sectors.[15] He found that, in 1980–1986, average weekly earnings increased by 12.4% per year in the modern sector while the rate of increase was almost as high at 11.2% per year in the traditional sector. At the same time, he found that the volume of net output per person engaged grew by 11.0% per year in the modern sector but at a much slower rate of 4.9% per year in the traditional sector.

However, this situation looks rather different if we also consider the growth rate of the *value* of net output per person engaged, for the purpose of comparing with earnings increases that are measured in current values. In fact, the value of net output per person engaged increased by 14.1% per year in the traditional sector in 1980–1986, which was more than the 11.2% per year increase in average weekly earnings. The value of net output per person engaged increased at an even higher rate of 18.1% per year in the modern sector.[16] Thus, rather than wage increases being too high for the traditional sector because they were more appropriate for the modern sector with its faster productivity growth, wage increases were in fact low enough to enhance the profitability of the traditional sector while being of even greater benefit to the profitability of the modern sector because of its faster productivity growth. Consequently, these wage trends do not help to explain the decline of traditional/indigenous industry in the years before the Celtic Tiger boom.

[15] The "modern" sectors were pharmaceuticals, office & data processing machinery, electrical engineering, instrument engineering and miscellaneous foods, while the "traditional" sectors were all other manufacturing sectors. Because of data constraints regarding the distinction between foreign-owned and Irish-owned industry per se, the modern category is sometimes used as a representative of foreign-owned industry while the traditional category is taken to be more representative of Irish-owned industry.

[16] Data from *Census of Industrial Production*.

Foreign-Owned Industry

The main source of growth of industry in Ireland from the 1960s to the 1980s was new investment by export-oriented foreign-owned MNCs.[17] By 1987 foreign firms accounted for 43% of manufacturing employment, 52% of manufacturing output and 74% of manufactured exports (*Census of Industrial Production*, 1987).

Until about the end of the 1960s, most FDI was in production of technologically mature, labour-intensive products such as clothing, footwear, textiles, plastic products and light engineering. Mature industries such as these, with standardised products, were most capable of being located in industrially undeveloped countries because they did not require close contact with the specialised skills, suppliers and services found in advanced industrial areas (Vernon 1966). Because they were generally quite labour-intensive, they had a motivation to move to relatively low-wage locations. The international relocation of such industries began quite early in relatively low-income countries on the periphery of the developed world, such as Puerto Rico and Ireland. Part of the attraction of Ireland was its tax concessions and grants while its wage levels were also lower than in the UK and much of Western Europe in the 1960s. From about the mid-1960s, such internationally mobile industries went increasingly to less-developed economies with much lower wages.

From about the late 1960s, export-oriented FDI in Ireland increasingly involved newer, more technologically advanced products, such as electrical and electronic products, machinery, pharmaceuticals and medical instruments and equipment. Typically, these industries placed only certain stages of production in Ireland, which were usually not the most technically demanding on local inputs and skills.

Again, there were some similarities here to the type of mobile industry that began going to less-developed countries from about the late 1960s (Helleiner 1973). However, the industries arriving in Ireland included some more highly skilled activities, particularly in electronics and pharmaceuticals, even though they usually lacked the most important business functions of the firm. Thus, in the early 1980s, the electronics industry in Ireland employed a significantly higher proportion of engineers and technicians than the electronics industries in Singapore or Hong Kong. At the

[17] See O'Malley (1989, Chapter 7) and O'Malley (1998b) for more details on developments outlined in this section.

same time, the industry in Ireland had a substantially lower proportion of engineers and technicians than the industries in the USA or UK, while the industry in Ireland undertook much less R & D in relation to sales than in the USA or UK (O'Brien 1985).

As regards the motivation for export-oriented FDI in Ireland, at first the main attractions were tax concessions, grants and relatively low-wage costs. After Ireland joined the EEC in 1973 there was the further significant attraction of assured access to the large EEC market, which was a major draw for growing numbers of companies from the USA. The basic objective of many of the foreign investors after that time was to establish a factory somewhere within the EEC (and later the EC or EU), to produce for sale in European markets, and then they selected Ireland as suitable for that purpose. Consequently, Ireland's main competitors in attracting such industries were usually other Western European countries rather than developing countries with far lower wages.

Another influence in attracting FDI to Ireland was the fact that the Industrial Development Authority (IDA) was doing an effective job in marketing Ireland as a location for expanding multinational companies. At the same time, the Irish education system managed to produce a good supply of graduates with the types of qualifications that were in strong demand for some rapidly growing industries internationally, e.g., electronics, pharmaceuticals and software. More generally, the fact that the Irish labour force is English-speaking was also an attraction for many overseas investors, particularly those from the USA.

Whereas employment in foreign-owned manufacturing grew almost continuously in the 1960s and 1970s, it reached a peak at 88,400 in 1980 and then fell continuously to 78,700 by 1987. Although this was a distinctly lower rate of decline than in the indigenous sector, it amounted to a decline of 11% over seven consecutive years.

The output of foreign-owned firms continued to grow quite fast for much of the 1980s, even while their employment was declining. But a problem as regards the contribution of this growth to the Irish economy was that most of the growth occurred in a small number of mostly foreign-owned sectors that had relatively limited linkages with the domestic economy. Thus, nearly all of the growth of industrial output in 1980–1987 was attributable to five sectors—pharmaceuticals, office & data processing machinery, electrical engineering, instrument engineering and "other foods"—while there was almost no growth in all other sectors combined (Baker 1988). These five sectors were importing a high proportion of their inputs and withdrawing very substantial profits from Ireland, so that data on their output alone would give a rather misleading impression of their impact on the economy.

What mattered for the Irish economy was not just the value of the output of foreign firms, but rather how much of that value was retained in Ireland, mainly in the form of payments of wages and taxes and purchases of Irish goods and services as inputs. Such expenditures in the Irish economy were a much lower proportion of the value of output in foreign-owned industry than in indigenous industry, and this was especially true of the five fast-growing sectors mentioned above. Thus in 1983 "Irish economy expenditures" amounted to 79% of the value of sales in indigenous industry compared with 44% in foreign-owned industry, while the figures for the five high-growth sectors ranged between 24 and 39%.[18] Therefore, although there was quite high growth of output in foreign-owned industry in 1980–1987, the declining trend in its employment was a serious indication that its contribution to Irish economic growth weakened in that period compared with the 1960s and 1970s.

Part of the reason for this weaker performance of foreign-owned industry was because the inflow of new foreign investment became somewhat weaker after 1981. This was partly because new US investment in Europe was declining or stagnating for much of the 1980s, while there was also growing competition from other European countries which were trying more actively to attract FDI.

Apart from the slowing down of new FDI in Ireland in the early 1980s, it had also become clear that foreign companies already established in Ireland tended to decline in employment eventually after an initial period of employment growth. This pattern was already established during the 1970s. For example, employment in foreign-owned manufacturing firms established before 1969 fell by 12% in 1973–1980, while total manufacturing employment was growing faster than in all other EC countries. This meant that the growth of total employment in foreign industry depended on a continuing strong inflow of new first-time foreign investors. As time went on, the overall employment trend in foreign-owned industry was increasingly influenced by the large stock of older plants with declining employment. Consequently, a continuously increasing inflow of new first-time investors was needed to maintain a

[18] Industrial Development Authority (1985), Table 2.1, and unpublished data from the survey reported in the same study.

given growth rate. In the 1980s, when new FDI was reduced, the result was that employment declined in most sectors in foreign-owned industry and in the foreign sector as a whole.

Industrial Policy Developments in the 1980s

In the early 1980s, the Telesis (1982) report to the National Economic and Social Council (NESC) made a number of criticisms of the practice of relying so heavily on FDI, and this point was largely taken on board by the NESC (1982). Trends in industry in the 1980s tended to support the view that more should be done to develop the indigenous sector, since heavy reliance on foreign industry was no longer producing the sort of results seen previously.

Beginning in the mid-1980s, a number of significant changes were made in industrial policy. The White Paper on *Industrial* Policy (1984) and subsequent official policy statements put an increased emphasis on the aim of developing Irish indigenous industry. This did not by any means imply an actual rejection of foreign-owned industry, but it did reflect some acceptance that there were limits to the benefits that could be expected from FDI and that the relatively poor long-term performance of indigenous industry called for a greater focus on addressing that problem.

More specifically, policy statements referred to a need for policy towards indigenous industry to be somewhat more selective, aiming to develop larger and stronger firms by building on those with a good record, rather than assisting a very large number of start-ups and very small firms indiscriminately. Policy was also intended to become more focused on specific areas of weakness that would be common in indigenous firms, such as technological capability, export marketing and management skills. It was intended to shift expenditures on industrial policy from simply supporting capital investment towards greater support for technology, export marketing and management (Industrial Policy 1984, Chapters 1 and 5; Department of Industry and Commerce 1987, Chapter 2).

Another prominent theme in statements of industrial policy objectives after the early 1980s, in a context of serious concern about the growing public debt, was an emphasis on making industrial policy measures more cost-effective in order to obtain better value for money. And a further notable theme was the objective of promoting greater integration of foreign-owned industry into the Irish economy. This meant aiming to have them purchase more of their inputs from Irish sources and to undertake in Ireland functions such as R&D and marketing, so as to increase their expenditures in Ireland and to generate greater technical spillovers for the domestic economy.

The introduction of policy changes in pursuit of these objectives was somewhat hesitant and gradual, and indeed there was some questioning about the real strength of commitment to the objectives. However, quite a number of relevant policy changes—of an incremental rather than a radical nature—were introduced over a period of some years.[19]

For example, the Company Development Programme was introduced in 1984. This involved staff of state development agencies with a range of expertise working with selected relatively promising indigenous companies on formulating and implementing strategic development plans. In addition, the National Linkage Programme commenced in 1985 with the aim of building on selected indigenous sub-supply companies which could supply components to the foreign MNCs. This programme also involved participation by development agency staff with a range of expertise. The role of the state agencies in these programmes was not to dictate development plans to the companies involved. Rather their role was to act as catalysts, sharing opinions, acting as information brokers and making suggestions on how they could assist a company's long-term development through their financial supports and services.

After the mid-1980s capital investment grants were awarded more selectively to firms with relatively good prospects for growth in international markets, in order to concentrate more on building larger firms. Thus, the group of existing firms (i.e., excluding new start-ups) that were awarded grant assistance in 1990 was only about half as large as the group awarded grants in 1984 (O'Malley et al. 1992, Chapter 3). Significantly, too, the award of such grants was increasingly made dependent on firms having prepared overall company development plans. In order to obtain better value for state expenditure, the average rate of capital grant was reduced after 1986 and a shift began towards repayable forms of financial support such as equity financing rather than capital grants. Given these constraints, together with the focus on relatively promising indigenous

[19] The relevant policy changes are summarised very briefly here. Further details can be found in official documents such as *Industrial* Policy (1984) and Department of Industry and Commerce (1987, 1990) and in O'Malley et al. (1992).

firms, the share of the industrial policy budget going to support capital investment declined from 61% in 1985 to 47% in 1992.

There was a corresponding shift towards measures other than capital grants. From 1985, new initiatives were introduced to strengthen export marketing capabilities of Irish firms, and expenditure on marketing measures increased from 11% of the industrial policy budget in 1985 to 17% in 1992. Such marketing measures were redirected from short-term operational support towards developing companies' long-term potential, and this support was focused more selectively on indigenous firms. Science and technology policies for industry were also substantially reorganised and new measures were introduced such as technology acquisition grants, subsidised technology audits of firms and subsidised placement of graduates and experienced technologists in firms. Expenditure on science and technology measures increased from 11% of the industrial policy budget in 1985 to 21% in 1992. Other new measures introduced starting in the mid-1980s included management development grants to strengthen the quality of management in indigenous firms.

In addition to these policy changes, there was also a substantial reorganisation of the institutional arrangements for implementing policy. Responsibility for promoting indigenous industry was separated from the task of encouraging FDI, to ensure that there would be a body of state agency staff focusing their full attention on the indigenous sector.[20]

Another type of initiative beginning in the mid-1980s was the formulation of sectoral development strategies or plans for some selected sectors. The purpose of these strategies was to identify development opportunities, and to help to focus the state agencies on building on areas of actual or potential competitive advantage and on correcting identified weaknesses.

It was argued above that Irish indigenous industry often faced various barriers or obstacles to its development arising from the established advantages of competitors in advanced countries such as superior scale, technological capabilities, marketing, etc. If so, then some of the changes in Irish industrial policy in the 1980s look like relevant responses—including the measures to build larger and stronger firms and to focus assistance more on improving specific capabilities such as technological

[20] This was done initially in 1988 by an internal reorganisation within the Industrial Development Authority (IDA) that established separate divisions for indigenous and overseas industry. Since 1993 there have been separate agencies for these two functions.

and marketing capabilities rather than just providing general support for investment.

While policies to develop Irish indigenous industry changed quite significantly after the early 1980s, there was less change in policies for foreign-owned industry. The National Linkage Programme, as mentioned above, was relevant for foreign-owned companies since it aimed to strengthen the local purchasing linkages between foreign multinationals and indigenous suppliers. More generally, policy placed more emphasis on the desirability of attracting foreign firms which would establish key business functions in Ireland such as R&D or marketing, rather than production alone. To this end, the IDA had flexibility to negotiate on the rate of grant assistance it would offer to foreign investors. The rate of grant assistance offered to a project could be made to depend on the expected level of linkages with Irish suppliers and on the type and quality of business functions that would be located in Ireland, as well as other factors.

2.3 Macroeconomic Trends 1960s–1980s

For much of the 1960s and 1970s overall economic growth in Ireland was quite strong, but this was followed by a period of persistent recession or slow growth in 1980–1986. Table 2.1 shows the main trends in output, employment and income per head in these decades before the Celtic Tiger boom. In 1961–1973 GDP grew by 4.4% p.a. and the growth of GNP was almost identical. However, the growth of employment in industry and services was barely sufficient to offset a decline in agricultural employment so that there was only a slight increase in total employment. As noted in Sect. 2.1, this resulted in a rate of net emigration amounting to about one-quarter of the annual number of school leavers.

Table 2.1 Annual percentage change in output, employment and income per head

	GDP	*GNP*	*Employment*	*Population*	*GNP per head*
1961–1973	4.4	4.3	0.2	0.7	3.5
1973–1980	4.0	3.4	1.2	1.5	1.9
1980–1986	1.5	0.0	−1.1	0.7	−0.7

Source Derived from Department of Finance, *Budgetary and Economic Statistics*, October 2012

With the arrival of the oil crisis in 1973 there was a marked slowdown in growth across the international economy but growth in Ireland slowed relatively little. Thus, GDP grew by 4.0% p.a. while GNP grew by 3.4% p.a. in 1973–1980. In addition, this period was exceptional compared to Ireland's previous experience in the sense that there was considerable growth in total employment and the traditional pattern of net emigration was replaced by net immigration.

All the main trends worsened substantially in 1980–1986. Growth of GDP was much slower while there was no growth in GNP, employment declined considerably, population growth slowed down, GNP per head declined and net emigration resumed. However, the scope for emigration was relatively limited in this period because of rising unemployment in the UK and other countries.[21] The combination of constraints on emigration, declining employment and natural growth of the labour force resulted in an unprecedented increase in the unemployment rate to 17% in 1986. In addition, the current account of the balance of payments was in deficit by more than 10% of GNP from 1979 to 1982, and the public finances became a serious cause for concern as high levels of public borrowing pushed the national debt up to 115% of GNP by 1986 and further to 118% in 1987.

Although the economic crisis in 1980–1986 looks very different from the relatively good times that preceded it in the 1960s and 1970s, there were weaknesses in the economic performance of the earlier period that are not very evident in the principal macro-level trends, and there were connections or continuities between the crisis in the 1980s and developments in the preceding period.

For one thing, as was discussed above in Sect. 2.2, the internationally traded branches of Irish indigenous industry had generally not fared well in the transition to free trade in the late 1960s and 1970s since they experienced a net loss of market share. This point was recognised by the National Economic and Social Council (1989) who concluded:

"… the economic performance in the first period of EC membership (1973–1980) was not as strong as is suggested by growth rates of aggregates, such as income or consumption or even manufactured production.

[21] Although the 1980s seems to be remembered by many in Ireland as a time of particularly high emigration, the rate of net emigration in 1981–86 was 4.1 per thousand of population which was a little less than the rate of 4.7 per thousand in 1961–1971 and far less than the rate of 14.1 per thousand in 1951–1961.

In particular, the position of indigenous industry in traded sectors was disturbing. But this implies a distinct *continuity* between the seventies and eighties – for indigenous manufacturing suffered even greater losses in the later period." (NESC 1989, pp. 207, 208).

The growth of FDI was more than sufficient to outweigh the weakness of indigenous industry and to generate strong industrial growth in the 1970s. Ireland's EEC membership from 1973 onwards encouraged a surge of new FDI by US companies aiming to produce for the EEC market. As was outlined in Sect. 2.2, however, the overall process of industrial expansion had become very dependent on obtaining a continuously increasing inflow of new first-time FDI. Consequently, if the inflow of new FDI were to weaken the result was always going to be a much poorer performance for the industrial sector as a whole. Such a weakening of new FDI eventually happened after 1981, reflecting the fact that new US investment in Europe was declining or stagnating while there was also increased competition from other European countries who wanted to attract FDI.

Another connection between economic developments in the 1970s and the 1980s was the conduct of fiscal policy. An important but ultimately unsustainable factor that enhanced the growth of output and employment in the 1970s was the growth of public borrowing and public service employment. In response to recessionary trends in the international economy the current budget deficit was first increased from 0.4% of GNP in 1973/1974 to 6.8% in 1975 while the total exchequer borrowing requirement (EBR) rose from 7.5 to 15.8% of GNP. Public borrowing was then reduced in 1976 and 1977 as the international economy improved. However, with Irish unemployment remaining relatively high by previous standards, the current budget deficit was pushed up again from 3.6% of GNP in 1977 to 6.8% or more in 1979 and the early 1980s while the EBR rose from 9.7% of GNP in 1977 to over 15% in the early 1980s.

This debt-financed expansion of public expenditure had a major impact on employment. While total employment grew by 8.3% in 1973–1980, employment in "non-market services" (public administration & defence, health and education) grew by 34.2% and employment in the rest of the economy grew by just 4.2%.[22] This meant that almost 60% of the

[22] Derived from ESRI Databank.

increase in total employment was in public services. Expansionary public spending would also have been partly responsible for the employment increase in other sectors through its impact on domestic demand so that probably at least three-quarters of the increase in total employment was attributable to the growth of public spending. Consequently, in the absence of this growth of public expenditure, 1973–1980 would not have been a particularly exceptional period for employment growth and net emigration would probably have continued or else unemployment would have increased more rapidly.

However, high levels of public borrowing to fund growing expenditure led to a growing national debt as well as large current balance of payments deficits. It became accepted in the 1980s that these trends were not sustainable. Consequently, tax increases and spending cuts were implemented during the 1980s and this had a depressing effect on domestic demand, which contributed to the severity of the 1980s recession.

A further connection between events in the 1970s and the crisis in the 1980s lay in the experience of the agriculture sector. As a large net exporter of agricultural products, a major motivation for Ireland in joining the EEC in 1973 had been to gain access to the large EEC market, which had high prices for agricultural output under the Common Agricultural Policy (CAP). Although there were some initial complications and setbacks, Ireland's EEC membership led to strong progress in Irish farm incomes between 1973 and 1978 as prices for Irish products were aligned upwards during a transition period. However, this progress in farm incomes was subsequently reversed in 1978–1986 as product prices weakened under a more restrictive CAP while the cost of agricultural inputs rose more rapidly (NESC 1989, pp. 89–92). The operation of the CAP involved a considerable net transfer of resources into the Irish economy. The value of these net transfers into Ireland rose from zero before 1973 to almost 10% of GNP by 1979 according to one definition, but then dipped to little more than 5% of GNP in 1981–1983 with a partial recovery towards 8% in 1985 and 1986 (NESC 1989, pp. 92–96).

To summarise, three significant factors combined to outweigh the weakness of indigenous industry and to boost the Irish economy temporarily in the 1970s—a surge in FDI on joining the EEC, debt-financed expansion of public expenditure and an initial boom in the agriculture sector as EEC membership took effect. All three factors contributed something to the exceptional growth of employment in the

1970s, but the expansion of public expenditure was the major influence in that regard. Without these factors, especially the growth of public spending, the old weakness concerning poor employment trends and constant emigration or unemployment would have continued to be evident.

The long period of recession or slow growth in 1980–1986 was partly caused by the international recession that followed the second oil crisis in 1979. But Ireland's recession in the 1980s was a good deal more severe and prolonged than in most other countries, mainly because of the continuing weakness of Irish indigenous industry combined with the weakening or reversal of the three factors outlined above that had boosted growth temporarily in the 1970s.

Incidentally, some of the same trends discussed above also explain (see Box 2.1) why the growth rates of GDP and GNP began to diverge in the 1970s and diverged even further in the 1980s, as was seen in Table 2.1.

Box 2.1: Why GDP and GNP Diverged

The values of GNP and GDP were the same in 1973 but GNP amounted to just 97% of GDP by 1980 and 91% by 1986.

The difference between GDP and GNP is the net flow of factor incomes from or to the rest of the world. Such factor incomes consist of items such as interest payments, profits and dividends that can flow either into or out of the country. If there is a net inflow of such factor incomes, GNP is higher than GDP and the country's income is higher than the value of its production, whereas a net outflow of such factor incomes makes GNP lower than GDP and the country's income is lower than the value of its production.

In most countries GDP and GNP are usually almost equal. In Ireland's case GNP was falling increasingly below GDP mainly because there was an increasing outflow of profits, dividends and royalties from foreign-owned companies as the sales and profits of such companies grew, and because there was an increasing outflow of national debt interest arising from the part of the national debt that had been raised abroad. By 1987 the gross outflow of profits, dividends and royalties amounted to over 6% of GDP while the gross outflow of national debt interest came to 4% of GDP.

Some economists (for example, Honohan and Walsh 2002) have offered an interpretation of the experience of the Irish economy in the 1960s–1980s that differs significantly from the account outlined above.

In particular, some suggest that the economy was performing well under broadly orthodox policies until about 1973, and the future outlook for the economy was promising with the potential for living standards to catch up with UK or other advanced European levels. However, the economy was then driven into major difficulties by a series of fiscal policy errors, which derailed the potential for such a rise in living standards.

In this account the fiscal policy errors involved borrowing in order to increase public expenditure, especially the decision to respond to continuing high unemployment with a highly expansionary fiscal policy from 1977 onwards. It was argued that this helped to drive up wages, undermining competitiveness and deterring investment. The rising public debt eventually led to tax increases in the 1980s, placing more upward pressure on wages and causing a reduction in domestic demand, while high-interest rates were a further deterrent to investment. This made Ireland's recession in the 1980s more severe than the general international experience.

This view is fairly widespread, and indeed Honohan and Walsh (2002) were probably quite right in suggesting that many people in 1973 felt that the economy was doing well and had good prospects. Economic growth had been quite strong since about 1960 and there was undoubtedly a general awareness that trends in employment and emigration had been much more favourable in 1960–1973 than in the 1950s. Nevertheless, the fact remains that there had been virtually no employment growth over the period 1960–1972 which resulted in a rate of net emigration amounting to about one-quarter of the annual number of school leavers. This was relatively good by comparison with Ireland's experience in the 1950s, but it was still very unsatisfactory compared with common experience in many other European countries. It is particularly significant that employment as a percentage of the population in Ireland had declined from 37.1% in 1960 to 34.8% in 1973. As long as that trend continued, there could be no realistic prospect of a convergence in living standards to reach the level of the UK and other advanced European economies, since such a convergence would have required Ireland's output per person employed to rise far above the levels attained in those countries—probably about 35–50% above their levels.

In addition, looking deeper than such macro-level trends, there were weaknesses in the industrial sector as discussed above. These were only beginning to emerge in the early 1970s, but they were set to become increasingly evident regardless of fiscal policy decisions. Fiscal policy in the

1970s was not the primary or essential cause of major difficulties in the economy, since the economy already had real problems that were quite independent of fiscal policy.

The fiscal policy of the 1970s mainly had the effect of postponing problems, by alleviating real difficulties in the 1970s while pushing the costs of doing so back into the 1980s. Thus, if there had been a more conservative and essentially neutral fiscal policy in the 1970s, growth would probably have been slower in that decade and there would have been very little employment growth with consequent continuation of net emigration and/or more rapidly rising unemployment. The policy that was adopted in the 1970s increased the rate of economic growth and particularly boosted employment growth directly and indirectly. The price that had to be paid for this was the growing national debt which eventually led to fiscal retrenchment in the 1980s with consequent reduction in domestic demand. This was one of a number of factors that reduced the rate of economic growth and put downward pressure on employment in the 1980s.

The costs of this fiscal policy on the downside in the 1980s were somewhat greater than the benefits on the upside in the 1970s because debts have to be repaid with interest, and interest rates were rising internationally. However, the evidence does not support the contention that expansionary fiscal policy was more damaging than that because it drove up wages and deterred investment.

As was discussed in Sect. 2.1, Irish wages had been close to the UK level for a few decades before the Second World War, had dropped well below that level in the 1940s and had then risen again towards the UK level during the post-war period. This rising trend flattened out as Irish wages arrived fairly close to parity with the UK level in the late 1970s. From the late 1970s until after 2000, Irish labour costs fluctuated around 90% of the UK level, with the fluctuations mainly arising from changes in the exchange rate (FitzGerald 2004).

Rather than fiscal expansion generating exceptional increases in labour costs, it can be seen in a chart presented by FitzGerald (2004) that the long-term rise in Ireland's labour costs relative to the UK stopped temporarily in 1973–1975 coinciding with the first phase of fiscal expansion. That long-term rise stopped more permanently as the second phase of fiscal expansion began in 1977, apart from subsequent fluctuations caused mainly by the exchange rate.

Similarly, the National Economic and Social Council (1989, Fig. 5.10) showed that Ireland's hourly earnings in manufacturing, adjusted for exchange rate changes, were rising relative to the UK until 1977 but then flattened out and declined somewhat relative to the UK in the early 1980s. Looking at the same indicator relative to all main trading partners, NESC (1989, Fig. 5.12) found a slowly rising trend in most of the 1970s but no further rise from 1978 to 1985. NESC (1989) also reported that if one examines unit labour costs, so as to take account of productivity growth, Ireland's relative unit labour costs generally rose more slowly or declined more rapidly than the trends in its relative earnings—with favourable implications for Ireland's cost competitiveness.

In addition, in Sect. 2.2 above it was noted that average earnings rose more slowly than the value of net output per person engaged in both the "modern" and "traditional" branches of Irish manufacturing in 1980–1986. This trend would have enhanced profitability and it could have been of some benefit for competitiveness. Specifically, average weekly earnings increased by 12.4% per year in the "modern" sector while the value of its net output per person engaged increased by 18.1% per year. In the "traditional" sector average weekly earnings increased by 11.2% per year while the value of its net output per person engaged increased by 14.1% per year.

2.4 Conclusion

In the mid-1980s, just before the Celtic Tiger period began, the Irish economy had very serious problems. The longstanding failure to generate sufficient employment was very much in evidence as there was a substantial rate of emigration together with an unprecedented level of unemployment. Consequently, the proportion of the population that was in employment was exceptionally low at just 31%. Largely reflecting that situation, average incomes (GNP per head of population) were relatively low at little more than 60% of the UK or EU levels, and there had been little sign of convergence towards EU levels for decades. In addition, the national debt as a percentage of GNP was very high and still rising until 1987 despite measures that had been taken to cut budget deficits since the early 1980s.

An important factor underlying these problems was an industrial sector that appeared to be in crisis. Much of Irish indigenous industry had been experiencing major difficulties as a result of stronger competition under free trade. Reliance on FDI as a substitute had perhaps seemed like a viable strategy in the 1970s but looked increasingly inadequate in the 1980s. Some new industrial policy measures had been introduced in the mid-1980s but it remained to be seen if they would make any difference.

Despite this unpromising situation, the Irish economy was about to begin two decades of extraordinary growth. That remarkable experience has naturally prompted many people to try to explain what caused this growth. The next chapter provides a survey of the literature that has aimed to explain what caused the boom, including some preliminary assessment of the explanations that have been suggested.

References

Baker, T.J. 1988. *Industrial Output and Wage Costs 1980–87*. Quarterly Economic Commentary, October. Dublin: The Economic and Social Research Institute.

Barry, Frank. 1996. Peripherality in Economic Geography and Modern Growth Theory: Evidence from Ireland's Adjustment to Free Trade. *World Economy* 19 (3): 345–365.

Barry, Frank. 1999. Irish Growth in Historical and Theoretical Perspective. In *Understanding Ireland's Economic Growth*, ed. Frank Barry, 25–44. London: Macmillan and New York: St Martin's Press.

Committee on Industrial Organisation. 1965. *Final Report*. Dublin: Stationery Office.

Department of Industry and Commerce. 1987. *Review of Industrial Performance 1986*. Dublin: Stationery Office.

Department of Industry and Commerce. 1990. *Review of Industrial Performance 1990*. Dublin: Stationery Office.

FitzGerald, John. 2004. Lessons from 20 Years of Cohesion. ESRI Working Paper No. 159. Economic and Social Research Institute, Dublin.

Helleiner, G.K. 1973. Manufactured Exports from the Less Developed Countries and Multinational Firms. *Economic Journal* 83 (329): 21–47.

Honohan, Patrick, and Brendan Walsh. 2002. Catching Up with the Leaders: The Irish Hare. *Brookings Papers on Economic Activity* 2002 (1): 1–57.

Industrial Development Authority. 1985. *The Irish Economy Expenditures of the Irish Manufacturing Sector*. Dublin: IDA.

Industrial Policy. (1984). Government White Paper. Stationery Office, Dublin.

Kennedy, Kieran A., Thomas Giblin, and Deirdre McHugh. 1988. *The Economic Development of Ireland in the Twentieth Century*. London: Routledge.

Mac Sharry, Ray, and Padraic White. 2000. *The Making of the Celtic Tiger: The Inside Story of Ireland's Boom Economy*. Cork and Dublin: Mercier Press.

National Economic and Social Council. 1982. Policies for Industrial Development: Conclusions and Recommendations. Report No. 66. NESC, Dublin.

National Economic and Social Council. 1989. Ireland in the European Community: Performance, Prospects and Strategy. Report No. 88. NESC, Dublin.

O'Brien, Ronan. 1985. Technology and Industrial Development: The Irish Electronics Industry in an International Context. In *Perspectives on Irish Industry*, ed. J. Fitzpatrick and J. Kelly. Dublin: Irish Management Institute.

O'Farrell, P.N., and R. Crouchley. 1984. An Industrial and Spatial Analysis of New Firm Formation in Ireland. *Regional Studies* 18 (3): 221–236.

Ó Gráda, Cormac. 1994. *Ireland: A New Economic History 1780–1939*. Oxford: Oxford University Press.

Ó Gráda, Cormac, and Kevin O'Rourke. 1996. Irish Economic Growth, 1945–88. In *Economic Growth in Europe Since 1945*, ed. N.F.R. Crafts and G. Toniolo. Cambridge: Cambridge University Press.

O'Leary, Eoin. 2015. *Irish Economic Development: High-Performing EU State or Serial Under-Achiever?* Abingdon and New York: Routledge.

O'Malley, Eoin. 1981. The Decline of Irish Industry in the Nineteenth Century. *Economic and Social Review* 13 (1): 21–42. Reprinted in Cormac Ó. Gráda, ed. 1994. *The Economic Development of Ireland Since 1870*. Aldershot: Edward Elgar.

O'Malley, Eoin. 1989. *Industry and Economic Development: The Challenge for the Latecomer*. Dublin: Gill and Macmillan.

O'Malley, Eoin. 1998a, April. The Revival of Irish Indigenous Industry 1987–1997. In *Quarterly Economic Commentary*, ed. T.J. Baker, David Duffy and Fergal Shortall. Dublin: Economic and Social Research Institute.

O'Malley, Eoin. 1998b. Industrial Policy in Ireland and the Problem of Late Development. In *Latecomers in the Global Economy*, ed. Michael Storper, Stavros B. Thomadakis, and Lena J. Tsipouri. London and New York: Routledge.

O'Malley, Eoin. 1999. Ireland: From Inward to Outward Policies. In *European Industrial Policy: The Twentieth-Century Experience*, ed. James Foreman-Peck and Giovanni Federico. Oxford: Oxford University Press.

O'Malley, Eoin, Kieran A. Kennedy, and Rory O'Donnell. 1992. The Impact of the Industrial Development Agencies. Report to the Industrial Policy Review Group. Stationery Office, Dublin.

Porter, Michael E. 1980. *Competitive Strategy: Techniques for Analysing Industries and Competitors*. New York: Free Press.

Telesis Consultancy Group. 1982. A Review of Industrial Policy. National Economic and Social Council Report No. 64. NESC, Dublin.

Vernon, Raymond. 1966. International Investment and International Trade in the Product Cycle. *Quarterly Journal of Economics* 80 (2): 190–207.

Open Access This chapter is licensed under the terms of the Creative Commons Attribution 4.0 International License (http://creativecommons.org/licenses/by/4.0/), which permits use, sharing, adaptation, distribution and reproduction in any medium or format, as long as you give appropriate credit to the original author(s) and the source, provide a link to the Creative Commons license and indicate if changes were made.

The images or other third party material in this chapter are included in the chapter's Creative Commons license, unless indicated otherwise in a credit line to the material. If material is not included in the chapter's Creative Commons license and your intended use is not permitted by statutory regulation or exceeds the permitted use, you will need to obtain permission directly from the copyright holder.

CHAPTER 3

A Review of Explanations for the Boom

This chapter presents a survey of the literature that has aimed to explain what caused the boom.[1] Most of this literature agrees that there was no single explanation for the boom and that the boom was caused by some combination of a number of explanatory factors, but there are widely varying views on which factors were important. The aim in Sect. 3.1 of this chapter is to present virtually all of the economic explanations that have been advanced, but it will not be possible to refer to every individual item of literature that discusses these explanations.

This chapter does not aim to reach final conclusions on how much each explanatory factor contributed to causing the boom. However, Sect. 3.2 includes some assessment of the suggested explanations, concluding that a number of them are not convincing or not very important whereas the others will call for further consideration and assessment in later chapters in this book.

[1] Parts of this chapter are adapted from O'Malley (2012).

© The Author(s) 2024

E. O'Malley, *Ireland's Long Economic Boom*, Palgrave Studies in Economic History, https://doi.org/10.1007/978-3-031-53070-8_3

3.1 Explanations for the Boom

Fiscal Stabilisation

Fiscal stabilisation was often cited as one cause of the boom. This was against the background of rising public debt in the 1980s which culminated with the debt reaching a peak of 118% of GNP in 1987. The government cut current and capital expenditure in 1987, reducing the budget deficit and the debt/GNP ratio from that year onwards. Economic growth began to improve almost immediately after years of very poor performance.

Giavazzi and Pagano (1990) suggested that this could have been an example of expansionary fiscal contraction (EFC), meaning that the fiscal contraction stimulated economic expansion. In principle, an EFC could occur if the deflationary impact of fiscal contraction on demand is outweighed by a boost to private investment and consumption resulting from improved confidence and expectations concerning future taxation, etc. (See Considine and Duffy 2007, for more on the EFC concept).

Bradley and Whelan (1997) used a small open economy macro econometric model of Ireland to assess this issue and they concluded that it was unlikely that an EFC could have occurred in Ireland. Honohan (1999) showed that the actual sequence of events was in the wrong order for an EFC. The economic recovery was led by very strong growth of exports in 1987, followed by smaller increases in the growth of consumption in 1988 and 1989, with investment beginning to recover only in 1989. It became largely agreed among economists in Ireland that there was no EFC in the late 1980s. Rather, the economic recovery was led by export growth which was stimulated by various conditions (e.g., Bradley et al. 1997; Bradley and Whelan 1997; OECD 1999; Honohan 1999; FitzGerald 2000; Bergin et al. 2010).

Despite the scepticism about fiscal contraction being the immediate cause of economic recovery in the late 1980s, it was nevertheless widely held that fiscal stabilisation had substantial long-run benefits. For example, it was seen as the "main precondition for a sustained economic recovery" (Mac Sharry and White 2000), and it "injected a crucial element of long-term confidence about the direction of policy" (Honohan 1999). Similar views were expressed by the OECD (1999), Honohan and Walsh (2002), Gallagher et al. (2002), NESC (2003) and Leddin and Walsh (2003).

Tax Cuts, Smaller Government

In political debate and media commentary it was frequently claimed that tax cuts were a major cause of the boom, but this view is scarcer or more qualified in the academic literature on the subject. Leddin and Walsh (1997) noted that tax declined from 41% to 34% of GDP between 1986 and 1996 and they described this as a "growth promoting factor". Powell (2003) argued that cuts in government spending in the late 1980s reduced the size of the government's role in the economy and he linked this to the recovery in growth at that time. He also argued that later reductions in income tax rates, as well as some cuts in corporation tax (see below), helped to bring about higher growth rates in the 1990s. He pointed out that by 1999 tax amounted to just 31% of GDP, almost the lowest level in the EU. Haughton (2005) similarly argued that the relatively limited role of the state was a pro-growth factor, with tax at just 31% of GDP in the early 2000s compared to 42% for the EU.

Leddin and Walsh (2003, p.481) expressed a significantly qualified view on the role of tax cuts by referring to the question of cause and effect. They said, "rapid growth of the economy has facilitated tax reductions and it is difficult to disentangle cause and effect", and there was a "virtuous circle with faster growth leading to lower tax and public debt burdens" which in turn reinforced the economy's performance. Honohan and Walsh's (2002) view was similar. Walsh's (2000) emphasis seemed somewhat different when he wrote that "no dramatic changes in tax rates or in the structure of taxation occurred in the late 1980s that can be identified as the factor that triggered the boom. And it is obvious that the rapid decline in the tax: GDP ratio during the 1990s was primarily a reflection of the large inflow of FDI and the exceptional growth of GDP rather than vice versa".

Most of the other literature on causes of the boom does not mention tax cuts although some authors explicitly rejected the idea that tax cuts were a cause of the boom. They argued that strong economic growth came first—with rising employment, falling unemployment, etc.—and this made it possible to cut taxes (Ó Gráda 2002; Sweeney 2004).

In the specific area of corporation tax, a very low rate of tax had already applied to manufacturing and selected internationally traded services well before the late 1980s. However, Conefrey and FitzGerald (2011) pointed out that a low corporation tax rate was gradually extended to the remaining services sectors over the late 1990s and early 2000s. They estimated that this had the effect of increasing the level of GNP in 2005 by 3.7% above what it would have been otherwise. This may be compared to GNP growth of 90% over the decade prior to 2005.

Delayed or Belated Convergence

In the 1990s it was occasionally argued that one factor that made some contribution to the boom was a suggested natural tendency for the income level of poorer countries to catch up with, or to converge on, the level of broadly comparable richer countries—if they had adequate preconditions and sound policies (Leddin and Walsh 1997; Sachs 1997; de la Fuente and Vives 1997).[2]

Ó Gráda (2002) put more emphasis on this natural convergence argument. Referring to Ó Gráda and O'Rourke (2000), he pointed out that in 1950–1987 other relatively low-income members of the OECD were converging towards the OECD average level of GDP per head, but Ireland failed to do so. Then rapid Irish growth in the period 1987–1998 put Ireland back "on track", so that over the whole period 1950–1998 Ireland's record of convergence was comparable to general OECD experience. Ó Gráda (2002) argued that Ireland had many of the conditions necessary for faster growth in the period before 1987 but it was held back initially by protectionism, and subsequently by "wrong-headed fiscal policy" in the late 1970s and early 1980s. However, by 1987 Ireland was beginning to overcome the earlier fiscal policy mistakes. Together with an inflow of US FDI and a stronger international economy, this allowed the "Celtic Tiger interlude" to make up the ground that had been lost.[3]

Honohan and Walsh's (2002) main explanation for the boom was similar in some respects. They said that by 1973 Ireland had the

[2] Ó Gráda and O'Rourke (2000) discussed the theoretical reasons why such convergence could tend to occur, such as higher returns to investment in poorer countries and their ability to import capital and advanced technology from richer countries.

[3] A later article, by Ó Gráda and O'Rourke (2021), made little reference to correction of fiscal policy errors as a trigger for the boom. Rather, it mentioned a number of possible causes, such as currency devaluations, a booming European economy, social partnership and a favourable monetary policy—while highlighting the important role of FDI in combination with the single European market, which was "an important turning point for the country".

preconditions needed for convergence and many foresaw a steady convergence towards UK and European levels "within a generation". However, convergence was derailed for more than a decade by a series of fiscal policy errors in the 1970s. When these errors were eventually corrected, this allowed convergence to occur, facilitated by a pro-employment approach to wage bargaining. Honohan and Walsh also noted that, although GDP per head of population was far lower in Ireland than in the UK in the 1970s, non-agricultural GDP per person engaged was about the same in both countries. This meant that convergence, when it eventually occurred, was "a belated convergence not in productivity but in the share of the population at work outside low-income agriculture".

Responding to Honohan and Walsh, Blanchard (2002) said that they went too far in saying that it was a "simple, run of the mill, catch-up story". Ireland's economic performance since 1987 was too impressive for that since it looked "quite miraculous". Responding to Ó Gráda, Barry (2002) accepted that poor policy could inhibit convergence, but he argued that "there are few models that propose that inappropriate policies act merely as a dam behind which the thwarted convergence forces build up … so that when appropriate policies are eventually adopted the lost ground is made up for all the more rapidly". As a further objection to the delayed convergence explanation for the boom, Barry asked why Ireland had not converged during the 1960s. He did not accept that this was due to delays in removing protection and improving education, because Ireland was ahead of Spain, Portugal and Greece in these respects yet those countries had quite strong convergence in the 1960s while Ireland did not. He also asked why the average income in Ireland had still been at the same level relative to the UK in 1960 as it was in 1913.

Haughton (2005) found that although there was a general convergence tendency among OECD countries over the period 1960–2002, there was not a significant convergence tendency during the second half of that period, 1980–2002. Therefore, Ireland's rapid growth phase was exceptional and called for an explanation. NESC (2003, Chapter 1) also considered the delayed convergence perspective proposed by Ó Gráda (2002) and Honohan and Walsh (2002) but they decided that they were "not persuaded" by it.

Strong Demand Growth in Export Markets

It was often stated that rapid growth in overseas demand made a significant contribution to the boom. This point was made mainly in relation to the late 1980s and 1993–2000. It is commonly recognised that Ireland's economic recovery in the late 1980s was partly attributable to strong growth in demand for Irish exports particularly in the UK (Bradley et al. 1997; Honohan 1999; Mac Sharry and White 2000). As regards 1993–2000, Kennedy (2000/2001) observed that overseas demand for imports grew far more rapidly than might have been expected from looking at GDP growth of the countries concerned. For example, in the EU, GDP grew by 2.5% per year while imports grew by 8.1% per year, perhaps because of the Single European Market. The volume of Irish exports increased by 16.5% per year in 1993–2000, which could be broken down into 7.8% per year being attributable to Ireland's performance in gaining market share while 8.0% per year was attributable to the growth of the markets themselves (Kennedy 2000/2001; NESC 2003, Chapter 1).

Supply of Labour

Quite a number of studies observed that Ireland had the benefit of a plentiful supply of labour in the boom years. Some of them identified and quantified the principal sources of this growing labour supply—a relatively high birth rate until about 1980, a large number of unemployed people in the late 1980s, a large number of emigrants abroad many of whom were willing to return, and rising female participation in the labour force starting from an unusually low initial level (Bradley et al. 1997; FitzGerald 1998, 2000; OECD 1999). Some authors also noted that a plentiful labour supply in the past had commonly resulted in more emigration or unemployment, rather than rising employment (Bradley et al. 1997; FitzGerald 1998; NESC 2003, Chapter 1).

Education, Human Capital

Rising levels of education have been very widely mentioned as making a significant contribution to the boom (e.g., Sweeney 1998, 2008; Gallagher et al. 2002). There is plenty of evidence showing that there were increasing levels of educational attainment in the population and labour force before and during the boom years (e.g., Bradley et al. 1997;

Durkan et al. 1999; OECD 1999; Duffy et al. 2001). Using the higher earnings levels of more highly educated people as an indicator of their higher productivity, Durkan et al. (1999) estimated that the rising education level of the labour force in 1986–1996 added 1% p.a. to the effective labour force, in the sense of making the labour force more productive to that extent (see also FitzGerald 2000).

Kennedy (2000/2001) observed that the same type of analysis showed that rising education levels were having an even greater impact on productivity in the early 1980s than during the boom years. He argued that rising education levels therefore could not account for the *acceleration* in economic growth that occurred in the Celtic Tiger boom (unless human capital affected growth in ways that are not captured by this type of analysis). He concluded that the outstanding new feature of the boom was the increasing utilisation of labour rather than the increase in its quality. Honohan and Walsh (2002) noted that education attainment levels had been rising for a long time before the boom and there was "no significant inflection point in the 1980s". They said that, like some other long-standing factors, this was an important part of the policy environment, but it could not explain the boom.

It has sometimes been noted, with varying degrees of emphasis, that in order for increased education to have an impact on the economy there had to be a context of adequate demand for the resulting skilled labour (e.g., Breathnach 1998; NESC 2003, Chapter 1). In the past many skilled workers had emigrated, especially in the 1980s (Bradley et al. 1997; Breathnach 2004). As Ó Gráda and O'Rourke (2000) put it, "in an economy like Ireland, the key issue is not how many graduates can be created, but how many of them can be provided with jobs at home".

Relating to this issue of demand for skilled labour, a number of authors suggested that there was an important interaction between rising levels of education and FDI, because new FDI created demand for skilled labour while at the same time the availability of skilled labour was a significant feature attracting new FDI into Ireland (FitzGerald 1998, 2000; Kennedy 2000/2001; Duffy et al. 2001; Barry 2005; Mac Sharry and White 2000).

Some studies examined international comparative indicators of educational expenditure, standards, participation rates, graduation rates, etc. and they found rather mixed results for Ireland with some strengths and some weaknesses. The education system looked good in certain respects, but not especially impressive overall compared to the EU or OECD (Ó

Gráda 2002; Barry 2005; O'Malley et al. 2008). However, Barry (2005) and Crafts (2005) highlighted the apparent strength of the Irish system in meeting the specific requirements of foreign MNCs.

The Single European Market

In the late 1980s and early 1990s the EU implemented a programme of reforms aimed at establishing a Single European Market by 1992. This involved removing non-tariff barriers to cross-border business activity within the EU—barriers such as different national technical standards, nationalistic government procurement and different national regulatory regimes. The Single European Market is widely considered to have boosted Ireland's economic growth (e.g., Sweeney 1998, 2008; OECD 1999; Bradley 2000; FitzGerald 2000; O'Donnell 2000; Ó Gráda and O'Rourke 2000).

Barry et al. (1999a) drew together the findings from a number of studies on this. They found that Ireland benefited to some extent from the general stimulus to the EU economy, but Ireland also benefited more than most other EU countries because of its own industrial structure and because of its ability to attract FDI. As regards industrial structure, Ireland had a relatively strong competitive position in the particular sectors that had previously been most constrained by the non-tariff barriers. Consequently, Ireland was well placed to gain more than most countries from the removal of the barriers. As regards FDI, flows of US FDI into the EU expanded quite dramatically in the late 1980s, and there was also an increase in intra-EU FDI flows. Barry et al. (1999a) concluded that much of the expansion of US FDI was due to the Single Market programme making the EU market more attractive. Ireland gained more than most countries from the increase in FDI, partly because it already had an ability to attract a disproportionate share of FDI and partly because the Single European Market made it more feasible for many companies to produce in a small peripheral country for the core EU markets (Mac Sharry and White 2000; Barry 2005).

O'Donnell (2000) and NESC (2003) argued that the Single European Market also had some other specific effects such as energising certain service sectors which had been relatively protected, stimulating free movement of capital, reforming competition policy, limiting state aids to weak sectors and causing radical change in public utilities.

EU Structural Funds

From 1989 onwards, Ireland received a substantial increase in its allocation from the newly enlarged EU Structural Funds, and it is widely agreed that this helped to increase Ireland's growth (e.g., FitzGerald 1998; OECD 1999; O'Donnell 2000; Barry 2000). It has also been stated quite often that this positive effect was relatively small compared to the scale of growth during the Celtic Tiger boom (e.g., Bradley et al. 1997; Ó Gráda 2002; Burnham 2003; Honohan and Walsh 2002; FitzGerald and Honohan 2023).

Between 1989 and 1999, about IR£9.5 billion of structural funds (in 1994 prices) were transferred to the Irish exchequer. The bulk of this funding was spent on physical infrastructure, human resource development and aid to investment in the private sector. Barryet al. (1999a) reviewed some studies that assessed the impact of this EU funding. They concluded that it raised GNP by the late 1990s to a level about 4% above what it would otherwise have been, which was a contribution of about 0.5% per year to the GNP growth rate in the 1990s (when GNP was growing at about 8% per year). They acknowledged that this could be a somewhat conservative estimate.

Some authors made the point that the increased impact of the structural funds began at a very apposite time, because the drive to cut public expenditure had resulted in a severe reduction in public investment by 1989. The structural funds enabled a resumption of public investment to support future growth (Fitzgerald and Honohan 2023).

Some argued that the structural funds also had other more qualitative benefits for Ireland. It is said that the process of planning and administering the funds introduced more effective longer-term planning and consistent implementation of investment (Bradley et al. 1997; FitzGerald 1998, 2000 ; O'Donnell 2000; Honohan and Walsh 2002; Fitzgerald and Honohan 2023). In addition, Ó Riain and O'Connell (2000) considered that the structural funds facilitated the introduction of important new development programmes, particularly for the development of indigenous enterprises, without having to struggle for and win funding from established programmes.

A number of studies considered that the impact of the Single European Market was probably greater than the structural funds in boosting GNP over the long term (Bradley et al. 1997; FitzGerald 2000). In addition, Matthews (1994, Table 7) observed that Ireland's receipts under the EU's Common Agricultural Policy (CAP) were a good deal larger than its receipts of EU structural funds. He estimated that Ireland's CAP receipts were worth about 10% of its GNP in the early 1990s (including the transfer arising from EU consumers paying higher prices for Ireland's agrifood exports because of the CAP), while the structural funds were worth about 3% of GNP.

Social Partnership, Wage Moderation

From 1987 onwards, the social partners negotiated a series of multi-year national agreements covering various economic and social issues. The "social partners" initially included employers, trade unions, farmers and government and later broadened out to include other community and voluntary organisations. Many have argued that social partnership underpinned economic growth by delivering moderate and competitive national wage agreements together with industrial peace, as well as agreement on the public finances, tax reform, social welfare, health spending, public sector reform, social exclusion, exchange-rate policy, the Maastricht criteria, etc. (e.g. O'Donnell 1998, 2000; Mac Sharry and White 2000; OECD 1999; Ó Riain and O'Connell 2000; Ó Gráda and O'Rourke 2000, Leddin and Egan 2018/2019). It has been argued that social partnership made a significant contribution to the development of a coherent and consistent set of economic policies (NESC 2003). It has also been argued that social partnership led to a general acceptance of the importance of competitiveness as well as recognition of the many factors (not just labour costs) that combine to produce competitiveness (Sweeney 1998, 2008).

Disagreements about the importance of social partnership as a cause of the economic boom have generally focused on the issue of wage moderation or restraint. Some argued that partnership boosted growth by delivering wage moderation which enhanced competitiveness resulting in employment growth. This in turn generated additional tax revenues which were later partly used to reduce direct tax rates thereby facilitating further wage moderation (O'Donnell and O'Reardon 2000). Barry (2009) showed, at a theoretical level, how it is possible for national agreements that offer future tax reductions in exchange for current wage moderation to enhance wage competitiveness in a way that would not occur otherwise.

As evidence that wage moderation occurred, Leddin and Egan (2018/2019) showed that wages' share of the national economy fell very significantly, Kennedy (2000/2001) showed that profits were taking a rising share of net domestic product, Blanchard (2002) showed that real wages rose more slowly than the rate of technological progress, and NESC (2003) quoted Lane (1997/1998) to show that the rate of return on capital almost doubled between 1987 and 1996. At the same time, Kennedy and Blanchard mentioned that these trends in their respective indicators were already occurring years before the boom.

FitzGerald (1999) found that wage rates and labour costs in Irish industry had been rising a good deal faster than in the UK in the 1960s and 1970s, but then stabilised relative to the UK from around the late 1970s onwards, with labour costs having reached about 90–100% of the UK level. FitzGerald's econometric work included a role for UK wage rates (among other things) in influencing wage formation in Ireland. His findings led him to suggest that the "impact of the partnership approach to wage formation has been less significant than many have assumed", and "the partnership approach served more to validate the results which market forces had made inevitable". However, FitzGerald (1999, 2000) acknowledged that partnership had other significant benefits relating to better industrial relations and economic policy-making.

Leddin and Walsh (1997, 2003) argued that high unemployment had imposed wage moderation on the Irish labour market from the early 1980s onwards, although they accepted that partnership contributed to reinforcing wage moderation after 1987. They also observed that some other countries such as the UK and USA had wage moderation and declining unemployment under a quite different system of decentralised wage bargaining. Honohan and Walsh (2002) expressed similar views. However, O'Donnell (1998) argued that Ireland's experience with partnership was much more satisfactory than the UK's approach, which had seen short bursts of fast economic growth followed by deep recessions imposed in order to reduce inflation.

McGuinness et al. (2010) analysed firm-level data from the 2003 National Employment Survey. They found that, despite the national wage agreement (NWA) negotiated under social partnership, there were still many firms that mainly used other types of wage bargaining such as individual-level or firm-level bargaining. Average labour costs were higher in these other firms than in NWA firms. They also found that foreign-owned MNCs that implemented the NWA enjoyed a particularly noticeable labour cost advantage. They concluded that, as the NWA was designed to protect employment in indigenous companies with lower productivity levels, MNCs implementing the NWA were able to set wages at levels well below what would be the case for them under firm-level or individual-level wage bargaining.

Foreign Direct Investment

It has been widely observed that rapid growth of FDI was a very prominent or central feature of the Celtic Tiger boom (e.g., Sachs 1997; Krugman 1997; OECD 1999; O'Hearn 2001; Duffy et al. 2001; Barry 2002, 2005). Ireland already had a record of attracting substantial amounts of export-oriented FDI in the decades before the boom, but US manufacturing investment in Ireland began to increase noticeably after 1987 and Ireland's share of US manufacturing investment in the EU also began to rise (Barry 2005). Employment in foreign-owned manufacturing began to grow from 1987 onwards after declining for some years previously. By the late 1990s, foreign-owned MNCs accounted for over 45% of employment, about 65% of gross output and over 80% of exports in manufacturing industry (Barry et al. 1999b). Murphy (2000) estimated that, in the absence of the contribution coming from high-tech MNCs' exports, Ireland's GDP would have grown by only about 3.5% per year in 1990–96 instead of the actual rate of 7.6% per year. He also mentioned another estimate by McCarthy (1999) that inflows of FDI into Irish manufacturing boosted the growth rate of the economy by about 3% per year in 1993–1997.

Of the reasons that have been suggested to explain why FDI grew in Ireland, some are long-standing reasons that originally aimed to explain why Ireland had been relatively attractive for FDI long before the boom. Many commentators argued that most of these were still relevant during the boom. Such reasons included EU membership with access to large EU markets; low tax on profits; grant incentives; active and effective industrial development agencies; a suitable available labour force—English-speaking, reasonably well-educated, with labour costs below many other EU countries; historical and cultural links with the USA; and a less regulated business environment than many EU countries.

A number of further reasons were suggested to explain the acceleration of FDI in the boom years. These included the single European market; the development and rapid internationalisation of a number of important industries, originating particularly in the USA; declining tariff and transport costs; changing location requirements among MNCs in certain key sectors, with increasing emphasis on access to major markets combined with availability of technical skills; improvements in international communications and the benefits of the transformation of Ireland's telecommunications system in the 1980s (Burnham 2003); more selective and focused state agency policies for attracting FDI; increasing agglomeration economies among growing clusters of related companies in Ireland, partly as a result of the state agency policies; and "demonstration" and "cascade" effects, meaning that the location decisions of prospective newcomer MNCs were influenced by the perceived successful experience of growing numbers of others already in Ireland.[4]

Some authors also stressed that Ireland's investment in education and training, resulting in rapid growth in the supply of skilled labour, became an increasingly important factor in attracting MNCs because their requirements for high-level skills were increasing over time (e.g., Breathnach 1998; FitzGerald 1998). This argument concerning education does not necessarily amount to a claim that the Irish education system was superior to those of other European countries in a general overall sense. For it has been argued, much more specifically, that the Irish system was unusually effective at producing sufficient numbers of graduates with the particular types of skills that were required by MNCs in the industries that were growing rapidly internationally (Mac Sharry and White 2000; Barry 2005; O'Malley et al. 2008). Shortages of such skills were not at all unusual elsewhere.

There have been a number of critical analyses of FDI in Ireland (e.g., O'Sullivan 2000; O'Hearn 2001; Kirby 2010), but they generally did not disagree with the view that FDI was a major factor in generating the Celtic Tiger economy. Rather they highlighted disadvantages and weaknesses in a form of economic growth that depended so heavily on such foreign MNCs, so that they were not impressed by the nature or likely

[4] Many studies have discussed some or most of the reasons for FDI mentioned in the two foregoing paragraphs. These include Krugman (1997), Breathnach (1998 and 2004), OECD (1999), Barry et al. (1999b), Murphy (2000), Mac Sharry and White (2000), Gallagher et al. (2002), Ruane (2003), Barry (2005), Crafts (2005), Buckley and Ruane (2006), Romalis (2007), and O'Malley et al. (2008).

sustainability of this growth process. But they generally accepted that FDI was a major element in the growth that occurred.

A Small Open Economy—Like a Region

A number of authors argued that one reason for Ireland's exceptional boom was the fact that it is a small and very open economy, and like a regional economy in some respects. Nobody suggested that this in itself generates stronger growth, but the argument was that some factors that boosted growth were able to have a greater impact in the small/regional Irish economy than they could have in larger countries.

There are a few characteristics of a small/regional economy that are relevant for this view. First, external trade is relatively large and very important for the economy. Second, inward FDI can occur on a scale that is great enough to be far more influential than in larger countries. Third, the labour market is very open so that relatively large-scale migration occurs easily. Given this type of economy, it was argued that rapid export growth, largely driven by export-oriented FDI, was the major driver of the Irish boom. The very open labour market meant that the return of former emigrants and the growth of new immigration facilitated and prolonged the boom, by preventing labour shortages from emerging and by moderating wage increases (Krugman 1997; Barry 1999, 2002, 2005). It was argued that booms quite like this had occurred in regions within larger countries rather than in entire large countries. NESC's (2003) interpretation of the boom was mostly consistent with this perspective, as was O'Leary's (2011), although NESC added that alongside the leading role of FDI there was also a very significant improvement in the performance of Irish indigenous firms.

O'Leary (2015, Chapter 7) also suggested that Ireland's small size was one reason why it was able to achieve EU agreement for its very favourable corporate tax regime, taking advantage of "the importance of being unimportant".

Blanchard (2002) presented a somewhat different version of the same type of story, in which the main distinctive element was the emphasis that he put on wage moderation as being the principal cause of strong investment including FDI. Wage moderation in turn, he considered, was probably quite largely a result of the very open labour market and the consequent influence of UK wage levels in restraining Irish wage increases, while the same open labour market provided the extra labour supply needed to prolong the boom.

Using theoretical neo-classical modelling, Barry and Devereux (2006) found that an economy with very open capital and labour markets is affected more substantially than a less open economy by shocks such as an increase in the economy's attractiveness to FDI, a reduction in labour market distortions, or an increase in total factor productivity.

Honohan and Walsh (2002), Leddin and Walsh (2003) and Crafts (2005) also mentioned the effects of the small/regional nature of the Irish economy, although with less emphasis than the other studies cited above.

Irish Indigenous Industry

Some studies stated, with varying degrees of emphasis, that a substantial improvement in the performance of Irish-owned or indigenous industry was a significant component of the boom (e.g., O'Malley et al. 1992; O'Malley 1998, 2004; Sweeney 1998; Barry 1999; Mac Sharry and White 2000; NESC 2003; Ó Riain 2004a, 2004b; OECD 2006).

Following years of very poor performance, Irish indigenous industry began to grow considerably faster than industry in the EU from 1987 onwards in terms of output and from 1988 in terms of employment. This trend continued throughout most or all of the boom. Exports of indigenous industry also grew relatively rapidly compared with the EU in the late 1980s, but then did no more than match the pace of EU export growth in the 1990s. It was suggested that the export comparison with the EU in the 1990s looked less impressive than the output comparison partly because EU exports were growing unusually fast in the 1990s (perhaps because of the Single European Market), and partly because Irish companies' incentive to increase exports was diminished when the domestic market began to grow very rapidly in the 1990s (O'Malley 1998, 2004). Indigenous industry also showed other signs of increasing strength such as rising profitability and productivity, rapidly growing R&D, above-average levels of innovation by EU standards, increasing professionalisation, and particularly rapid growth (including export growth at above EU rates) in high-tech and medium-tech sectors rather than the more mature traditional sectors (Ó Riain 2004a, 2004b; O'Malley 1998, 2004; O'Malley et al. 2008).[5]

A number of explanations were suggested for this performance of Irish indigenous industry, including the EU structural funds, rising education levels, social partnership, the secondary effects of FDI growth, etc. However, this literature generally put a particular emphasis on the role of the state's industrial policy as a factor behind the improvement. It pointed out that industrial policy, from the mid-1980s onwards, had an increased focus on the development of Irish indigenous industry and that a series of new policy measures and approaches were implemented to further this aim. It also argued that the evidence indicated that such measures were successful (O'Malley et al. 1992; O'Malley 1998; Ó Riain and O'Connell 2000; NESC 2003; Ó Riain 2004a, 2004b).

Some authors doubted whether there had been a really significant improvement in indigenous industry (e.g., O'Sullivan 2000; O'Hearn 2001; Enterprise Strategy Group 2004). They cited concerns such as an unconvincing export performance, insufficient evidence of innovation capabilities and limited development of sales to foreign MNCs in Ireland, all leading to questions about the sustainability of this growth.

Other Explanations

A number of other explanations for the boom have occasionally been suggested. These include progress towards peace in Northern Ireland (Gray 1997), local development policies and active labour market policies (NESC 2003), new forms of work organisation (Sweeney 1998) and currency devaluations in 1986 and 1993 (Leddin and Walsh 1997, 2003; Honohan and Walsh 2002; Gallagher et al. 2002). Most of these suggestions were proposed by no more than two or three authors, sometimes with rather little supporting discussion. In most of these cases, it seems clear that the authors did not consider them to be among the more important explanations for the boom.

Some also argued that Ireland's transition to participation in EMU helped economic growth (O'Donnell 2000; Leddin and Walsh 2003; NESC 2003). However, Honohan and Walsh (2002) argued that the

[5] Ó Riain's analysis also found indications of such industrial "upgrading" in foreign-owned as well as indigenous industry.

stimulatory effects of the resulting lower interest rates came in the late 1990s which was relatively late and not very helpful timing.

Honohan (2006) considered whether financial sector development might have been a driver of Ireland's twenty-year growth success but concluded that there was little evidence to support this idea.

Although privatisation and deregulation were a major focus for economic policy in much of Europe during the time of the boom, they were seldom mentioned as causes of the Irish boom. However, the specific case of airlines was mentioned sometimes. In the mid-1980s, deregulation introduced more competition in the Irish airline industry, and it has been argued that this provided a major stimulus for a subsequent tourism boom (Barry 1999, 2000; Murphy 2000; Burnham 2003). It has also been argued that stronger promotion and improved price competitiveness contributed to that growth of tourism (Honohan and Walsh 2002; Leddin and Walsh 2003).[6]

It was also sometimes argued that the transformation of Irish telecommunications in the 1980s proved to be very important for attracting FDI in the service sector (Burnham 2003; Barry 2000). However, this transformation was carried out under the control of the state monopoly company Telecom Éireann, which was not privatised until much later.

Some authors suggested different types of explanation for the boom, of a social or political nature, but these are mostly outside the scope of this book which focuses on economic explanations. If these other explanations made an important contribution, they probably had their effects on economic growth mainly by means of driving or influencing some of the explanatory factors that are included here.

3.2 Assessment of the Explanations

This section undertakes a preliminary assessment of the explanations discussed above. It argues that a number of the suggested explanations are not convincing or not very important and that it will not be necessary to consider them further, whereas the others will call for further consideration and assessment in later chapters.

[6] Tourism accounted for just 4% of GNP by 2000. Outward tourism expenditure grew at a similar rate to inward tourism after the mid-1980s (Honohan and Walsh 2002).

Necessary But Normal Conditions

Among the explanations for the boom discussed in Sect. 3.1, a few refer to conditions that could be described as necessary but normal. Rather like a reliable electricity supply or a functioning legal system, for example, these conditions would be necessary for the attainment of a satisfactory or average growth performance, while they have also been quite normal or common across many countries and time periods. Because they have been so normal in many places and times, they cannot actually help much to explain why Ireland had such a highly exceptional boom, which involved departing substantially from the contemporaneous experience of most other countries and from Ireland's own previous experience.

Fiscal stabilisation is in this "necessary but normal" category. If the expansionary fiscal contraction argument is rejected, as seems to be largely agreed, fiscal stabilisation refers to the establishment of a condition that was necessary but was also quite normal or common. It could reasonably be argued that fiscal stabilisation was an important precondition for a return to moderate or average growth in Ireland after the slump of the 1980s. However, like the example of a reliable electricity supply, it is difficult to see how such a normal condition could help to explain why Ireland's economic growth was much faster than average for a very long time.

Ireland's plentiful supply of labour in the boom years was another necessary condition, but this was a condition that was also quite normal in the sense that many other European countries had plenty of labour available. In the years when the boom was occurring in Ireland, the unemployment rate in the EU-15 was usually above 8% (as was seen in Fig. 1.4), and many of those EU countries could also have attracted additional immigrant labour if they had required it. Furthermore, a plentiful supply of labour had been normal in Ireland itself for generations before the boom, but the previous results had always been a good deal of emigration and/or unemployment rather than exceptional growth of employment and the economy. What was new and distinctive about the boom period in Ireland was not the availability of a plentiful supply of labour, but the fact that there was strong demand within the country for the available labour.

As regards education or human capital, it is necessary to make a distinction between (a) the general process of raising the educational standards of the population and labour force and (b), within the broader system, the particular activity of producing a supply of graduates with the specific skills and qualifications that were required by rapidly growing and internationally mobile industries. The more general process was necessary but, as discussed in the literature on this topic cited in Sect. 3.1, it was also quite normal in the sense that it had already been going on for years before the boom and there does not appear to have been an acceleration or intensification that could be seen as a cause of the boom. It was also normal in the sense that the standards being attained do not seem to have been very exceptional for the most part, compared with other developed countries.

However, the more specific activity of deliberately providing for the skill requirements of fast-growing and mobile target industries was more exceptional in an international context, and was consciously intended to take advantage of new opportunities as they emerged and expanded. Hence this was potentially a cause of exceptional growth outcomes, in conjunction with changing patterns of industrial growth and FDI.

Delayed or Belated Convergence

If correct, the argument concerning delayed or belated convergence would be important. It could, on its own, provide much of the explanation for the boom. It would also transform the significance of fiscal stabilisation—described above as simply a "necessary but normal" condition—since the delayed convergence argument holds that Ireland was naturally overdue for relatively rapid growth as soon as such normal conditions for growth prevailed.

However, there are a number of problems with the delayed convergence argument. For one thing, as was outlined in Sect. 3.1, Barry (2002) identified significant problems with it.

Perhaps more fundamentally, the basic premise of the delayed convergence argument is questionable, i.e., the premise that there is a general tendency for convergence of average income levels among broadly comparable economies. There are conflicting theories on this matter—Ó Gráda and O'Rourke (2000) outlined some examples—so that the validity of the basic premise cannot be taken for granted. As regards empirical evidence, a convergence tendency certainly has been observed among some countries in some periods, but there is also other evidence that shows no such tendency, which calls into question the idea that convergence is the general tendency.

For example, Haughton (2005) found that although there was a general convergence tendency among OECD countries over the period 1960–2002, there was actually no significant convergence tendency during the second half of that period, 1980–2002. This means that there was a marked convergence tendency over one two-decade period, 1960–1980, but such a tendency was absent over the following two decades.

Ó Gráda and O'Rourke (1996) generally accepted the view that convergence was the prevailing tendency, at least among developed countries, but findings that they presented look consistent with the idea that convergence may actually have been confined to certain periods. Their Fig. 13.2 showed that, among Western European countries, GDP per head did tend to converge over the long period 1950–1988. However, when this is broken down into sub-periods, convergence was weak in 1950–1960, strong in 1960–1973 and absent in 1973–1988.

It was already seen in Fig. 1.2 in Chapter 1 of this book that there was no sign of convergence between the USA and the EU-15 during the period 1980–2007. In addition, Pain (2000/2001) showed that the EU's GDP per head had risen from less than half of the USA's level in 1950 to two-thirds of the US level by 1973, but then little further convergence occurred over the next 25 years, 1973–1998, as the EU's GDP per head stayed within a range of about 65–72% of the US level. Thus, the overall story here—concerning the two largest economic blocs in the world—is that there was quite strong convergence between them in the 23-year period 1950–1973 followed by no further convergence in the 34-year period 1973–2007.

Taking account of the various observations outlined above, it may be concluded that the evidence here is too inconsistent to support the theory that convergence of average income levels has been a generally prevailing tendency. It seems more likely, from this evidence, that convergence may have been quite a common tendency among developed market economies from about the 1950s until the early 1970s, but there was no obvious convergence tendency after that time. Consequently, the evidence here would not justify the assumption that Ireland must necessarily have benefited from a strong convergence tendency in 1973–1986 if only it had adopted sound fiscal policies. There is also little support here for the argument that the Irish boom after 1986 was caused by the eventual arrival of the general convergence tendency.

Another type of problem with the delayed convergence argument arises from the fact that the theory underlying the suggested tendency to convergence (as outlined by Ó Gráda and O'Rourke 2000) actually applies largely to factor incomes. This means that the theory says that remuneration per unit of labour or capital should tend to converge. Even if this is true, the problem is that it does not necessarily mean that incomes per head of population have to converge. For example, Pain (2000/2001) showed that the EU's GDP per hour worked rose from two-thirds of the US level in 1973 to almost 100% of the US level by the late 1990s. This would have provided a basis for convergence in hourly wage rates. But despite this, there was no convergence trend in GDP per head of population in that period because of differences between the EU and USA with respect to the proportion of the population in employment and hours worked per employee.

This point is relevant for Ireland because, as mentioned above, non-agricultural GDP per person engaged was actually about the same in Ireland and the UK in 1973, although Ireland's GDP per head of population was 27% below the UK level. Thus, Ireland's output per employee (and hence potentially wages per employee) across the bulk of the economy had already converged on the UK level by that time, while Ireland's relatively low GDP per head of population was mainly due to a low proportion of the Irish population being in employment. Given this situation, it is not clear that Ireland had anything to gain from the convergence of factor incomes that is envisaged by the theory underlying the suggested general tendency to convergence.

In Honohan and Walsh's (2002) version of the delayed convergence argument, they explicitly recognised that Ireland's productivity had largely converged with the UK by 1973, and they recognised that convergence for Ireland in terms of GDP per head of population would require a large increase in employment, and more specifically non-agricultural employment, as a percentage of the total population. They believed that in 1973 the conditions in Ireland were right for such a convergence to occur by around the end of the century, before the convergence was derailed by fiscal policy errors.

As Honohan and Walsh made no explicit reference either to international evidence or to any generalised theory in order to justify their belief that Ireland in 1973 was on the way to convergence, their view is not undermined by the problems discussed above with the international evidence and the theory relating to convergence. However, this also means that the only rationale for their view appears to be a judgement that trends in Ireland were moving in the right direction, with rising participation by a better-educated workforce in non-agricultural sectors. This looks like an inadequate basis for their view because there were important trends in Ireland in the years leading up to 1973 that did not provide support for their argument.

A key point here is that total employment in Ireland had scarcely grown at all in 1960–1973, with an increase of just 0.2% per year, as discussed in Chapter 2. In that context, employment as a percentage of the population in Ireland had declined from 37.1% in 1960 to 34.8% in 1973—far below the corresponding figure for the UK. This trend was the opposite of the essential trend that was required for Ireland to achieve convergence in terms of GDP per head of population. Unless this trend could be reversed, there could be no prospect of Ireland's average living standards reaching the level of the UK and other advanced European economies, because such a convergence in those circumstances would require Ireland's output per person employed to rise far above the levels found in those countries.

Honohan and Walsh (2002) focused particularly on non-agricultural employment. If we look at the trend in non-agricultural employment as a percentage of the population, there was a clear rising trend in this indicator during 1960–1973, but this trend was of limited significance because it was too weak. In a context where the agricultural labour force was in secular decline, there would have needed to be a sizeable compensating increase in non-agricultural employment as a percentage of the population just to maintain total employment at a constant percentage of the population. In fact, the growth of non-agricultural employment in 1960–1973 was not even sufficient to do that since we have seen that there was a decline in total employment as a percentage of the population in 1960–1973.

Honohan and Walsh (2002) presented a chart which showed the rising trend in non-agricultural employment as a percentage of the population. If we extrapolate the rising trend seen in 1960–1973 forward in time, it seems that non-agricultural employment was heading towards about 33 or 34% of the population by the end of the century. However, this rising trend was well below what was needed to bring about convergence by the end of the century. When GNP per head converged on the EU level at the end of the century, non-agricultural employment had actually reached about 42% of the population, much higher than where it had been heading during 1960–1973.

Finally, there is another problem with the delayed convergence argument. The delayed convergence argument holds that the rise in Ireland's GNP per head from about 65% of the EU level in the early 1970s to almost 100% by 2000 was primarily a natural convergence process. This convergence process would have been occurring more evenly throughout that period but for the fact that it was prevented from happening in the 1970s and early 1980s because of fiscal policy mistakes, with the result that the eventual convergence took the form of an exceptional boom from the late 1980s onwards.

To put this suggestion in perspective, consider some quantitative estimates by FitzGerald (2000) that are relevant here. FitzGerald's Fig. 3.10 indicated that the expansionary impetus imparted by fiscal policy in 1977–1979 amounted to about 2.5% of GNP and this was followed by a deflationary impact of around 6% of GNP in 1980–1987, giving a net deflationary impact of about 3.5% of GNP by 1987. Similarly, FitzGerald's Fig. 3.11 indicated that if a neutral fiscal policy had been pursued from 1974 onwards, GNP could have been 3 or 4% higher by 1987 than it actually was.

This implies that, with more orthodox fiscal policies, Ireland's GNP per head could have reached about 66% of the EU level by 1987 instead of the actual figure of 64%. This gives little support to the suggestion that there was a convergence tendency present all the time that was strong enough to raise Ireland from about 65% to almost 100% of the EU level within a few decades provided that Ireland avoided policy errors. It is more consistent with the idea that there was no convergence tendency of any significance applying to Ireland.

Tax Cuts

Those who argued that tax cuts were an important cause of the boom generally supported this view by stating that there was a substantial decline in tax as a percentage of GDP between about 1986 and the late 1990s. However, this argument is questionable because the decline in taxation actually occurred relatively late in this period, long after the boom began.

Figure 3.1 shows tax as a percentage of GNP and GDP each year from 1982 to 2007. It can be seen that there was no clear declining trend in either of these series before 1995. In 1994 tax as a percentage of GNP or GDP was actually higher than in 1986 when the boom was about to begin and, even if we deduct the exceptional revenue received from a tax amnesty in 1994, tax as a percentage of GNP or GDP in that year was at just the same level as in 1986. Thus, it was not until 1995—the ninth year of relatively fast economic growth—that the overall tax level began a declining trend.[7]

Much of the discussion about tax cuts as a cause of the boom focused more specifically on taxes that have a bearing on labour costs. A useful way to examine trends in such taxation is to consider trends in the "tax wedge", which measures the difference or gap between the cost to an employer of employing someone and the take-home pay received by the employee. The size of this wedge or gap is determined by the amount of social insurance (PRSI) paid by the employer plus the amount of income tax and social insurance paid by the employee. Figure 3.2 shows the trend in the tax wedge in 1982–2007, as measured by the average cost to the employer divided by the average take-home pay of the employee. Thus, a reading of 1.5 in Fig. 3.2 would mean that on average it costs the employer 1.5 times the amount that the employee receives.

Rather like the trend already seen with respect to overall taxation in Fig. 3.1, there was no declining trend in the tax wedge before 1995. The figures for 1993 and 1994 were somewhat higher than the figure for 1986 when the boom was about to begin, and it was not until 1995—nine years into the boom—that the tax wedge began a declining trend.

It is clear from Figs. 3.1 and 3.2 that tax cuts did not help to start the boom or to sustain it through its first decade or so. Therefore, the boom was generated by other factors. When the declining trend in tax began, it was an effect or a consequence of the boom since fast growth of incomes and employment had led to a declining unemployment rate, a declining dependency ratio and a declining national debt burden—all of which facilitated tax reductions.

[7] In addition to the total tax data series depicted in Fig. 3.1, there is also a somewhat broader measure of total government revenue that includes other non-tax revenue. According to that data series total revenue as a percentage of GNP did decline by one percentage point between 1986 and 1994. However, that apparent decline was actually caused by a discontinuity in the non-tax revenue data in 1988. A related more general point concerning the data for tax, GNP and GDP is that there were a number of such discontinuities, as well as some quite substantial revisions over the years, which can potentially lead to some misinterpretation of trends. For this reason, Fig. 3.1 is based on a single data source that provides long series of data incorporating the most up-to-date revisions, with discontinuities being highlighted or corrected.

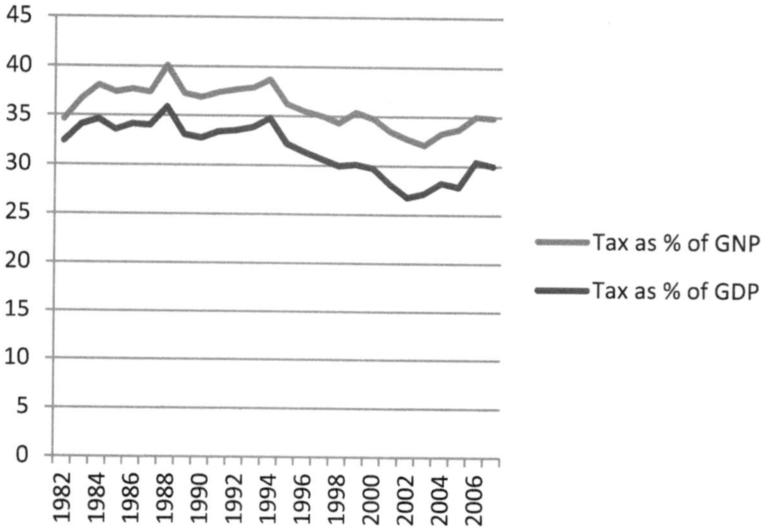

Fig. 3.1 Tax as a percentage of GNP and GDP, 1982–2007 (*Note:* Once-off receipts under tax amnesties increased the tax yield by 2.1% of GNP in 1988 and by 0.7% of GNP in 1994. Tax here is defined to include taxes, employers' and employees' social insurance contributions and health and training fund contributions. It does not include other exchequer non-tax revenue. *Source* Derived from Department of Finance, *Budgetary and Economic Statistics*, October 2012, Tables 4 and 12)

In the literature discussed in Sect. 3.1, it was suggested by a couple of authors that a "virtuous circle" effect could have developed, such that tax cuts were initially a consequence of the boom but the tax cuts then helped to stimulate further growth, which in turn facilitated further tax cuts and so on. However, this suggestion is not convincing. The economy had already proved capable of prolonged rapid growth without tax reductions being part of the explanation, so evidently that could have continued to be the case. At the same time, no evidence was offered to support the suggestion that tax cuts could have helped to stimulate growth further.

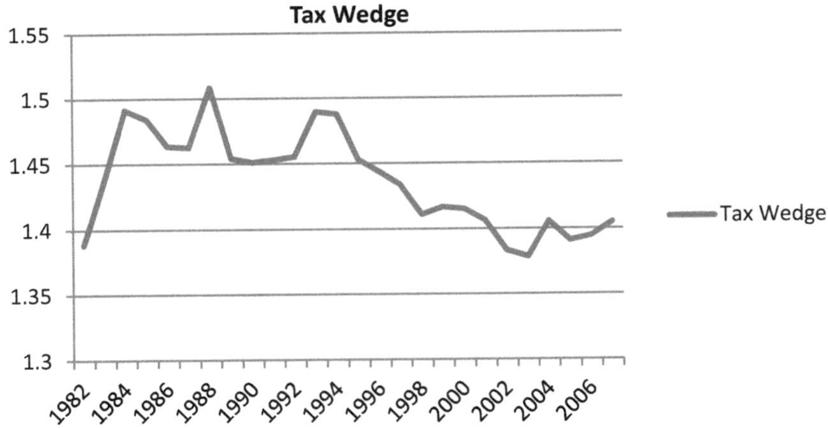

Fig. 3.2 Irish labour market tax wedge, 1982–2007 (*Note* The tax wedge is defined here as (1 + RGTYSE)/(1 − RTYPTOT) where RGTYSE is the average rate of employer social insurance contributions and RTYPTOT is the average rate of personal taxation, including social insurance, paid by employees. *Source* Derived from Economic and Social Research Institute (ESRI) databank, based on data from the Central Statistics Office (CSO). Creative Commons Attribution BY 4.0)

Minor Explanations

The range of "other explanations" for the boom that were mentioned at the end of Sect. 3.1 were clearly of no more than minor importance even if there was some truth in them. Most of them were mentioned by few authors, and it seems clear that nobody considered most of them to be among the more important explanations for the boom. Here we briefly consider two of them that were mentioned more than most—currency devaluation in 1986 and 1993, and deregulation of airlines.

It was suggested that the devaluation of the Irish pound in August 1986 helped to stimulate the growth of Irish industry's exports over the following years. However, any such effect must have been minimal. The main reason is because the devaluation was relative to the ECU (European Currency Unit) while there was no significant devaluation relative to other currencies that were important for Irish industrial exports. If we go by the trade-weighted exchange-rate index for the Irish pound published by the Central Bank of Ireland, the value of the Irish pound changed rather little each year in 1986–1989 declining by an average of just 1.1% per year. Since it then rose the following year, it ultimately increased slightly by 0.6% per year over the period 1986–1990.

The devaluation at the end of January 1993 had a more substantial effect at first, with an initial decline of about 10% in the Irish pound's effective exchange rate, but most of this decline was reversed over the next few years so that the net decline over the period 1993–1996 was just 3%. It seems unlikely that this could have been of significant lasting benefit for the economy.

It was claimed that deregulation and greater competition in the airline industry led to the growth of air traffic and consequent benefits for the tourism industry. However, since tourism accounted for just 4% of GNP by 2000, its growth cannot have contributed very substantially to the overall boom. Perhaps more importantly, since the growth of air traffic facilitated outward tourism as much as inward tourism, the net contribution to Ireland's GNP would have been significantly less than the contribution coming from the growth of inward tourism.

3.3 Conclusion

For the reasons discussed in Sect. 3.2, it may be concluded that a number of the explanations for the boom that were proposed in the literature are not convincing or not very important. Consequently, those proposed explanations will not be considered further in this book, whereas the others will call for further consideration and assessment in later chapters.

The suggested explanations that will not be considered further are fiscal stabilisation, a plentiful supply of labour, the general process of education (other than education specifically for fast-growing industries), delayed convergence, tax cuts and the "other explanations" that were mentioned at the end of Sect. 3.1.

The rest of the suggested explanations remain as potentially significant causes of the boom and they will be considered and assessed further in later chapters in this book. These remaining suggestions are strong demand growth in export markets, foreign direct investment, the Single European Market, education for fast-growing industries, the small/regional nature of the economy, Irish indigenous industry, EU structural funds and social partnership/wage moderation.

References

Barry, Frank. 1999. Irish Growth in Historical and Theoretical Perspective. In *Understanding Ireland's Economic Growth*, ed. Frank Barry, 25–44. London: Macmillan and New York: St Martin's Press.

Barry, Frank. 2000. Convergence Is Not Automatic: Lessons from Ireland for Central and Eastern Europe. *The World Economy* 23 (10): 1379–1394.

Barry, Frank. 2002, Summer. The Celtic Tiger Era: Delayed Convergence or Regional Boom? In *Quarterly Economic Commentary*, ed. Daniel McCoy, David Duffy, Adele Bergin, J. Eakins, Jonathan Hore, and Conall MacCoille. Dublin: Economic and Social Research Institute.

Barry, Frank. 2005, Winter. Future Irish Growth: Opportunities, Catalysts, Constraints. In *Quarterly Economic Commentary*, ed. Alan Barrett, Ide Kearney, Shane Garrett, and Yvonne McCarthy. Dublin: Economic and Social Research Institute.

Barry, Frank. 2009. Social Partnership, Competitiveness and Exit from Fiscal Crisis. *Economic and Social Review* 40 (1): 1–14.

Barry, Frank, John Bradley, and Aoife Hannan. 1999a. The European Dimension: The Single Market and the Structural Funds. In *Understanding Ireland's Economic Growth*, ed. Frank Barry, 99–118. London: Macmillan and New York: St Martin's Press.

Barry, Frank, John Bradley, and Eoin O'Malley. 1999b. Indigenous and Foreign Industry: Characteristics and Performance. In *Understanding Ireland's Economic Growth*, ed. Frank Barry, 45–74. London: Macmillan and New York: St Martin's Press.

Barry, Frank, and Michael B. Devereux. 2006. A Theoretical Growth Model for Ireland. *Economic and Social Review* 37 (2): 245–262.

Bergin, Adele, Thomas Conefrey, John FitzGerald, and Ide Kearney. 2010. The Behaviour of the Irish Economy: Insights from the HERMES Macro-Economic Model. Working Paper No. 287. Economic and Social Research Institute, Dublin.

Blanchard, Olivier. 2002. Comments on 'Catching Up with the Leaders: The Irish Hare'. *Brookings Papers on Economic Activity* 2002 (1).

Bradley, John. 2000. The Irish Economy in Comparative Perspective. In *Bust to Boom? The Irish Experience of Growth and Inequality*, ed. Brian Nolan, Philip J. O'Connell, and Christopher T. Whelan, 4–26. Dublin: Institute of Public Administration.

Bradley, John, John FitzGerald, Patrick Honohan, and Ide Kearney. 1997. Interpreting the Recent Irish Growth Experience. In *Medium-Term Review: 1997–2003*, , ed. David Duffy, John FitzGerald, Ide Kearney, and Fergal Shortall, Chapter 3. Dublin: Economic and Social Research Institute.

Bradley, John, and Karl Whelan. 1997. The Irish Expansionary Fiscal Contraction: A Tale from One Small European Economy. *Economic Modelling* 14: 175–201.

Breathnach, Proinnsias. 1998. Exploring the 'Celtic Tiger' Phenomenon: Causes and Consequences of Ireland's Economic Miracle. *European Urban and Regional Studies* 4 (4): 305–316.

Breathnach, Proinnsias. 2004. Explaining Ireland's Inward Investment Surge in the 1990s: The Role of Changing FDI Location Trends. Mimeo.

Buckley, Peter J., and Frances Ruane. 2006. Foreign Direct Investment in Ireland: Policy Implications for Emerging Economies. *The World Economy* 29 (11): 1611–1628.

Burnham, James B. 2003. Why Ireland Boomed. *The Independent Review* VII (4, Spring): 537–556.

Conefrey, Thomas, and John D. FitzGerald. 2011. The Macro-Economic Impact of Changing the Rate of Corporation Tax. *Economic Modelling* 28: 991–999.

Considine, John, and David Duffy. 2007. Tales of Expansionary Fiscal Contractions in Two European Countries: Hindsight and Foresight. Working Paper 07-07. Department of Economics, University College Cork.

Crafts, Nicholas. 2005. Interpreting Ireland's Economic Growth. Industrial Development Report 2005 Background Paper Series, UNIDO.

de la Fuente, Angel, and Xavier Vives. 1997. The Sources of Irish Growth. In *International Perspectives on the Irish Economy*, ed. Alan W. Gray. Dublin: Indecon Economic Consultants.

Duffy, David, John FitzGerald, Jonathan Hore, Ide Kearney, and Conall MacCoille. 2001. Growth in the 1990s. In *Medium-Term Review: 2001–2007*, Chapter 2. Dublin: Economic and Social Research Institute.

Durkan, Joseph, Doireann FitzGerald, and Colm Harmon. 1999. Education and Growth in the Irish Economy. In *Understanding Ireland's Economic Growth*, ed. Frank Barry, 119–135. London: Macmillan and New York: St Martin's Press.

Enterprise Strategy Group. 2004. *Ahead of the Curve: Ireland's Place in the Global Economy*. Dublin: Forfas.

FitzGerald, John. 1998. An Irish Perspective on the Structural Funds. *European Planning Studies* 6 (6): 677–694.

FitzGerald, John. 1999. Wage Formation and the Labour Market. In *Understanding Ireland's Economic Growth*, ed. Frank Barry, 137–165. London: Macmillan and New York: St Martin's Press.

FitzGerald, John. 2000. The Story of Ireland's Failure—And Belated Success. In *Bust to Boom? The Irish Experience of Growth and Inequality*, ed. Brian Nolan, Philip J. O'Connell, and Christopher T. Whelan, 27–57. Dublin: Institute of Public Administration.

FitzGerald, John, and Patrick Honohan. 2023. *Europe and the Transformation of the Irish Economy*. Cambridge: Cambridge University Press.

Gallagher, Liam A., Eleanor Doyle, and Eoin O'Leary. 2002, Spring. Creating the Celtic Tiger and Sustaining Economic Growth: A Business Perspective. In *Quarterly Economic Commentary*, ed. Daniel McCoy, David Duffy, Jonathan Hore and Conall MacCoille. Dublin: Economic and Social Research Institute.

Giavazzi, F., and M. Pagano. 1990. Can Severe Fiscal Contractions Be Expansionary? Tales of Two Small European Countries. In *NBER Macroeconomics Annual 1990*, ed. O.J. Blanchard and S. Fischer, 75–111. Cambridge: MIT Press.

Gray, Alan W. 1997. Foreword: Irish Economic Challenges and International Perspectives. In *International Perspectives on the Irish Economy*, ed. Alan W. Gray. Dublin: Indecon Economic Consultants.

Haughton, Jonathan. 2005. Growth in Output and Living Standards. In *The Economy of Ireland: National and Sectoral Policy Issues*, ed. John O'Hagan and Carol Newman. Dublin: Gill & Macmillan.

Honohan, Patrick. 1999. Fiscal Adjustment and Disinflation in Ireland: Setting the Macro Basis of Economic Recovery and Expansion. In *Understanding Ireland's Economic Growth*, ed. Frank Barry, 75–98. London: Macmillan and New York: St Martin's Press.

Honohan, Patrick. 2006, Winter. To What Extent Has Finance Been a Driver of Ireland's Economic Success? In *Quarterly Economic Commentary*, ed. Alan Barrett, Ide Kearney, and Yvonne McCarthy. Dublin: Economic and Social Research Institute.

Honohan, Patrick, and Brendan Walsh. 2002. Catching Up with the Leaders: The Irish Hare. *Brookings Papers on Economic Activity* 2002 (1): 1–57.

Kennedy, Kieran. 2000/2001. Reflections on the Process of Irish Economic Growth. Symposium on Economic Growth in Ireland. *Journal of the Statistical and Social Inquiry Society of Ireland* XXX: 123–139.

Kirby, Peadar. 2010. *Celtic Tiger in Collapse: Explaining the Weaknesses of the Irish Model*. London: Palgrave Macmillan.

Krugman, Paul R. 1997. Good News from Ireland: A Geographical Perspective. In *International Perspectives on the Irish Economy*, ed. Alan W. Gray. Dublin: Indecon Economic Consultants.

Lane, Philip. 1997/1998. Profits and Wages—Ireland, 1987–1996. *Journal of the Statistical and Social Inquiry Society of Ireland* XXVII: Part V.

Leddin, Anthony, and Paul Egan. 2018/2019. Ireland's National Wage Agreements and Macroeconomic Performance: 1988–2008. *Journal of the Statistical and Social Inquiry Society of Ireland* XLVIII: 71–101.

Leddin, Anthony and Brendan Walsh. 1997. "Economic Stabilisation, Recovery and Growth: Ireland 1979–96", *Irish Banking Review*, Spring.

Leddin, Anthony J., and Brendan M. Walsh. 2003. *The Macroeconomy of the Eurozone: An Irish Perspective*. Dublin: Gill & Macmillan.
McCarthy, John. 1999, Winter. Foreign Direct Investment: An Overview. Central Bank of Ireland Quarterly Bulletin.
McGuinness, Seamus, Elish Kelly, and Philip J. O'Connell. 2010. The Impact of Wage Bargaining Regime on Firm-Level Competitiveness and Wage Inequality: The Case of Ireland. *Industrial Relations: A Journal of Economy and Society* 49 (4): 593–615.
Mac Sharry, Ray, and Padraic White. 2000. *The Making of the Celtic Tiger: The Inside Story of Ireland's Boom Economy*. Cork and Dublin: Mercier Press.
Matthews, Alan. 1994. *Managing the EU Structural Funds*. Cork: Cork University Press.
Murphy, Antoin E. 2000. The 'Celtic Tiger'—An Analysis of Ireland's Economic Growth Performance. EUI Working Paper RSC No. 2000/16. European University Institute.
National Economic and Social Council. 2003. An Investment in Quality: Services, Inclusion and Enterprise. Report No. 111. NESC, Dublin.
O'Donnell, Rory. 1998. Ireland's Economic Transformation: Industrial Policy, European Integration and Social Partnership. Working Paper No. 2. University of Pittsburgh, Centre for West European Studies.
O'Donnell, Rory. 2000. The New Ireland in the New Europe. In *Europe—The Irish Experience*, ed. Rory O'Donnell. Dublin: Institute of European Affairs.
O'Donnell, Rory, and Colm O'Reardon. 2000. Social Partnership in Ireland's Economic Transformation. In *Social Pacts in Europe—New Dynamics*, ed. Giuseppe Fajertag and Phillipe Pochet. Brussels: European Trade Union Institute/Observatoire Social Europeen.
OECD. 1999. *OECD Economic Surveys: Ireland*. Paris: OECD.
OECD. 2006. *OECD Economic Surveys: Ireland*. Paris: OECD.
Ó Gráda, Cormac. 2002, Spring. Is the Celtic Tiger a Paper Tiger? In *Quarterly Economic Commentary*, ed. Daniel McCoy, David Duffy, Jonathan Hore, and Conall MacCoille. Dublin: Economic and Social Research Institute.
Ó Gráda, Cormac, and Kevin O'Rourke. 1996. Irish Economic Growth, 1945–88. In *Economic Growth in Europe Since 1945*, ed. N.F.R. Crafts and G. Toniolo. Cambridge: Cambridge University Press.
Ó Gráda, Cormac, and Kevin O'Rourke. 2000. Living Standards and Growth. In *The Economy of Ireland: Policy and Performance of a European Region*, ed. John O'Hagan, 178–204. London: Macmillan.
Ó Gráda, Cormac, and Kevin O'Rourke. 2021. The Irish Economy During the Century After Partition. *The Economic History Review* 75 (2): 336–370.
O'Hearn, Denis. 2001. *The Atlantic Economy: Britain, the US and Ireland*. Manchester and New York: Manchester University Press.

O'Leary, Eoin. 2011. Reflecting on the 'Celtic Tiger': Before, During and After. *Irish Economic and Social History* 18 (1): 73–88.

O'Leary, Eoin. 2015. *Irish Economic Development: High-Performing EU State or Serial Under-Achiever?* Abingdon and New York: Routledge.

O'Malley, Eoin. 1998, April. The Revival of Irish Indigenous Industry 1987–1997. In *Quarterly Economic Commentary*, ed. T.J. Baker, David Duffy, and Fergal Shortall. Dublin: Economic and Social Research Institute.

O'Malley, Eoin. 2004, Winter. Competitive Performance in Irish Industry. In *Quarterly Economic Commentary*, ed. Daniel McCoy, David Duffy, Adele Bergin, Shane Garrett, and Yvonne McCarthy. Dublin: Economic and Social Research Institute.

O'Malley, Eoin. 2012. *A Survey of Explanations for the Celtic Tiger Boom*. IIIS Discussion Paper No. 417. Institute for International Integration Studies, Trinity College, Dublin.

O'Malley, Eoin, Nola Hewitt-Dundas, and Stephen Roper. 2008. High Growth and Innovation with Low R&D: Ireland. In *Small Country Innovation Systems: Globalization, Change and Policy in Asia and Europe*, ed. Charles Edquist and Leif Hommen. Cheltenham: Edward Elgar.

O'Malley, Eoin, Kieran A. Kennedy and Rory O'Donnell. 1992. *The Impact of the Industrial Development Agencies*. Report to the Industrial Policy Review Group. Dublin: Stationery Office.

Ó Riain, Seán. 2004a. State, Competition and Industrial Change in Ireland 1991–1999. *Economic and Social Review* 35 (1): 27–53.

Ó Riain, Seán. 2004b. *The Politics of High-Tech Growth: Developmental Network States in the Global Economy*. Cambridge: Cambridge University Press.

Ó Riain, Seán, and Philip J. O'Connell. 2000. The Role of the State in Growth and Welfare. In *Bust to Boom? The Irish Experience of Growth and Inequality*, ed. Brian Nolan, Philip J. O'Connell, and Christopher T. Whelan, 310–339. Dublin: Institute of Public Administration.

O'Sullivan, Mary. 2000. The Sustainability of Industrial Development in Ireland. *Regional Studies* 34 (3): 277–290.

Pain, Nigel. 2000/2001. Openness and Growth: An International Perspective. Symposium on Economic Growth in Ireland. *Journal of the Statistical and Social Inquiry Society of Ireland* XXX: 140–158.

Powell, Benjamin. 2003. Economic Freedom and Growth: The Case of the Celtic Tiger. *Cato Journal* 22 (3): 431–448.

Romalis, John. 2007. Capital Taxes, Trade Costs and the Irish Miracle. *Journal of the European Economic Association* 5 (2/3): 416–435.

Ruane, Frances. 2003. Foreign Direct Investment in Ireland. Lancaster University Management School Working Paper 2003/005.

Sachs, Jeffrey D. 1997. Ireland's Growth Strategy: Lessons for Economic Development. In *International Perspectives on the Irish Economy*, ed. Alan W. Gray. Dublin: Indecon Economic Consultants.

Sweeney, Paul. 1998. *The Celtic Tiger: Ireland's Economic Miracle Explained*. Dublin: Oak Tree Press.

Sweeney, Paul. 2004. *Tax Cuts Did Not Create the Celtic Tiger*. Dublin: Irish Congress of Trade Unions.

Sweeney, Paul. 2008. *Ireland's Economic Success: Reasons and Lessons*. Dublin: New Island.

Walsh, Brendan. 2000. The Role of Tax Policy in Ireland's Economic Renaissance. *Canadian Tax Journal* 48 (3): 658–673.

Open Access This chapter is licensed under the terms of the Creative Commons Attribution 4.0 International License (http://creativecommons.org/licenses/by/4.0/), which permits use, sharing, adaptation, distribution and reproduction in any medium or format, as long as you give appropriate credit to the original author(s) and the source, provide a link to the Creative Commons license and indicate if changes were made.

The images or other third party material in this chapter are included in the chapter's Creative Commons license, unless indicated otherwise in a credit line to the material. If material is not included in the chapter's Creative Commons license and your intended use is not permitted by statutory regulation or exceeds the permitted use, you will need to obtain permission directly from the copyright holder.

CHAPTER 4

Sectoral Growth and Export Earnings

This chapter analyses the contributions made by different sectors to economic growth during the boom. It aims to clarify what was the relative importance of sectors such as manufacturing, construction or services in driving economic growth, and it examines how their importance changed over time. Since this book ultimately aims to explain why the boom occurred, it is useful at this stage to identify which sectors had particularly important roles in driving economic growth in order to establish the context for further inquiry in later chapters.

A significant factor that complicates consideration of this issue is the fact that there were very large outflows of profits from foreign-owned multinational companies. As was mentioned in Chapters 1 and 2, these outflows of profits from the country were the main reason why GNP was a good deal smaller than GDP. At the sectoral level, the profit outflows came disproportionately from certain sectors and this naturally raises the question whether those sectors were really as important for the Irish economy as they might have appeared to be at first sight. This chapter aims to clarify this issue as part of the process of identifying which sectors were the key drivers of growth.

Section 4.1 examines the changing contribution of the different sectors to the growth of output (taking account of profit outflows) and to the growth of employment. Section 4.2 then focuses on the contributions of different sectors to exports. As an essential part of this it also examines the

© The Author(s) 2024

E. O'Malley, *Ireland's Long Economic Boom*, Palgrave Studies in Economic History, https://doi.org/10.1007/978-3-031-53070-8_4

net foreign earnings that accrued to the Irish economy after deducting the profit outflows and the payments for imported inputs that were associated with the exports of each sector.

4.1 Sectoral Growth

Gross Value Added (GVA)

Table 4.1 and Fig. 4.1 show each sector's share of total gross value added (GVA) in 1986, 1993, 2000 and 2007. Since GDP is essentially the sum of all value-added in the economy, a sector's GVA is similar to its contribution to GDP.[1]

A couple of sectors had generally below average growth as seen in their declining share of total GVA, namely agriculture, forestry & fishing and non-market services, which includes predominantly public sector activities such as public administration, defence, education, health and social welfare. Two other sectors had approximately average growth with no very strong trends in their share of total GVA, namely Distribution and Transport & Communications.

Table 4.1 Sectoral shares of gross value added (%)

	1986	*1993*	*2000*	*2007*
Agriculture, forestry & fishing	8.7	8.3	3.7	2.4
Manufacturing	26.0	26.9	32.8	22.0
Building & construction	5.8	5.2	7.3	9.3
Other industry	3.0	1.9	0.9	1.4
Distribution	11.9	11.1	9.3	10.7
Transport & communications	5.7	5.3	6.3	4.8
Financial services	5.8	7.2	7.2	10.3
Other market services	13.4	15.6	18.8	22.9
Non-market services	19.6	18.5	13.8	16.3
Total gross value added	100	100	100	100

Source Derived from Economic and Social Research Institute (ESRI) databank, based on data from the Central Statistics Office (CSO). Creative Commons Attribution BY 4.0

[1] The sum of GVA in all sectors, after an adjustment for product taxes and subsidies, equals GDP.

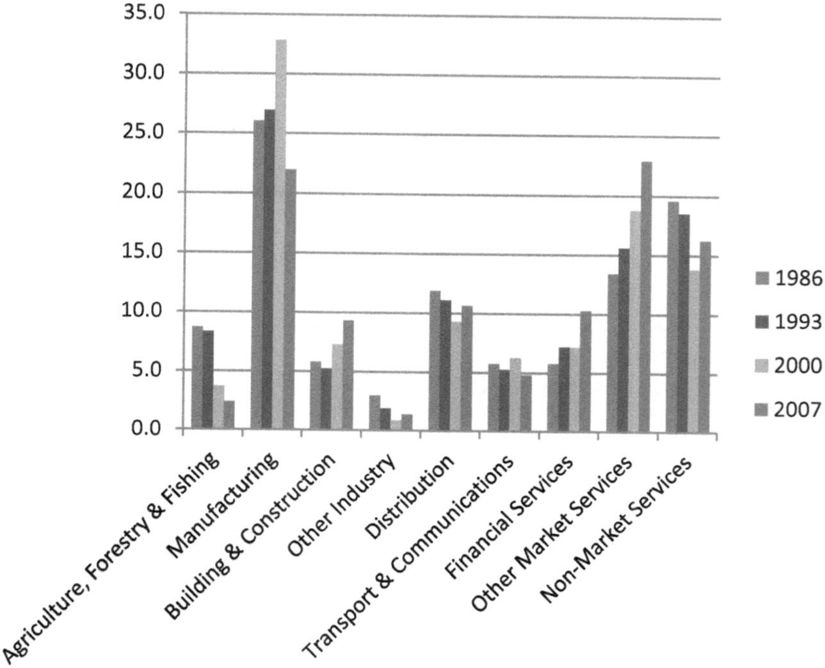

Fig. 4.1 Sectoral shares of gross value added (%) (*Source* Derived from Economic and Social Research Institute (ESRI) databank, based on data from the Central Statistics Office (CSO). Creative Commons Attribution BY 4.0)

On the other hand, there were four sectors that had well above average growth at some stage during the boom although the timing of their particularly rapid growth varied. In the case of "other" market services there was relatively rapid growth throughout the two decades. Manufacturing grew exceptionally fast before 2000, especially in 1993–2000, but its share of total GVA then slumped in 2000–2007. Meanwhile, building & construction and financial services did not grow exceptionally fast in the earlier stages of the boom, but they then grew much faster than most sectors later on.

"Retained GVA"

The GVA figures depicted in Table 4.1 and Fig. 4.1 include the profits of any foreign-owned companies that were present in each sector. Since those profits generally did not accrue to residents of Ireland it is naturally of interest to ask what were the contributions of different sectors to the economy if the profits of foreign companies are deducted. There are no regular official data that show the value of each sector's output excluding such profits, but it is possible to make reasonably good estimates. Table 4.2 shows estimates of "retained GVA" in 2000, by which we mean the GVA that is retained in Ireland after profit outflows from foreign companies are deducted.

The first two columns of Table 4.2 show GVA by sector and each sector's percentage share of total GVA. The third column shows estimates of profit outflows from foreign-owned MNCs in manufacturing and market services. As explained in Appendix, the total profit outflow figure of €22,298 million in the third column of the table is not an estimate since that is an official figure published by the Central Statistics Office, but some estimation was required for the purpose of allocating that total amount between manufacturing and market services. There are no estimates in the table for profit outflows from the other sectors because of a

Table 4.2 GVA adjusted to remove profit outflows, 2000

	GVA, 2000 € million	*GVA %*	*Estimated Profit Outflow € million*	*Retained GVA € million*	*Retained GVA %*
Agriculture, forestry & fishing	3,498	3.7		3,498	4.9
Manufacturing	30,809	32.8	16,568	14,241	19.9
Building & construction	6,811	7.3		6,811	9.5
Other industry	841	0.9		841	1.2
Market services	38,931	41.5	5,730	33,201	46.4
Non-market services	12,972	13.8		12,972	18.1
Total	93,862	100.0	22,298	71,564	100.0

Source Derived from Economic and Social Research Institute (ESRI) databank, based on data from the Central Statistics Office (CSO). See Appendix for details. Creative Commons Attribution BY 4.0

lack of relevant data, and because there are good reasons to believe that profits of foreign MNCs in those sectors would be so small that they can reasonably be ignored. (See Appendix for more detailed discussion of the derivation and interpretation of Table 4.2).

The final two columns of Table 4.2 show "retained GVA" by sector, and the sectoral proportions of the total, after deducting profit outflows from GVA. Whereas a sector's GVA is similar to its contribution to GDP (apart from an adjustment for product taxes and subsidies), its retained GVA as shown in Table 4.2 is more like its contribution to GNP (see Appendix for more clarification).

Compared to the original GVA figures in the first two columns of Table 4.2, the greatest difference in the retained GVA figures is the large reduction in the size of the manufacturing sector after profit outflows are deducted, while the reduction in the market services sector is a good deal smaller. Most of the reduction in market services was because of profit outflows from financial businesses.

In the years before 2000, retained GVA grew significantly less than GVA in manufacturing, because profit outflows were taking a rising proportion of its GVA. This was because there was particularly rapid growth in a small number of sectors within manufacturing which were predominantly foreign-owned and highly profitable. The sectors concerned—namely pharmaceuticals, office & data processing machinery, electrical engineering, instrument engineering, and soft drink concentrates—were identified in the 1980s and early 1990s as being the source of most of the profit outflows from manufacturing (O'Malley and Scott 1987, 1994). Because of their fast growth these five sectors accounted for a rapidly increasing percentage of total manufacturing GVA in the 1990s, with a rise from 33.5% of total manufacturing GVA in 1991 to 59.8% by 2000.[2] Since these major sources of profit outflows accounted for a rapidly growing proportion of the manufacturing sector, profit outflows from manufacturing were rising as a proportion of its GVA.

In financial services, there had been a traditional presence of some foreign-owned companies long before the boom began in the late 1980s,

[2] In fact, the industrial classification system was changed from 1991 onwards, so the figures mentioned here refer, not to exactly the same five sectors as those identified by O'Malley and Scott, but to their nearest equivalents in the new NACE Rev.1 system. These are NACE Rev.1 categories, 154, 156, 1588, 1589, 2414, 2441, 2442 and 30–33.

but there was also a substantial new effort to attract foreign direct investment (FDI) into export-oriented financial service activities, beginning with the establishment of the International Financial Services Centre (IFSC) in Dublin in 1987. This effort had a good deal of success. Consequently, many of the foreign-owned financial businesses that existed by 2000 were relatively new and had developed quite rapidly over the previous 13 years or so—together with an associated profit outflow.

At the macroeconomic level, it was seen in Chapter 1 that GNP generally grew more slowly than GDP in the 1980s and 1990s, primarily because profit outflows were taking a rising proportion of GDP. Since about three-quarters of the total profit outflow was coming from manufacturing by 2000, with most of the rest coming from financial services, these must have been the main sectors that were giving rise to those macroeconomic trends.

The macroeconomic trends changed in the 2000s. Profit outflows stopped taking a rising proportion of GDP, and GNP no longer grew more slowly than GDP during much of the period up to 2007. This reflected some changing trends at the sectoral level. In particular, there was a substantial decline in the importance of profit outflows from manufacturing relative to GDP or total GVA. At the same time profit outflows increased quite significantly in market services—but the increase there was not sufficient to outweigh the declining importance of the outflows from manufacturing.

To be more specific, between 2000 and 2005, the total profit outflow from the whole economy declined from 23.8% to 21.4% of total GVA. At the same time our estimated profit outflow from manufacturing fell substantially from 17.7% to 11.3% of the whole economy's GVA.[3] This change in manufacturing was a result of relatively slow growth in that sector compared to the rest of the economy (as seen in Fig. 4.1), slower growth in foreign-owned manufacturing than in total manufacturing, and lower profitability within foreign-owned manufacturing.

While profit outflows from manufacturing were declining in relative importance in 2000–2005, the opposite trend was happening in market services, including a wider range of services apart from just financial companies. In all market services combined the estimated profit outflow increased from 6.1% of the total economy GVA in 2000 to 10.1% in

[3] The method used for estimating sectoral profit outflow figures for 2005 was the same as that already described with respect to the figures for 2000 in Table 4.2.

2005. This was a general reflection of the increasing involvement of foreign-owned MNCs in market services.

It is worth noting that the sharp change seen in the manufacturing sector's share of GVA after 2000 (Table 4.1 and Fig. 4.1) looks less substantial when seen in terms of "retained" GVA after profit outflows are deducted. Much of the decline in its share of GVA, or GDP, reflected a decline in the profits and profit outflows of foreign-owned manufacturing MNCs, and this particular trend did not reduce manufacturing's retained GVA, or its share of GNP.

In market services in the same period, 2000–2005, the opposite effect occurred, meaning that its share of retained GVA rose by less than its share of GVA because of the growing influence of profit outflows.

In the building & construction sector there was no significant influence of profit outflows and consequently the increase seen in its share of GVA was matched by a similar increase in its share of retained GVA,

Employment

Turning to trends in employment by sector, Table 4.3 and Fig. 4.2 show each sector's share of total employment in 1986, 1993, 2000 and 2007. In some respects, the changing trends here are quite different to those seen in the case of GVA in Table 4.1 and Fig. 4.1.

Table 4.3 Sectoral shares of employment (%)

	1986	*1993*	*2000*	*2007*
Agriculture, forestry & fishing	16.0	12.9	7.8	5.2
Manufacturing	19.8	19.4	17.6	13.0
Building & construction	6.3	5.8	9.5	12.8
Other industry	1.5	1.0	0.7	0.6
Distribution	14.1	15.1	14.2	14.1
Transport & communications	5.7	5.7	5.7	5.4
Financial services	3.7	4.2	4.4	4.8
Other market services	12.9	15.1	20.9	21.6
Non-market services	20.0	20.8	19.1	22.4
Total employment	100.0	100.0	100.0	100.0

Source Derived from Economic and Social Research Institute (ESRI) databank, based on data from the Central Statistics Office (CSO). Creative Commons Attribution BY 4.0

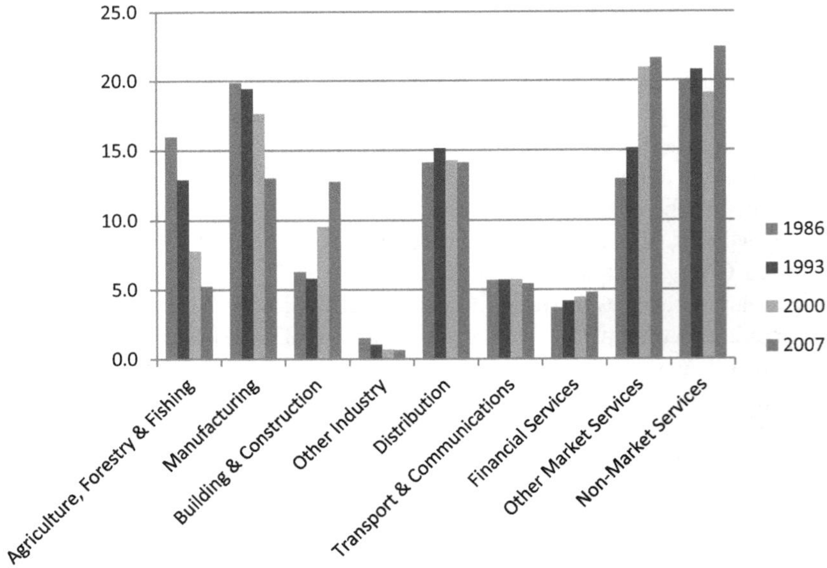

Fig. 4.2 Sectoral shares of employment (%) (*Source* Derived from Economic and Social Research Institute (ESRI) databank, based on data from the Central Statistics Office (CSO). Creative Commons Attribution BY 4.0)

Probably the most striking difference is in the manufacturing sector. In terms of GVA, manufacturing had much stronger growth than the total economy before 2000 followed by much weaker than average growth in 2000–2007, so that its share of total GVA rose substantially before 2000 followed by a very sharp decline in 2000–2007. However, in terms of employment, manufacturing did not have a growing share of the national total before 2000. Furthermore, the decline in its share of total employment in 2000–2007 was much less than in the case of its share of GVA, with a reduction of 4.6 percentage points for its share of employment as compared to 10.8 for its share of GVA.

The trend in manufacturing's share of employment after 2000 was actually quite similar to the trend in its share of retained GVA, rather than its share of GVA. This is not really surprising. GVA essentially consists of labour costs and profits. When profit outflows are deducted from GVA, most of the profits are removed (at least this was true in Ireland in the boom years). Thus, the retained GVA that is left consists very largely of labour costs—and one could reasonably expect trends in a sector's share of total labour costs to show some relationship to trends in its share of total employment.

Looking at some of the market services sectors in Table 4.3 and Fig. 4.2, it is noticeable again that the changing trends in employment were somewhat different to the trends seen in GVA—at least in the period after 2000. There was a common tendency for the trends in their share of employment to be weaker than the trends in their share of GVA. The weaker trends in employment than in GVA tend to be consistent with the fact that the trends in their retained GVA were weaker than the trends in their GVA.

On the other hand, building & construction increased its share of GVA considerably in 1993–2007 and there was also a large rise in its share of employment. There was no significant rise in the influence or distorting effect of profit outflows in that sector.

Summary

To summarise, this Sect. 4.1 has aimed to examine the contributions made by different sectors to economic growth during the boom, in terms of growth of output (while taking account of profit outflows) and growth of employment.

Seen in terms of GVA alone there is a reasonably clear story whereby four sectors had well above average growth at some stage during the boom. "Other" market services had relatively rapid growth throughout the two decades. Manufacturing grew exceptionally fast before 2000, especially in 1993–2000, but it then grew much more slowly than average in 2000–2007. Meanwhile, building & construction and financial services had not grown particularly fast in the earlier stages of the boom, but they then grew much faster than most sectors later on.

However, part of this story breaks down to some extent when we take account of profit outflows and focus on "retained GVA" and also on employment. Seen in those terms, it is doubtful whether manufacturing grew significantly faster than average before 2000, and its growth in 2000–2007 was not as weak as it seems in terms of GVA. In market services, growth in the period after 2000 was weaker in terms of retained GVA and employment than it looks when seen in terms of GVA, because of the rising influence of profit outflows.

4.2 Sectoral Export Earnings

In examining the contribution of different sectors to a small and very open economy like Ireland it is particularly important to consider each sector's exports and foreign earnings, because the sectors that export and have positive foreign earnings make an essential contribution that helps to sustain the rest of the economy.

The Importance of Exports

The importance of exports derives from the fact that a large part of the economy's expenditure is used to purchase imports.[4] Whenever the economy grows there usually tends to be increasing demand for imports, including imports of materials, equipment and fuel required as inputs for growing production sectors, and also imports of consumer goods to meet growing demand from consumers. When Ireland had its own national currency before 1999, it was quite clear that export growth was needed to pay for the increasing imports. If exports did not grow sufficiently, a balance of payments deficit tended to open up, and hence the value of the Irish currency tended to decline. A declining currency tended to result in inflation as prices of imports rose in terms of Irish currency, and at the same time it reduced the country's purchasing power when it came to paying for the imports of inputs required for production, which became an obstacle to economic growth.

From 1999 onwards, Ireland had the euro as its currency and, given the small size of the Irish economy relative to the entire eurozone, its own balance of payments position could have no effect on the value of the euro. It was sometimes suggested that this meant that Ireland's international trade performance and balance of international payments no longer mattered much. However, although the mechanism became somewhat different, a good performance in international trade continued to be essential for the health of the economy.

At any given time, a certain proportion of expenditure in Ireland is used to purchase products and services that can be traded internationally, and the rest is used to purchase "non-traded" products and services that generally have to be produced locally to meet domestic demand. If Ireland

[4] In Ireland expenditure on imports generally amounted to about 40–60% of GNP during the boom.

has a competitive and successful performance in international trade, its internationally traded sectors can grow, employment in those sectors can grow, and this increases demand for the products of the non-traded sectors which allows them to grow too and to increase their employment. Thus, in these circumstances total employment can grow, and emigration can decline or become net immigration. On the other hand, if Ireland imports a growing proportion of the internationally traded products and services that it requires, and if it fails to increase exports to the same extent, production and employment in the internationally traded sectors are reduced. As the internationally traded sectors decline, that in turn reduces demand for the output of the non-traded sectors which forces them into decline too, with adverse consequences for total employment and migration.

In his article on the Celtic tiger boom, Krugman (1997) outlined a similar view of the Irish economy as seen from an American perspective. He considered that the Irish economy had a good deal in common with a regional economy such as the Boston area rather than a large national economy such as the USA. In the US national economy, he argued, the size of the labour force is quite predictable looking, say, 15 years ahead so that economic growth over such a period is essentially determined by productivity trends alone. But at the level of a region such as the Boston area things are quite different:

> "What, then, do economists trying to forecast growth in Boston (or any other metropolitan area) look at? The usual answer is that they look at the prospects for the region's 'export base', the industries that sell to customers outside the region itself." (Krugman 1997)

He explained further that a regional economy is more open to and dependent on external trade than the economy of a large nation and, even more important, factors of production—especially labour—move much more freely into and out of a regional economy than they do in most national economies. Consequently, if Boston's "export" industries are successful this boosts employment in those industries, and hence also in other local sectors providing services to those industries and to their growing labour force, and this gives rise to inward migration of workers. Consequently, the success or failure of externally trading industries is a major determinant of the rate of growth of the labour force and of inward or outward migration of workers in a particular region.

In a similar vein, Barry (1999) considered that since the 1840s Ireland has,

> ... functioned more as a regional economy, whose population expands or contracts as economic conditions dictate, than as a national economy whose population size is largely determined by demographic factors. ... The size of a regional economy ... is crucially determined by its export base....

Consequently, Barry (1999) concluded that the fundamental economic issue for Ireland has generally been the need to achieve competitive success in internationally tradeable sectors besides agriculture.[5]

The view that the Irish economy is largely driven by the growth or decline of its internationally traded sectors is a common feature in a good deal of the analysis and research undertaken by Irish economists, although it may not always be stated and justified very explicitly. It seems worthwhile to spell it out explicitly here mainly because, after the introduction of the euro, it was sometimes claimed in Ireland that the country's international trade performance and balance of international payments no longer mattered very much.

However, it should be acknowledged that there are some circumstances in which the particular importance of exporting sectors may not hold true, but such circumstances tend to be temporary or quite specific in nature. For example, growth of imports could be paid for by an inflow of loans or investment from abroad rather than by growing exports, but that would ultimately be unsustainable unless much of the inflow is invested in productive activities that generate foreign earnings. Alternatively, the importance of maintaining a strong performance in international trade could be reduced for a time if the composition of domestic demand is shifting away from purchasing internationally traded goods and towards non-traded products such as housing or locally oriented services. However, unless there is reason to believe that there will be a continuing series of shifts further in that direction, it will ultimately be necessary to have a good international trade performance.

[5] Chapter 2 in this book outlined a brief account of the history of the Irish economy which is consistent with the perspective discussed above. It focused particularly on the role of the industrial sector—as the main internationally traded sector apart from agriculture—and it concluded by referring to the main issues confronting the industrial sector in the 1980s immediately before the boom.

Sectoral Export Earnings During the Boom

For the reasons discussed above it is usually essential for the Irish economy to have some competitive and successful internationally trading sectors. More specifically, some sectors must export sufficient amounts to pay not only for their own imported inputs but also for many other imports, because the non-traded sectors and consumers purchase imports without being able to contribute to exports. Thus, sectors that have a positive and growing surplus of exports in excess of their own import requirements make an essential contribution that helps to sustain growth in the rest of the economy. Conversely, sectors that do not export, or that export less than their own import requirements, may look vibrant in terms of strong trends in production or employment, but their continuing prosperity usually depends on the success of the sectors that have a surplus of exports over imports.

During most of the Celtic Tiger boom, Ireland's exports grew very rapidly—much faster than the rest of the economy—although in the final six or seven years of the boom export growth slowed down. In 1986–2001, total exports of goods and services increased by 13.6% per year when measured in constant prices and by 15.6% per year in terms of current prices. In 2001–2007, the growth rate slowed down to 5.2% per year in constant prices and to 4.5% per year in current prices.[6]

From the start of the boom until the end of the 1990s, merchandise accounted for four-fifths or more of the value of total exports while services accounted for no more than one-fifth of the total. However, that pattern changed from about 2000 onwards as the share of services rose very rapidly up to 2007 (see Fig. 4.3). Both merchandise and services exports had grown rapidly before the 2000s as merchandise exports grew by 14.8% per year in 1986–2001 while services exports grew by 19.1% per year, in terms of current prices. The main change that happened after that was a very sharp deterioration in the growth rate of the value of merchandise exports to -0.6% per year in 2001–2007. The growth of services exports also slowed down somewhat compared with 1986–2001 but it nevertheless continued at a very high rate of 14.7% per year in 2001–2007, again in current prices.

[6] Data from ESRI Databank.

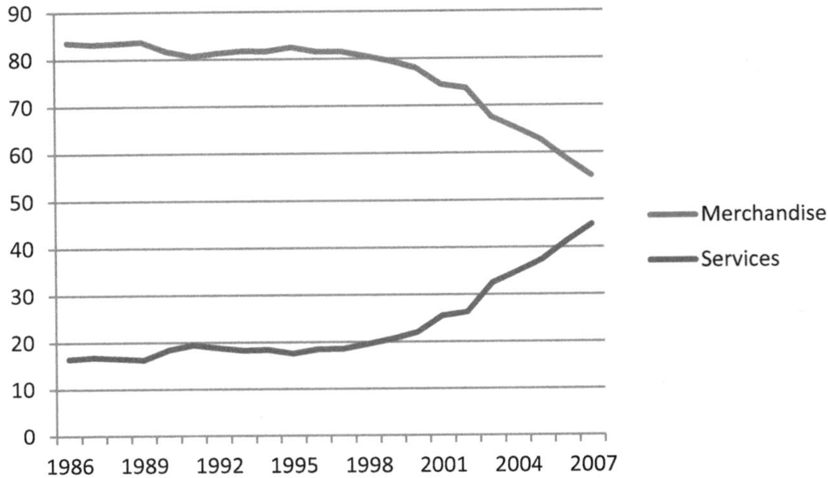

Fig. 4.3 Merchandise and services shares of total exports, 1986–2007 (%) (*Source* Derived from Economic and Social Research Institute (ESRI) databank, based on data from the Central Statistics Office (CSO). Creative Commons Attribution BY 4.0)

Products of the manufacturing sector accounted for the vast majority of merchandise exports—generally 95% or more—with some primary products such as live cattle and metal ores making up the remainder. However, the agriculture sector also made an important indirect contribution to merchandise exports since most of its output was processed through companies in the manufacturing sector, such as meat and dairy processors, before being exported. It can be seen in Table 4.4 that food accounted for 21% of merchandise exports at the start of the boom, with meat and dairy products accounting for 12%. The value of these exports increased during the boom, but their share of total merchandise exports declined substantially as some other categories grew much more rapidly.

The strongest growth in merchandise exports occurred in chemicals, particularly in the two categories of pharmaceuticals and organic chemicals, which include finished pharmaceutical products as well as ingredients for pharmaceuticals. As shown in Table 4.4 these products combined accounted for 8.7% of merchandise exports in 1986 rising continuously to 38.5% by 2007. Electronic and electrical products also grew particularly

Table 4.4 Composition of merchandise exports, 1986–2007 (%)

	1986	*1993*	*2000*	*2007*
Food	20.7	19.1	6.6	8.2
Meat & dairy products	12.0	9.8	3.5	4.3
Other food	8.6	9.3	3.1	3.9
Chemicals	13.3	19.3	32.6	48.3
Organic chemicals	6.6	9.4	20.1	22.0
Pharmaceutical products	2.1	4.9	6.3	16.5
Other chemicals	4.7	5.0	6.1	9.7
Machinery, transport equipt.	30.4	29.0	40.5	24.4
Electronic & electrical products[a]	25.5	25.1	37.3	21.1
Other machinery & transport equipt.	4.9	3.9	3.3	3.4
Other merchandise	35.6	32.6	20.3	19.1
Total merchandise	100.0	100.0	100.0	100.0

Note [a]"Electronic & Electrical Products" here includes the following SITC categories: (75) Office machines and data processing equipment; (76) Telecommunications and sound recording, reproducing equipment; (77) Electrical machinery, appliances etc., n.e.s.
Source Derived from CSO, External Trade statistics. Creative Commons Attribution BY 4.0

fast before 2000 and they accounted for 37% of merchandise exports by that date. However, the value of these exports then declined substantially between 2000 and 2007 and their share of merchandise exports slumped back to below their 1986 level. The decline in this category of exports in the 2000s was a major reason why the growth of merchandise exports deteriorated so sharply in that period.

As regards services exports, at the start of the boom they initially consisted largely of transport services (41% of total services exports) and lodging & catering (23%), with smaller contributions coming from business services (7%), financial and insurance services (4%) and a variety of other smaller amounts (totalling 25%).[7] During the boom there was growth in the exports of the transport and tourism services which had initially dominated services exports but the fastest growth occurred in other areas—particularly computer services, business services, insurance and financial services—so that the share of transport and tourism in total services exports declined substantially.

[7] Derived from CSO, *Input–Output Tables for 1985*.

It can be seen in Table 4.5 that the share of transport and tourism in total services exports was much reduced by 1998 compared with the mid-1980s, and this trend continued to the end of the boom. Meanwhile computer services, business services, insurance and financial services became the dominant categories of services exports and they accounted for 86% of total services exports by the end of the boom. It is noticeable in Table 4.5 that there was a particularly sharp rise in the share of business services in total services exports between 2000 and 2007. This was mainly due to a sharp increase in two types of business service that had been much less prominent before that time, merchanting/trade-related services and operational leasing.[8]

Tables 4.4 and 4.5 show data on exports, but we are interested here in looking deeper than this to establish the amount of net foreign earnings that accrued to the Irish economy from each sector. This means that it is necessary to deduct from each sector's exports the value of its imported

Table 4.5
Composition of services exports, 1998–2007 (%)

	1998	*2000*	*2007*
Transport	9.2	6.9	4.3
Tourism & travel	18.4	13.2	6.5
Communications	1.9	4.7	0.8
Insurance	15.0	12.6	12.9
Financial services	7.2	10.4	10.9
Computer services	29.7	37.5	32.0
Business services	15.0	9.6	30.3
Merchanting/trade-related	*0.4*	*2.1*	*15.0*
Operational leasing	*4.0*	*2.8*	*8.5*
Other business services	*10.7*	*4.7*	*6.7*
Other services	3.5	5.1	2.3
Total	100.0	100.0	100.0

Source Derived from CSO, Balance of Payments, current account.
Creative Commons Attribution BY 4.0

[8] "Merchanting/trade-related services" consisted very largely of "merchanting". Merchanting means sales (net of purchases), by Irish resident enterprises, of foreign goods bought from and sold to non-residents without the goods entering or leaving Ireland. Other "trade-related" services are services provided by resident agents to non-residents in connection with importing and exporting. Operational leasing covers leasing, by residents to non-residents, of aircraft, ships or other plant and equipment, without operators being provided. In Ireland this referred very largely to aircraft leasing.

inputs as well as its profit outflows. For this purpose, it is necessary to use data from official input–output tables. These tables use the classification system that is used for production sectors, rather than the system that is used for international trade data as seen in Tables 4.4 and 4.5. The input–output tables include data by sector on exports as well as imported inputs.

Table 4.6 shows the changing sectoral composition of all exports using data derived from input–output tables, and Fig. 4.4 shows the same data leaving out the few sectors that had zero exports—electricity, gas & water, construction, and non-market services. Since the input–output tables were published infrequently—usually at five-year intervals—there is a limited choice of years available for this purpose, but the years 1985, 2000 and 2005 shown in Table 4.6 and Fig. 4.4 are reasonably suitable. The period 1985–2000 corresponds quite well to the phase of very rapid export growth during the boom, while the period 2000–2005 is quite similar to the final phase of the boom when export growth was slower.

Despite the differences in classification systems and the details of time periods, most of the major trends seen in Tables 4.4 and 4.5 are also evident in Table 4.6 and Fig. 4.4. Thus, among the manufacturing sectors in Table 4.6 and Fig. 4.4 the strongest export growth was in chemical products. There was also relatively fast growth in metal products, engineering & electronics up to 2000 and its share of total exports then slumped after 2000; this sector would include most of the category "electronic & electrical products" seen in Table 4.4, as well as metal products and agricultural & industrial machinery. Exports of food, beverages & tobacco grew relatively slowly during most of the boom so that its share of the total dropped substantially.

Most other manufacturing sectors in Table 4.6 and Fig. 4.4 also had relatively slow export growth with declining shares of the total. An obvious exception to this was "other" industry which grew rapidly in 1985–2000—largely because it included the production of recorded media which in Ireland mainly meant software products. Exports of software were growing very fast. In 2000–2005 the growth of "other" industry exports slowed down to average pace, as software was increasingly being transmitted to customers by electronic means rather than being sold on a physical medium such as a disk. This change meant that

Table 4.6 Composition of total exports, 1985–2005 (%)

	1985	*2000*	*2005*
Agriculture, forestry & fishing	3.4	0.8	0.5
Food, beverages & tobacco	26.5	7.4	9.8
Textiles, clothing, leather products	5.1	0.7	0.4
Chemical products	12.4	26.4	24.2
Rubber & plastics	2.3	0.7	0.6
Non-metallic mineral products	3.1	0.9	0.3
Metal products, engineering, electronics[a]	29.4	33.1	20.1
Vehicles, Other Transport Equipment	0.8	1.0	0.7
Other industry	4.6	10.6	10.5
Electricity, gas & water	0.0	0.0	0.0
Construction	0.0	0.0	0.0
Wholesale & retail	3.4	0.5	4.7
Hotels & restaurants	2.3	1.8	2.0
Transport services	4.7	1.6	1.8
Communication services	0.2	1.1	0.3
Financial services & insurance	0.4	4.4	10.2
Business services	0.7	8.8	13.4
Non-market services	0.6	0.0	0.0
Other services	0.3	0.2	0.3
Total	100.0	100.0	100.0

Note [a]"Metal Products, Engineering & Electronics" here includes metal products, agricultural & industrial machinery, office machinery & computers, other electrical and electronic products and medical, precision & optical instruments

Source Derived from CSO, ***Input–Output Tables for 1985; 2000 Supply and Use and Input–Output Tables; Supply and Use and Input–Output Tables for Ireland—2005***. Creative Commons Attribution BY 4.0

software exports were increasingly being classified as exports of business services rather than manufactured products.[9]

Summing up all the categories of merchandise exports seen in Table 4.6 and Fig. 4.4, their combined share of total exports was 88% in 1985, declining slowly to 82% in 2000, and falling far more rapidly to

[9] It is not possible to show a more detailed disaggregation of "other" industry, or some of the other large categories in Table 4.6 and Fig. 4.4, because there was a major revision of the classification system used for production sectors between 1985 and 2000/2005. This means that, for the purpose of making comparisons between 1985 and 2000/2005, it is necessary to use some categories only at high levels of aggregation.

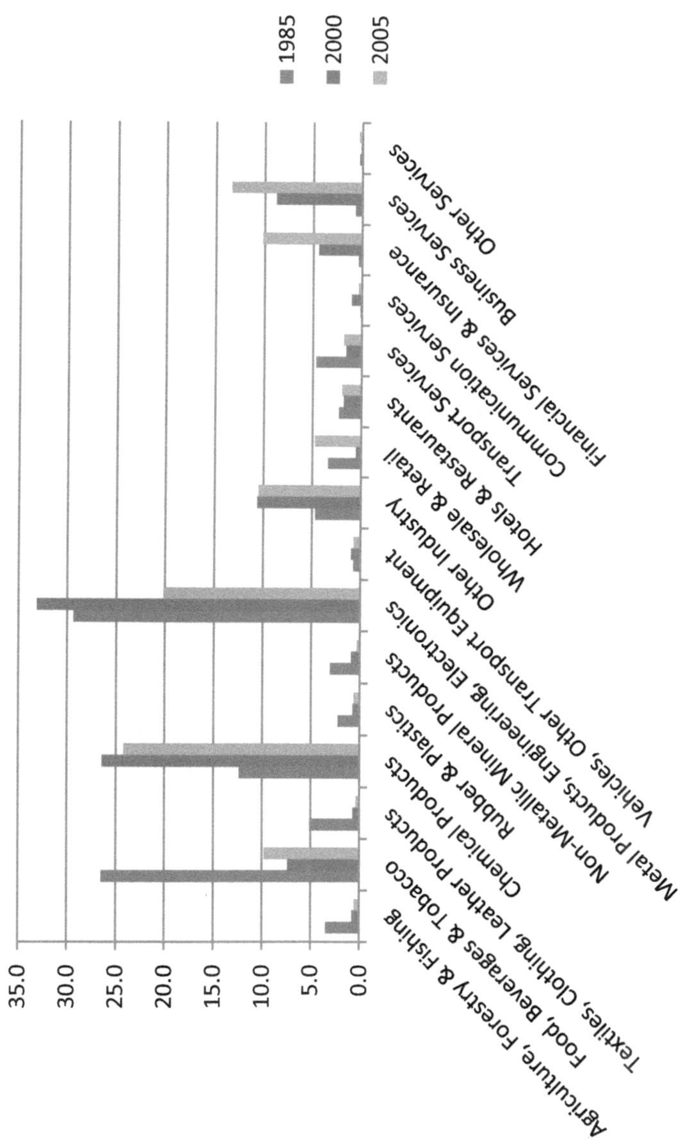

Fig. 4.4 Composition of Total Exports, 1985–2005 (%) (*Sources* and *Notes* As for Table 4.6. Creative Commons Attribution BY 4.0)

67% by 2005. This is similar to the trend seen above in Fig. 4.3, which is based on international trade data.

As regards exports of the services sectors, the main trends mentioned above when discussing Table 4.5 are also evident in Table 4.6 and Fig. 4.4. These trends include the particularly rapid growth of exports from financial services & insurance and from business services, and the decline in the relative importance of transport services and hotels & restaurants. In Table 4.6 and Fig. 4.4, business services include computer and related services, which were a separate category in Table 4.5. It is noticeable in Table 4.6 and Fig. 4.4 that there was a sharp increase in the share of exports held by wholesale & retail distribution between 2000 and 2005. This partly corresponds to the increase in the importance of "merchanting" in Table 4.5, which was mentioned above.

In order to look deeper than the data on exports to see how much net foreign earnings accrued to the Irish economy from each sector, it is necessary to subtract from each sector's exports the value of its imported inputs and its profit outflows. This is a significant issue in the case of the Irish economy, because imported inputs and profit outflows can be quite large relative to exports, and sectors can differ substantially in terms of their import content and their outflows of profits. Table 4.7 and Fig. 4.5 show data by sector for the year 2000 on exports, net exports and net foreign earnings. To clarify the terminology that is employed here, a sector's "net exports" is defined here as the value of its exports minus the value of the imported inputs that are used in producing the exports. Its "net foreign earnings" is defined here as the value of its net exports minus the profit outflows that arise from production of the exports. In 2000, total net foreign earnings were worth 34% of the value of total exports (Table 4.7).

Table 4.7 and Fig. 4.5 show that some sectors—construction, non-market services and electricity, gas & water—had no exports and no net foreign earnings, although these sectors all had imported inputs. These sectors depended on the success of other industries in international markets in order to facilitate growth of their imports, growth of the economy and growth of domestic demand for their output. Consequently, although the construction industry looked particularly vibrant in terms of strong trends in production and employment during most

Table 4.7 Exports, net exports and net foreign earnings, by sector, 2000 (€ million)

	Exports	*Net exports*	*Net foreign earnings*
Agriculture, forestry & fishing	750	642	642
Food, beverages & tobacco	7,165	5,894	4,986
Textiles, clothing, leather products	684	468	423
Chemical products	25,664	12,065	3,779
Rubber & plastics	714	449	393
Non-metallic mineral products	852	647	621
Metal products, engineering & electronics	32,139	11,126	7,016
Vehicles, other transport equipment	943	482	402
Other industry	10,337	5,168	3,165
Electricity, gas & water	0	0	0
Construction	0	0	0
Market services	17,854	14,582	11,229
Non-market services	0	0	0
Total	97,104	51,526	32,659

Notes "Net Exports" here means the value of a sector's exports minus the value of the imported inputs that are used in producing the exports. "Net Foreign Earnings" means the value of its net exports minus the profit outflows that arise from production of the exports

"Metal Products, Engineering & Electronics" here includes metal products, agricultural & industrial machinery, office machinery & computers, other electrical and electronic products and medical, precision & optical instruments

Source Exports and net exports derived from CSO, *2000 Supply and Use and Input–Output Tables*. Profit outflows estimated using the method discussed in Sect. 4.1 and in Appendix. Creative Commons Attribution BY 4.0

of the boom, it could not be seen as a significant independent driver of economic growth for this reason.[10]

The sectors that had the capability to be significant independent drivers of economic growth were those that had substantial exports and, more important, substantial net foreign earnings. It can be seen in Table 4.7 and Fig. 4.5 that the sectors with the most exports in 2000 were metal products, engineering & electronics, followed by chemical products, with

[10] This does not mean that the non-exporting sectors are not important. In fact, all of them include activities that are essential for the welfare and even the survival of a modern society. However, the point here is that they do not have the same capability as exporting sectors to drive the process of economic growth.

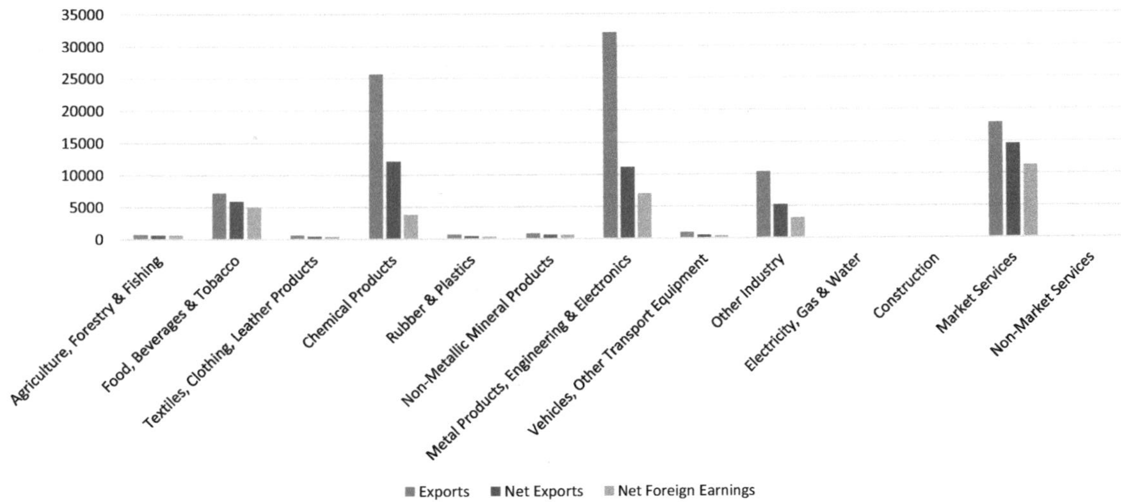

Fig. 4.5 Exports, net exports and net foreign earnings, by Sector, 2000 (€ million) (*Notes* "Net Exports" here means the value of a sector's exports minus the value of the imported inputs that are used in producing the exports. "Net Foreign Earnings" means the value of its net exports minus the profit outflows that arise from production of the exports; "Metal Products, Engineering & Electronics" here includes metal products, agricultural & industrial machinery, office machinery & computers, other electrical and electronic products and medical, precision & optical instruments. *Source* As for Table 4.7. Creative Commons Attribution BY 4.0)

market services, "other" industry and food, beverages & tobacco some way behind. However, in some of those sectors foreign ownership was very common and there were high levels of imported inputs and profit outflows. Consequently, net foreign earnings amounted to only 15–31% of the value of exports in metal products, engineering & electronics, chemical products and "other" industry. In contrast, net foreign earnings amounted to 70% of the value of exports in food, beverages & tobacco and 63% of the value of exports in market services. As a result, market services were a more important source of net foreign earnings than chemical products or metal products, engineering & electronics.

To be clear, the "market services" sector in Table 4.7 and Fig. 4.5 combines together all of the service sectors that were separate categories in some previous tables and charts, with the exception of non-market services. They are grouped together here because of data constraints when estimating profit outflows from service sectors (see Appendix).

Box 4.1: How Reliable Are the Estimates of Net Foreign Earnings?
It may seem surprising that the estimates of net foreign earnings for some sectors in Table 4.7 and Fig. 4.5 are so low relative to their exports. How reliable are these estimates?

All the figures presented for net exports were derived using only official CSO data—so no estimation was involved in deriving those figures. When deducting profit outflows from net exports to arrive at net foreign earnings, the total profit outflow figure was also obtained from official CSO data, without requiring any estimation. The need for making estimates arose only when allocating the total profit outflow among the different sectors to derive sectoral net foreign earnings.

There is a way to check the estimates for some of the most important sectors. The Annual Business Survey of Economic Impact (ABSEI) published by Forfas presented figures, by manufacturing sector, on "direct expenditure in the Irish economy", which was defined as expenditure on total payroll costs, Irish-sourced material inputs, Irish-sourced services inputs and the profits of Irish-owned companies (e.g., see Forfas 2006). Thus, a sector's sales minus its "direct expenditure in the Irish economy", from that survey, should be almost equivalent to the sector's total "outflows" from the economy in the form of expenditure on imported inputs plus profit outflows, as derived for Table 4.7 and Fig. 4.5.

Comparing sectoral outflows as a percentage of sales derived from the Forfas ABSEI data with figures for outflows as a percentage of production derived by our own estimation procedure produces the following results for the year 2000:

Chemical products: 86% from ABSEI and 85% from our own estimates.

Metal products, engineering & electronics: 74% from ABSEI and 79% from our own estimates.

Food, beverages & tobacco: 27% from ABSEI and 28% from our own estimates (after an adjustment to ensure that excise tax is counted as an expenditure in Ireland in both cases).

Total manufacturing: 66% from ABSEI and 69% from our own estimates.

Since there ought to be some small differences between figures from the two sources, these results from two independent sources look close enough to give some assurance that both sets of figures are quite reasonable. However, it should probably be assumed that there could be errors of up to about four percentage points in our sectoral estimates.

(The ABSEI survey did not cover most services, and its definition of "other" industry was very different to that in Table 4.7).

The three "modern" or "high-tech" manufacturing sectors—metal products, engineering & electronics, chemical products and "other" industry—accounted for a dominant 70% share of exports in 2000. However, their share of total net foreign earnings was a good deal lower at 43%. At the same time market services and food, beverages & tobacco combined accounted for just 26% of exports but as much as 50% of net foreign earnings.

It is clear that a sector's contribution to exports does not necessarily give a good indication of the relative importance of its contribution to net foreign earnings, which actually matters more than exports for sustaining the growth of the economy.

To show the trends in net foreign earnings over time, Table 4.8 presents estimates of net foreign earnings by sector in 1985, 2000 and 2005, together with the increases in net foreign earnings in 1985–2000 and 2000–2005. Figure 4.6 shows the increases in net foreign earnings compared to increases in exports for selected sectors in 1985–2000, while Fig. 4.7 similarly shows the increases in net foreign earnings and exports in selected sectors in 2000–2005. The selected sectors that are included in Figs. 4.6 and 4.7 are all the sectors that had significant increases in exports or net foreign earnings or both, in at least one of the two periods.

Table 4.8 Net foreign earnings, 1985–2005, million Euros, current values

	1985	*2000*	*2005*	*Increase 1985–2000*	*Increase 2000–2005*
Agriculture, forestry & fishing	433	642	554	209	−88
Food, beverages & tobacco	2,896	4,986	7,189	2,090	2,203
Textiles, clothing, leather products	408	423	238	16	−185
Chemical products	596	3,779	6,104	3,183	2,325
Non-metallic mineral products	239	621	308	382	−313
Metals & engineering	1,494	7,418	7,190	5,924	−228
Other industry	367	3,558	4,134	3,191	576
Electricity, gas & water	0	0	13	0	13
Construction	0	0	0	0	0
Market services	1,434	11,229	25,936	9,795	14,707
Non-market services	80	0	34	−80	34
Total	7,946	32,659	51,700	24,713	19,041

Note "Net Foreign Earnings" here means the value of a sector's exports minus the value of the imported inputs that are used in producing the exports, minus the profit outflows that arise from production of the exports

Source Exports and imported inputs data derived from CSO, *Input–Output Tables for 1985; 2000 Supply and Use and Input–Output Tables;* and *Supply and Use and Input–Output Tables for Ireland - 2005.* Profit outflow figures by sector for 2000 and 2005 were estimated using the method discussed in Sect. 4.1 and in Appendix. For 1985, profit outflow figures by sector were estimated using a different method which is outlined in a separate section in Appendix. Creative Commons Attribution BY 4.0

Table 4.8 shows that there were some sectors—namely electricity, gas & water, construction, and non-market services—that had very low or zero exports throughout the period. The imported inputs required by these sectors generally grew as their production grew. Thus, positive growth in net foreign earnings was required from other sectors in order to make the growth of these sectors sustainable.

In 1985–2000 the greatest increase in net foreign earnings came from market services. This was followed by metals & engineering, "other" industry, chemical products and food, beverages & tobacco (Table 4.8 and Fig. 4.6). This was different to the pattern of contributions to the growth of exports since metals & engineering and chemical products had by far the largest increases in exports (Fig. 4.6).

The three "modern" or high-tech manufacturing sectors—metals & engineering, chemical products and "other" industry—accounted for 76% of the total increase in exports in 1985–2000. However, their share of the

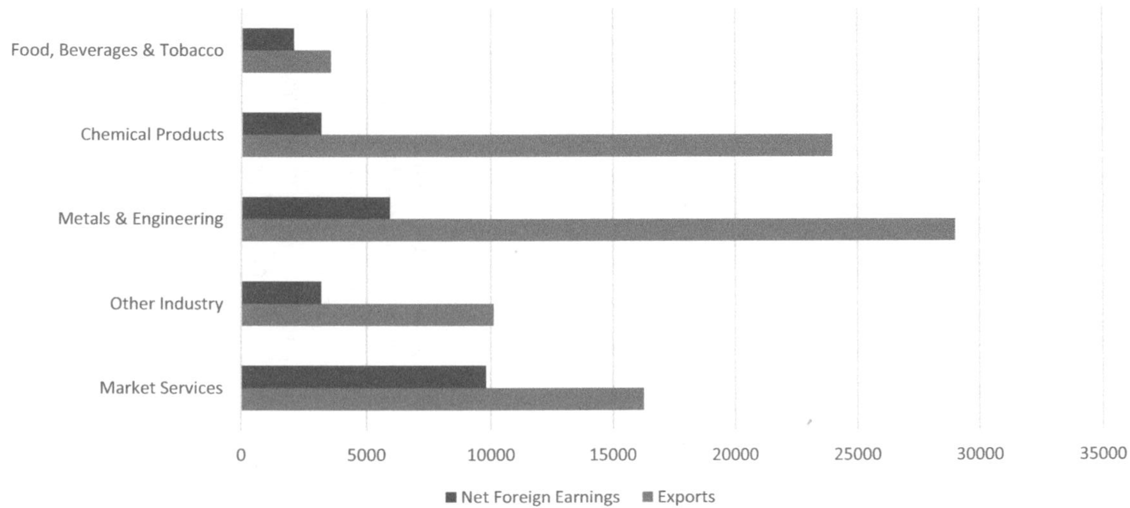

Fig. 4.6 Increase in the value of exports and net foreign earnings, selected sectors, 1985–2000, million Euros (*Note* "Net Foreign Earnings" here means the value of a sector's exports minus the value of the imported inputs that are used in producing the exports, minus the profit outflows that arise from production of the exports. *Source* Exports and imported inputs data derived from CSO, *Input–Output Tables for 1985*, and *2000 Supply and Use and Input–Output Tables*. Profit outflow figures by sector for 2000 were estimated using the method discussed in Sect. 4.1 and in Appendix. For 1985 profit outflow figures by sector were estimated using a different method which is outlined in a separate section in Appendix. Creative Commons Attribution BY 4.0)

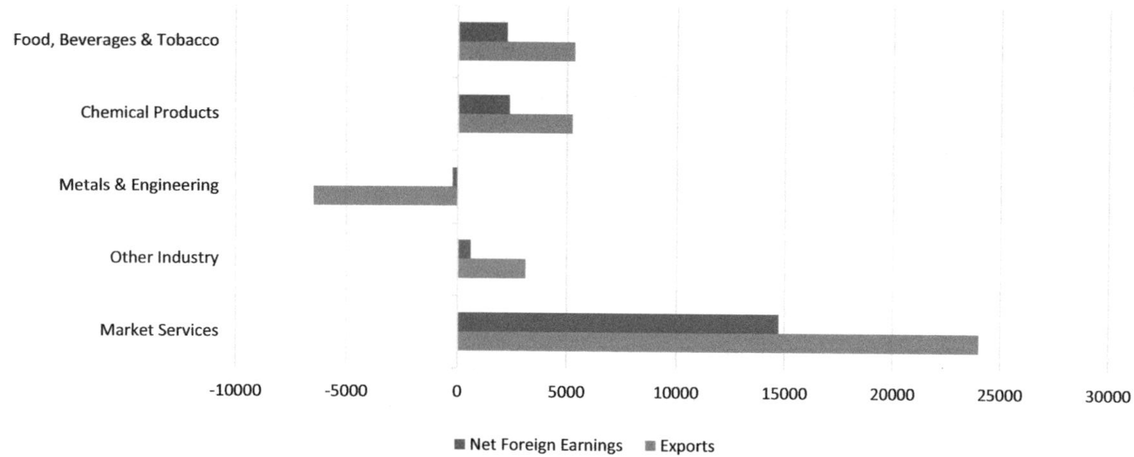

Fig. 4.7 Increase in the value of exports and net foreign earnings, selected sectors, 2000–2005, million Euros (*Note* "Net Foreign Earnings" here means the value of a sector's exports minus the value of the imported inputs that are used in producing the exports, minus the profit outflows that arise from production of the exports. *Source* Exports and imported inputs data derived from CSO, *2000 Supply and Use and Input–Output Tables,* and *Supply and Use and Input–Output Tables for Ireland - 2005*. Profit outflow figures by sector for 2000 and 2005 were estimated using the method discussed in Sect. 4.1 and in Appendix. Creative Commons Attribution BY 4.0)

total increase in net foreign earnings was a good deal lower at 50%. At the same time, market services together with food, beverages & tobacco accounted for just 24% of the total increase in exports but they accounted for as much as 48% of the total increase in net foreign earnings.

As regards the period after 2000, it was noted earlier in this chapter that a feature of that period was a weakening in manufacturing exports in contrast to the strong growth of services exports. The most important reason for the weakness in manufacturing exports was because of a sharp decline in exports of electronic & electrical products. Accordingly, Fig. 4.7 shows a large decline in exports of metals & engineering products (a broader category than electronic & electrical products) in 2000–2005. Since net foreign earnings were low relative to exports in that sector, Fig. 4.7 also shows that the decline in its net foreign earnings was far less significant than the decline in its exports.[11] The small decline in net foreign earnings in metals & engineering was outweighed by some other trends among the manufacturing sectors—an acceleration in the growth of net foreign earnings in the food, beverages & tobacco sector as a result of acceleration in its exports, while there was also continuing substantial growth in chemical products.

As regards the strong growth of market services exports in the period after 2000, net foreign earnings were tending to decline somewhat as a proportion of exports as the relative importance of foreign-owned MNCs in the sector increased, but the increase in net foreign earnings in market services was still much greater than in any other sector.

To focus on the overall outcome of these sectoral trends, it was already noted above that the growth of total exports slowed down very markedly after 2000. However, this weakening trend in exports did not result in a similar weakening of the trend in total net foreign earnings. Table 4.9 shows that the rate of growth of exports was 14.0% p.a. in 1985–2000, declining to just 5.6% p.a. in 2000–2005, valued in current prices. At the same time, the rate of growth of net foreign earnings was 9.9% p.a. in

[11] Actually, the decline in net foreign earnings in metals & engineering was extremely small relative to the decline in its exports, and this was partly an effect of changing composition within that sector—with steep export decline occurring in a part of the sector with particularly low net foreign earnings relative to exports (namely electronic products), while some export growth was occurring in other parts of the sector with higher net foreign earnings relative to exports (such as mechanical engineering).

Table 4.9 Growth rates of exports, net foreign earnings and GNP (% p.a.), current values

	1985–2000	*2000–2005*
Exports	14.0	5.6
Net foreign earnings	9.9	9.6
GNP	9.7	9.0

Source Exports data derived from CSO, *Input–Output Tables for 1985; 2000 Supply and Use and Input–Output Tables;* and *Supply and Use and Input–Output Tables for Ireland—2005.* Net foreign earnings from Table 4.8. GNP from Department of Finance, *Budgetary and Economic Statistics*, October 2012. Creative Commons Attribution BY 4.0

1985–2000 and virtually the same rate at 9.6% p.a. in 2000–2005, again in current prices.

The explanation for these contrasting trends in exports and net foreign earnings lies in the sectoral developments outlined above. In 1985–2000 net foreign earnings grew much more slowly than exports mainly because most of the export growth at that time was occurring in sectors where net foreign earnings were a relatively low proportion of exports. Then, after 2000 exports grew a good deal more slowly than net foreign earnings mainly because most of the weakness in exports occurred in a sector where net foreign earnings were a relatively low proportion of exports, so that the dramatic decline in its exports was of limited significance for the overall trend in net foreign earnings.

The opening part of this Sect. 4.2 outlined the reasons why it would be expected, in a small and very open economy, that the growth of exports would be the main determinant of economic growth. That view is a useful first approximation and it would generally be valid whenever net foreign earnings are growing at about the same rate as exports. However, it seems clear that, if there are periods when net foreign earnings and exports are growing at very different rates, then it is net foreign earnings rather than exports that have the main influence on economic growth. Table 4.9 indicates that Ireland's GNP growth tended to be similar to the growth of net foreign earnings rather than exports when the growth rates of net foreign earnings and exports diverged because of rapidly changing sectoral composition.

There is a common view which holds that the sustainable export-led boom that had been occurring in Ireland up to about 2000 really came to an end at around that time, because export growth became so much weaker, while economic growth became very dependent on unsustainable factors such as the speculative housing boom.

The findings of this section indicate that this view is not tenable with respect to the first four or five years after 2000. The weakening of export growth after 2000 was not as serious for the economy as it appeared to be. The continuing growth of net foreign earnings accruing to the economy from export growth in 2000–2005 was quite capable of sustaining the economic growth that was occurring, which continued to be relatively fast economic growth by international standards.

Property-related lending and the growth of construction probably did start to become excessive and unsustainable some time during 2001–2004.[12] However, it is not clear that this activity increased the growth rate of the economy in those years over and above the growth rate that was going to happen anyway if there had been no such property boom. In that period, 2001–2004, the property boom was still very largely financed by Ireland's own domestic savings rather than by additional funding sourced from abroad. This indicates that economic growth could have happened at about the same rate if the excessive investments that went into property had been spent instead in more usual ways. Also, balance of payments current account deficits were small in the period 2001–2004, averaging just 0.7% of GNP. In that sense, the overall rate of economic growth was not too high to be sustainable.

However, the final few years of the boom were different. In 2005–2007 the growth of our estimated net foreign earnings did slow right down—to 3.8% p.a. in current values—which was not sufficient to sustain GNP growth which continued at a high rate of 8.1% p.a. in current values. In those years the banks sourced large amounts of additional funding from abroad, mainly for property-related lending which increased very rapidly. This was reflected in a rise in the current balance of payments deficit from 0.7% of GNP in 2004 to 4.1% in 2005 and 2006 and 6.2% in 2007. Thus, in those years it was the case that a large inflow of finance from abroad for property-related lending was making it possible for the economy to grow at a rate that was unsustainable and that would not have been attained otherwise.

To sum up, the pace of growth of net foreign earnings was sufficient to sustain the growth that was occurring in the economy from 2000 to 2004 or 2005 (even if the property and construction boom was already heading towards serious problems). It was not until about 2005 that the growth

[12] We consider this further in Chapter 7.

of net foreign earnings ceased to be sufficient to support the growth that was happening in the economy.

4.3 Conclusion

The sectors that were most influential in driving economic growth were those that had the most substantial increase in net foreign earnings.

To concentrate first on the period from the mid-1980s until 2000, those most influential sectors were, in the following order: (1) market services—including business services, computer-related services, financial services, distribution, etc.; (2) metals & engineering—including electronic products; (3) "other" industry—including software products; (4) chemical products; and (5) food, beverages & tobacco.

This was different to the pattern of contributions to the growth of exports since metals & engineering and chemical products had by far the largest increases in exports. The three high-tech manufacturing sectors taken together accounted for 76% of the total increase in exports in 1985–2000 but their share of the total increase in net foreign earnings was a good deal lower at 50%. At the same time market services together with food, beverages & tobacco accounted for just 24% of the total increase in exports but they accounted for as much as 48% of the total increase in net foreign earnings.

Thus, the high-tech manufacturing sectors were considerably less important for growth than they appeared to be in the period up to 2000. Nevertheless, it must be recognised that, even after taking full account of the high levels of their imported inputs and their large profit outflows, they did make a very large contribution to the growth of net foreign earnings and hence the economy. They were an essential part of the Celtic tiger boom in the period up to 2000, although their role was not as dominant as it seemed.

Staying with the period before 2000, the building & construction sector had relatively fast growth in 1993–2000, whether its growth is considered in terms of GVA or in terms of employment. However, that sector did not export, so that it depended on the success of other industries in international markets in order to facilitate the growth of the economy and hence growth of domestic demand for its output. Consequently, although the growth of construction looked particularly vibrant, it could not be seen as a significant independent driver of economic growth.

Turning to the period after 2000, export growth weakened substantially then but the growth of net foreign earnings arising from exports remained strong enough for another four or five years to sustain the economic growth of that period, which continued to be relatively fast growth by international standards. Thus, relatively fast economic growth was still sustainable until about 2004 or 2005.

The most important sectors in terms of growth of net foreign earnings at that time were, in the following order: (1) market services; (2) chemical products; and (3) food, beverages & tobacco. Thus, the contribution of the high-tech manufacturing sectors was much less important than it had been before 2000, with only chemical products still having substantial growth of net foreign earnings while there was a decline in metals & engineering.

In the final few years of the boom, the economy continued to grow relatively fast but the pace of its growth was not genuinely sustainable. It was dependent on an excessive property and construction boom which was heavily supported by an inflow of debt finance from abroad.

It is clear from the findings of this chapter that there can be a good deal of variation between industries in terms of the scale of profit outflows and imported inputs. It is necessary to take account of these factors in order to recognise different industries' true contributions to the Irish economy. These variations between sectors are often related to differences between Irish indigenous companies and foreign-owned MNCs in Ireland, and the relative prevalence of these two groups within different sectors.

The distinction between indigenous and foreign-owned companies, and differences in their activities and their economic impacts, is a basic theme running through the next two chapters. Paying attention to this distinction will help to shed further light on some of the sectoral developments outlined in this chapter.

Appendix: Estimation of Profit Outflows, Retained GVA and Net Foreign Earnings

Profit Outflows and Retained GVA

Table 4.2 shows estimates of "retained GVA" in 2000, in which outflows of profits from the country are deducted from GVA in the sectors where the profit outflows mainly arise. The first two columns show GVA by sector and each sector's percentage of total GVA. The third column shows estimates of profit outflows from foreign-owned MNCs in manufacturing and market services.

While there are no estimates in the table for profit outflows from the other sectors because of a lack of relevant data, there are good reasons to believe that profit outflows from foreign MNCs in those sectors would be such a small proportion of sectoral GVA that they can reasonably be ignored. Thus, profits of foreign MNCs could scarcely be a significant proportion of GVA in Irish agriculture. In the case of the building & construction industry, it is known, from the *Census of Building and Construction*, that profits (after deducting capital expenditure) of firms employing over 20 people in that sector accounted for just 10% of the whole sector's GVA in 2001. Since it is likely that profit outflows from foreign companies would be only a small fraction of that 10% of GVA, this is not a significant issue in the building & construction sector. The "other industry" sector accounted for a very small proportion of total GVA, and the vast majority of its GVA came from Irish public sector activities in supply of electricity, gas, and water as well as peat extraction. Hence there was no scope here for substantial profit outflows from foreign companies. Finally, it is also clear that profits of foreign MNCs could not have been a significant part of GVA in non-market services such as public administration, defence, education and health services because they were generally part of the Irish public sector.

In the third column of Table 4.2, the total profit outflow figure comes from the official *Balance of International Payments* for 2000, published by the Central Statistics Office (CSO). To be precise, it is presented in the current account of the balance of payments as the debit or outflow side of "Direct Investment Income on Equity".

In order to determine profit outflows by sector, first a figure for profit outflows from financial businesses was obtained from Riordan (2008, Chapter 4 including Table 4a, and Table A.4). Riordan says that the profit outflow data in the balance of payments are subdivided into financial and non-financial businesses, without further sectoral detail. Although the financial/non-financial distinction does not actually appear in the official balance of payments publications for that period, Riordan presents the relevant figures for non-financial businesses in 2000–2005, which allows one to calculate figures for financial businesses since the total profit outflow figures are readily available.[13]

To derive estimates of profit outflows from manufacturing and non-financial market services, the total profit outflow from non-financial sectors was distributed among those sectors in proportion to estimates of the amount of profits of foreign-owned companies arising in those sectors. These estimates of profits of foreign companies were based on data from the *Census of Industrial Production (CIP)*, in the case of the manufacturing sector, or the *Annual Services Inquiry (ASI)*, in the case of services. The estimates of profits were based on GVA of foreign-owned firms minus their total labour costs.

This procedure was applied to estimate profit outflows from eight individual sectors within manufacturing and from three individual sectors in non-financial market services. These detailed estimates for individual manufacturing sectors are used in some of the later tables and charts. However, in all the later tables and charts, as well as in Table 4.2, the results for all market services including financial services are combined together. This is because the figures for profit outflows from financial businesses, obtained from Riordan (2008), partly arise from service companies which would be outside the financial services sector as defined in the NACE classification system used in the ASI and input–output tables. Consequently, there could be quite significant errors in our initial figures for "retained GVA" and net foreign earnings particularly in financial services and, to a lesser extent, in other services. Although it is not possible to say exactly how great are these errors, it is quite clear that they are reduced to a level that is not important for our purposes when the market services sectors are combined together. Incidentally, we did not have the option of estimating the profit outflow from financial services in the same way as for other service sectors, because financial services are not included in the ASI.

[13] More recently, the CSO has published some sectoral breakdown of profit outflows for years from 2012 on.

The method used to derive our estimates of sectoral profit outflows gave rise to a few issues. First, the data required from the ASI were not actually available classified by nationality of ownership in 2000, although the necessary data classified by nationality of ownership were published from 2001 on. We needed estimates for 2000 in order to link them with data from the input–output tables for 2000. Therefore, we first derived the necessary estimates of profits of foreign companies from the ASI for 2001, and then assumed that foreign profits would be the same proportion of a sector's GVA in 2000 as they were in 2001.

A second issue concerns interest, tax and depreciation. In view of the estimation methodology used (profits being equal to GVA minus total labour costs), our estimated profits of foreign companies were profits before deducting interest, tax and depreciation. We then distributed the relevant total profit outflow (which would be after interest etc.) across sectors in proportion to those estimates of profits. Consequently, this procedure involves an implicit assumption that interest, tax and depreciation would be proportionately about the same in each sector, or at least that differences between sectors in this respect would not be so large as to result in substantial errors to the estimates of "retained GVA" or net foreign earnings that are presented in this chapter.

Another issue that is worth considering concerns the relationship between the amount of profits of foreign-owned companies that arise in a sector and the amount of profits that flow out of the country from that sector. To clarify this, it must be pointed out that all the profits of foreign-owned companies (after interest and tax) were officially defined as debits or outflows of profits in the current account of the balance of international payments. Even if foreign-owned companies chose to reinvest some of their profits in Ireland, the full amount of their profits (after interest and tax) was still officially defined as a debit or outflow. The reinvestment was then treated as a separate matter and it was counted as a credit or inflow called "reinvested earnings" in the financial account, rather than the current account, of the *Balance of International Payments*

For the purpose of making our estimates, and in the associated discussion in this chapter, we followed this official practice in treating all foreign-owned companies' profits (after interest and tax) as being profit outflows, regardless of any reinvestments that might occur. This does not mean that we have simply ignored the contribution that their reinvested profits make to the Irish economy. The fact is that, if the reinvested profits of foreign MNCs contribute to maintaining or increasing their production in Ireland, that effect is automatically reflected in the size of their GVA. The GVA of such companies in any given year is the product both of their original investments and of their reinvestments to date. Thus, their GVA incorporates the contribution made by all their investments to generating income in Ireland and, in deducting their profits from their GVA, we are deducting the part of that income that does not accrue to residents of Ireland. While some of their profits in the current year may be reinvested in Ireland and may increase Irish incomes in the future, that will be reflected in future GVA, and it would not be appropriate to take it into account as an aspect of current Irish incomes if it does not contribute to current GVA.

Finally, it was stated in Sect. 4.1 that a sector's GVA is similar to its contribution to GDP (apart from an adjustment for product taxes and subsidies), whereas its "retained GVA" in Table 4.2 is more like its contribution to GNP. In saying this, it should be acknowledged that the difference between GDP and GNP is the net flow of factor incomes from or to the rest of the world. Such factor incomes consist of various items such as interest payments, profits, dividends and some wage payments, and they flow both into and out of the country. Consequently, there is more to the difference between GDP and GNP in Ireland than just profit outflows from foreign MNCs in Ireland. However, in Ireland these profit outflows have been the major component of the difference between GDP and GNP, and in fact the profit outflows were greater than the difference between GDP and GNP throughout most of the boom. Furthermore, many of the other factor income flows, such as interest on government bonds, are not associated with specific sectors of the Irish economy, whereas the profit outflows from foreign MNCs clearly do arise in specific sectors. For these reasons, it seems fair to say that a sector's "retained GVA" is quite like (but not exactly the same as) its contribution to GNP.

Net Foreign Earnings

Tables 4.7–4.9 and Figs. 4.5–4.7 present estimates of net foreign earnings for each sector, which is defined as the value of the sector's exports minus the value of the imported inputs that are used in producing the exports, minus the profit outflows that arise from production of the exports.

For this purpose, the sectoral export data were taken from the official input–output tables for the year concerned. The input–output tables also provided data on each sector's imported inputs. It was assumed that the percentage of each sector's imported inputs that were used in producing the sector's exports was equal to its exports as a percentage of its total output.

Each sector's profit outflows were estimated in the manner already outlined above (except for 1985, which is discussed separately below). It was assumed that the percentage of each sector's profit outflows that arose from producing exports was equal to the exports of foreign-owned companies in the sector as a percentage of the foreign-owned companies' total output.

A couple of further issues arose in estimating profit outflows by sector for Tables 4.7–4.9 and the associated charts, arising from the fact that they include a more detailed breakdown of sectors than Table 4.2.

First, in the food, beverages & tobacco sector, the drink and tobacco companies pay a substantial amount of excise tax, which is included in the sector's GVA in the Census of Industrial Production. Therefore, it was necessary to deduct the excise tax from foreign-owned companies' GVA in that sector when estimating the profits of foreign-owned companies for the purpose of estimating profit outflows.

A second issue arises from the fact that we obtained exports and imported inputs data from input–output tables, whereas the CIP or ASI were our basic data sources for estimating profits of foreign-owned companies. There are some differences between the input–output tables on the one hand and the CIP or ASI on the other hand as regards their definitions of what exactly they include in which sector. For the most part these differences were not significant for our purposes, but there was a substantial difference concerning the food, beverages & tobacco sector and the chemical products sector. The CIP classifies some products in the food sector which are counted as chemical products in the input–output tables, so that the CIP's food sector is relatively large compared to the input–output tables' food sector, while the CIP's chemicals sector is relatively small compared to the input–output tables' chemicals sector. Therefore, after estimating profit outflows from those sectors, using CIP data, we transferred part of the estimate for food to chemicals. In 2005 the amount transferred in this way was 15% of the initial estimate of profit outflows from food, beverages & tobacco and 4% of the initial estimate for chemical products.

Profit Outflows for 1985

In order to produce Table 4.8 and Fig. 4.6 estimates of profit outflows by sector had to be made for 1985. These estimates had to be based on a different method to the method for 2000 and 2005 outlined above, because data on GVA and labour costs of foreign-owned companies by sector were not available from either the *Census of Industrial Production* or the *Annual Services Inquiry* in 1985.

Instead, the estimates for 1985 used data on profits as a percentage of sales, for foreign-owned companies by sector, from the "Irish Economy Expenditures Survey", which was undertaken annually by the Industrial Development Authority (IDA) in the 1980s. (This survey later came to be organised by Forfás and became known as the Annual Business Survey of Economic Impact, or ABSEI; it was referred to in Box 4.1). The relevant 1980s profits data that were used here were originally provided for the study reported in O'Malley (1995).

The figures on profits as a percentage of sales from the survey were multiplied by data on foreign companies' gross output, by sector, from the 1985 *Census of Industrial Production* to give estimates of foreign companies' profits by sector. In a similar manner to the estimates for 2000 and 2005, the total profit outflow figure was taken from the official *Balance of International Payments* for 1985, and then that total profit outflow was distributed across the sectors in proportion to the estimates of foreign-owned companies' profits in each sector. In order to estimate the amount of profit outflows that arose from production of exports in each sector, it was assumed that the percentage of a sector's profit outflows that arose from producing exports was equal to the exports of foreign-owned companies in the sector as a percentage of the foreign-owned companies' total output.

The main defect of these estimates for 1985 as compared to the estimates for later years is the fact that they do not include any estimates for service sectors, because the Irish Economy Expenditures survey concentrated on manufacturing. Thus, in using these estimates there is effectively an assumption that profit outflows from service sectors were negligible at that time. In reality, that is probably not far from the truth since the flow of FDI into very profitable internationally traded services nearly all came later. Even as late as 2000, our estimates indicate that only about 6% of all profit outflows came from non-financial services and the figure for 1985 must have been a good deal lower. A larger amount of profit outflows was coming from financial services by 2000, but that would have been largely a result of a surge of FDI into the International Financial Services Centre (IFSC), which started after 1985.

Nevertheless, there is some bias here towards underestimating profit outflows from service sectors in 1985. That means that we overestimate net foreign earnings in service sectors in 1985 and hence underestimate the increase in net foreign earnings in service sectors in 1985–2000 to some extent. It is very unlikely that this bias could be large enough to invalidate the statements made when discussing Table 4.8 and Fig. 4.6.

References

Barry, Frank. 1999. Irish Growth in Historical and Theoretical Perspective. In *Understanding Ireland's Economic Growth*, ed. Frank Barry, 25–44. London: Macmillan and New York: St Martin's Press.

Forfas. 2006. *Annual Business Survey of Economic Impact 2004*. Dublin: Forfas.

Krugman, Paul R. 1997. Good News from Ireland: A Geographical Perspective. In *International Perspectives on the Irish Economy*, ed. Alan W. Gray. Dublin: Indecon Economic Consultants.

O'Malley, Eoin. 1995. An Analysis of Secondary Employment Associated with Manufacturing Industry. General Research Series Paper No. 167. Economic and Social Research Institute, Dublin.

O'Malley, Eoin, and Sue Scott. 1987. Determinants of Profit Outflows from Ireland. In *Medium-Term Review: 1987–1992*, ed. J. Bradley, J. Fitz Gerald, and R.A. Storey. Dublin: The Economic and Social Research Institute.

O'Malley, Eoin, and Sue Scott. 1994. Profit Outflows Revisited. In *Economic Perspectives for the Medium Term*, ed. Sara Cantillon, John Curtis, and John Fitz Gerald. Dublin: The Economic and Social Research Institute.

Riordan, Brendan. 2008. *The Net Contribution of the Agri-Food Sector to the Inflow of Funds into Ireland: A New Estimate*. Dublin: Department of Agriculture, Fisheries and Food.

Open Access This chapter is licensed under the terms of the Creative Commons Attribution 4.0 International License (http://creativecommons.org/licenses/by/4.0/), which permits use, sharing, adaptation, distribution and reproduction in any medium or format, as long as you give appropriate credit to the original author(s) and the source, provide a link to the Creative Commons license and indicate if changes were made.

The images or other third party material in this chapter are included in the chapter's Creative Commons license, unless indicated otherwise in a credit line to the material. If material is not included in the chapter's Creative Commons license and your intended use is not permitted by statutory regulation or exceeds the permitted use, you will need to obtain permission directly from the copyright holder.

CHAPTER 5

Irish Indigenous Companies

This chapter focuses on the role of Irish-owned or indigenous companies during the boom and Chapter 6 deals with the role of foreign-owned multinational companies. Of course, some sectors of the economy were almost entirely indigenous, including agriculture, non-market services and construction, and consequently the indigenous/foreign distinction is of little relevance for those sectors. Therefore, this chapter and the next concentrate on manufacturing and market services. These are the sectors where foreign-owned MNCs did have a substantial and distinctive role alongside indigenous companies, and they are also the sectors that were particularly influential in driving economic growth since they were the source of most exports and net foreign earnings, as seen in Chapter 4. In this chapter, Sect. 5.1 deals with indigenous firms in manufacturing and Sect. 5.2 goes on to look at indigenous firms in market services.

5.1 Growth and Development of Indigenous Manufacturing

It was seen in Chapter 2 that, before the boom began in the late 1980s, much of Irish indigenous manufacturing had been experiencing persistent difficulties in coping with foreign competition in the domestic market after the introduction of free trade in the 1960s and 1970s. This existing weakness was compounded by a sharp deterioration in domestic demand conditions in the 1980s, resulting in a slump in indigenous industry.

© The Author(s) 2024

E. O'Malley, *Ireland's Long Economic Boom*, Palgrave Studies in Economic History, https://doi.org/10.1007/978-3-031-53070-8_5

Against that background, there was a considerable improvement in the growth and development of indigenous manufacturing beginning in the late 1980s, although its performance was somewhat uneven with some strong points and some weak points. The growth of indigenous manufacturing looked quite good in some respects compared to other countries, although its performance was overshadowed for about half of the boom by much stronger growth in foreign-owned industry in Ireland.

Employment Trends

Table 5.1 shows employment trends in Irish indigenous and foreign-owned manufacturing in 1980–2006. Total manufacturing employment declined considerably during the recession of the 1980s with a particularly sharp decline in the indigenous industry which was reduced from 61.8% of the total in 1980 to 57.4% in 1988. Then from 1988 to 2000, there was strong growth in manufacturing employment. This growth was faster in foreign-owned industry than in indigenous industry so the indigenous share of the total declined further. Nevertheless, the employment growth seen in the indigenous industry was substantial, amounting to 1.9% p.a. in 1988–2000, which was in marked contrast to earlier in the 1980s and indeed was quite unprecedented in twentieth-century Ireland under free trade conditions. The decline that followed in 2000–2006 affected both foreign-owned and indigenous manufacturing employment, although the decline was a little less severe among the indigenous companies which slightly increased their share of the total over that period.[1]

Before the boom, the employment trend in indigenous manufacturing had been exceptionally weak compared to international experience among developed countries but after 1988 it became exceptionally strong compared to other countries. Thus in 1980–1988 employment declined by 3.2% p.a. in indigenous manufacturing and by 2.2% p.a. in total manufacturing in Ireland while it declined by 1.6% p.a. in the EU-15 and by 0.7% p.a. in the USA. It can be seen in Fig. 5.1 that the growth of indigenous manufacturing employment which followed in 1988–2000 contrasted with the still declining trend in the EU and USA. Employment in Irish indigenous industry was clearly growing more slowly than

[1] The indigenous share of the total actually reached a low point of 50.7% in 2005 and then increased to 52.2% in 2006.

Table 5.1 Employment in Irish indigenous and foreign-owned manufacturing, 1980–2006

	1980	*1988*	*1993*	*2000*	*2006*
Irish indigenous	137,200	106,200	111,167	132,666	114,744
Foreign-owned	84,700	78,900	88,836	122,978	105,078
Total	221,900	185,100	200,003	255,644	219,822
Indigenous percentage	61.8	57.4	55.6	51.9	52.2
Foreign percentage	38.2	42.6	44.4	48.1	47.8
Total	100.0	100.0	100.0	100.0	100.0

Source Primarily the *Census of Industrial Production*, supplemented by data from the IDA/Forfás Employment Survey to obtain the figures for 1980 and 1988, as explained in Appendix

employment in foreign-owned industry in Ireland, but it was growing quite rapidly by most other comparisons.

After 2000, there was a substantial decline in indigenous manufacturing employment. However, Fig. 5.1 shows that this trend was quite similar to international experience. By 2006, employment in indigenous industry was still 8% above its 1988 level whereas industrial employment was 19 or 20% below the 1988 level in the EU and the USA.

As regards sectoral trends within Irish indigenous manufacturing, it is necessary to consider 1988–1990 separately from the later years because of a change in the industry classification system after 1990 (as discussed in Appendix). In 1988–1990 total indigenous manufacturing employment grew by 1.3% p.a., compared to 1.0% p.a. for the EU and −0.7% p.a. for the USA. About three-quarters of the sectors within indigenous industry had growing employment in that period but it was noticeable that the growth rates were well above average in the "high-technology" sectors—pharmaceuticals (5.6% p.a.), office & data processing machinery (35.3% p.a.), electrical engineering (6.0% p.a.) and instrument engineering (4.1% p.a.). However, employment in most of those sectors, with the exception of electrical engineering, was still very small in absolute terms being numbered in hundreds rather than thousands (O'Malley 1998).

Table 5.2 shows subsequent trends in indigenous manufacturing employment by sector in 1991–2000 and 2000–2006. In 1991–2000, when total indigenous manufacturing employment growth was quite rapid at 2.1% p.a., there was growth in all sectors apart from two.

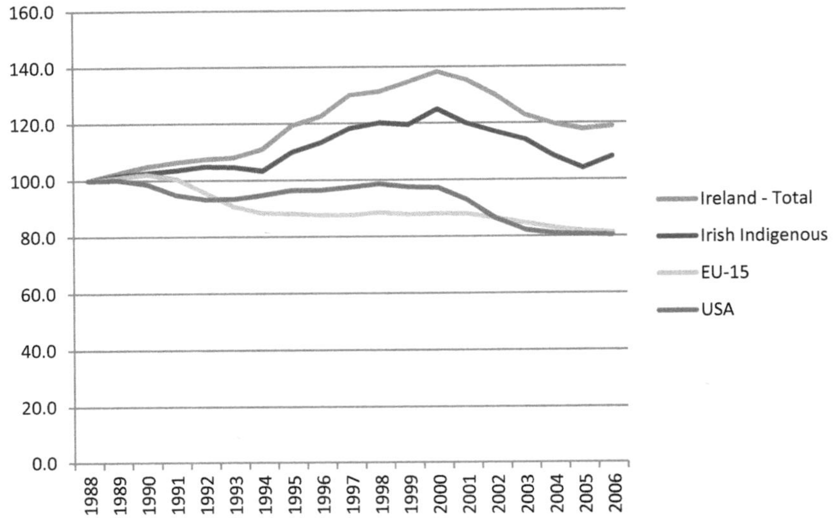

Fig. 5.1 Manufacturing employment index (1988 = 100), Ireland total, Irish indigenous, EU-15 and USA, 1988–2007 (*Source*: *Census of Industrial Production* for Irish data, with a few minor adjustments as explained in Appendix. EU-15 data from EUKLEMS database [euklems.net]. USA from OECD's STAN database. Creative Commons Attribution BY 4.0)

Nearly all the sectors that are classified by Eurostat as "high-technology" sectors grew exceptionally fast—communication equipment & technical instruments (14.2% p.a.), pharmaceutical products (8.3% p.a.) and office machinery & computers (7.6% p.a.). In addition, nearly all the sectors that are classified as "medium–high technology" grew at faster than average rates—electrical machinery & apparatus (9.8% p.a.), machinery & equipment (4.5% p.a.) and other chemicals (4.4% p.a.). In fact, the only sector that might possibly be seen as going against the general trend of above-average growth for the higher technology sectors was transport equipment.[2] Consequently, the composition of indigenous manufacturing

[2] The transport equipment sector was rather diverse so that it was not a clear-cut case of a higher technology sector. Within that sector, aircraft & spacecraft would conventionally be classified as high-technology, motor vehicles and railway equipment are classified as medium–high-technology, and shipbuilding and boatbuilding are medium–low-technology.

Table 5.2 Employment growth by sector in Irish indigenous manufacturing, 1991–2006

NACE Rev.1 Code	*Sector*	*Average growth (% p.a.) 1991–2000*	*Average growth (% p.a.) 2000–2006*	*Employment 2000*
15–16	Food, drink & tobacco	1.0	−0.8	34,932
17–18	Textiles & textile products	−5.8	−12.2	6,719
20	Wood & wood products	3.4	3.4	5,138
21	Pulp, paper & paper products	2.8	−7.4	4,030
22	Printing & publishing	2.0	−3.2	12,329
244	Pharmaceutical products	8.3	4.7	1,587
24 less 244	Other chemicals	4.4	−4.2	3,737
25	Rubber & plastics	7.0	−0.1	6,895
26	Non-metallic mineral products	1.7	−0.3	9,582
27–28	Metals & metal products	4.2	−0.1	13,330
29	Machinery & equipment	4.5	−4.0	7,960
30	Office machinery & computers	7.6	−13.3	2,420
31	Electrical machinery & apparatus	9.8	−11.4	5,703
32–33	Communication equipment, technical instruments	14.2	−5.7	4,983
34–35	Transport equipment	−5.9	−4.3	4,245
36, 37, 23, 19	Furniture, miscellaneous, recycling, oil, leather	3.3	−1.7	9,076
15–37	Total indigenous manufacturing	2.1	−2.4	132,666

Note In 2006, tobacco products (NACE 16) is not included with food & drink and is included with miscellaneous manufacturing. The employment involved (no more than a few hundred) has a negligible impact on the findings here

Source: *Census of Industrial Production*. Creative Commons Attribution BY 4.0

employment was shifting significantly towards higher technology sectors (Jacobson and O'Malley 2018).

In 2000–2006 total indigenous manufacturing employment declined. Table 5.2 indicates that there was a reversal of the earlier sectoral trends since the decline tended to be particularly severe among the high-technology and medium–high-technology sectors, with only pharmaceutical products among those sectors continuing to have a stronger than average record. However, these trends in 2000–2006 need to be interpreted with some care. The problem here is that, for the *Census of Industrial Production* (CIP) data used in Table 5.2, companies' nationality of ownership is defined according to their nationality in each year. Consequently, if some companies are Irish-owned at the start of a period and are then taken over by new foreign owners during that period, their employment is included in the indigenous category in the initial year but not in the final year. This can result in a weak trend in indigenous employment in that period although there may have been no real competitive or commercial weakness resulting in declining businesses.

In fact, there is evidence that this type of effect was very influential in the indigenous high-technology and medium–high-technology sectors in 2000–2006. In the Forfás *Annual Employment Survey*, companies' nationality of ownership was defined according to their latest nationality when responding to the survey, and then presentations of data on past trends in the survey reports applied each company's latest nationality to all previous years so that changes of nationality did not affect the trends over time. With nationality defined in this way, the Forfás *Annual Employment Survey 2008* (Appendix Table 5) indicated that total indigenous manufacturing employment declined by 1.2% p.a. in 2000–2006, which was less than the decline by 2.4% p.a. seen in the CIP data in Table 5.2. Furthermore, the Forfás survey data indicate that employment in the indigenous high-technology and medium–high-technology sectors declined by just 0.5% p.a. in 2000–2006, which was much less than the decline by 5.8% p.a. in the CIP data.[3] In the low-technology and medium–low-technology sectors the rate of decline was similar in both data sets, at 1.6% p.a. in the CIP and 1.3% p.a. in the Forfás survey.

Thus, the combination of the two sets of data shows that there were significant net transfers of ownership from Irish to foreign during 2000–2006, with nearly all of these transfers being among the high-technology and medium–high-technology sectors. In the absence of such net transfers of ownership, the overall trend in indigenous manufacturing employment would have looked considerably stronger and the high-technology and medium–high-technology sectors would probably have continued to increase their share of the total. Also, the slight increase in the indigenous share of total manufacturing employment in 2000–2006, which was seen

[3] Transport equipment is not included here among the high-technology and medium–high-technology sectors, in the figures from both data sets.

in Table 5.1, would have been greater in the absence of net transfers from Irish to foreign ownership.

Incidentally, the trends in indigenous manufacturing after the boom was over are of some relevance here because they show what happened when net foreign takeovers ceased for a while. In 2008–2014, the comparison between the CIP and the Forfás survey shows no significant net transfers from Irish to foreign ownership, perhaps because that period was dominated by the "great recession" in Ireland and elsewhere so that many multinational companies had to focus more on surviving in very difficult conditions rather than expanding by means of acquisitions. In the absence of net foreign takeovers, the trend of particularly rapid growth among the higher technology sectors resumed in Irish indigenous manufacturing. CIP data show that employment grew by 1.6% p.a. in the indigenous high-technology and medium–high-technology sectors in 2008–2014 despite the major international recession, while it declined by 2.9% p.a. in the low-technology and medium–low-technology sectors.[4]

To see how Irish indigenous employment compared to the EU, Table 5.3 shows indigenous industry's percentage share of EU-15 employment in each manufacturing sector in 1991, 2000 and 2006. Indigenous industry's share of total EU-15 manufacturing employment increased substantially from 0.32% in 1991 to 0.44% in 2000 and then declined a little to 0.42% in 2006. The net transfers of ownership from Irish to foreign in 2000–2006 were probably sufficient to account for the decline in the share of EU employment in that period.

At the sectoral level, Irish indigenous industry increased its share of EU employment in 1991–2000 in all manufacturing sectors apart from textiles & textile products and transport equipment. Initially in 1991, indigenous industry was relatively under-represented in the higher technology sectors compared to the EU. For example, indigenous industry had a 0.32% share of total manufacturing employment in the EU-15, but its share of EU-15 employment was a good deal lower in sectors such as pharmaceutical products (0.24%), machinery & equipment (0.14%), electrical machinery & apparatus (0.15%), and communication equipment & technical instruments (0.08%). That situation changed considerably during 1991–2000. Since Irish indigenous employment was growing

[4] The foregoing paragraphs draw from Jacobson and O'Malley (2018).

Table 5.3 Irish indigenous industry's share of EU-15 manufacturing employment, by sector, 1991–2006 (%)

NACE Rev.1	*Sector*	*1991*	*2000*	*2006*
15–16	Food, drink & tobacco	0.81	0.93	0.90
17–18	Textiles & textile products	0.34	0.30	0.19
20	Wood & wood products	0.35	0.52	0.68
21	Pulp, paper & paper products	0.38	0.59	0.41
22	Printing & publishing	0.50	0.65	0.60
244	Pharmaceutical products	0.24	0.33	0.42
24 less 244	Other chemicals	0.22	0.33	0.29
25	Rubber & plastics	0.27	0.48	0.51
26	Non-metallic mineral products	0.53	0.70	0.76
27–28	Metals & metal products	0.20	0.31	0.31
29	Machinery & equipment	0.14	0.25	0.20
30	Office machinery & computers	0.42	1.13	0.62
31	Electrical machinery & apparatus	0.15	0.41	0.22
32–33	Communication equipment, technical instruments	0.08	0.29	0.24
34–35	Transport equipment	0.25	0.16	0.13
36, 37, 23, 19	Furniture, miscellaneous, recycling, oil, leather	0.25	0.37	0.39
15–37	Total indigenous manufacturing	0.32	0.44	0.42

Source: *Census of Industrial Production* for Irish Indigenous. EU-15 data from EUKLEMS database (euklems.net). Creative Commons Attribution BY 4.0

particularly fast in most of the high-technology and medium–high-technology sectors, the Irish indigenous share of EU employment rose very rapidly in many of those sectors. In all of those sectors combined, indigenous industry more than doubled its share of EU employment from 0.14% in 1991 to 0.33% by 2000. The Irish indigenous share of EU employment in the low-technology and medium–low-technology sectors also increased in the same period but the rate of increase was slower, from 0.39% in 1991 to 0.49% in 2000.

As regards 2000–2006, if we focus on the CIP data that are used for Table 5.3, Irish indigenous industry's share of EU manufacturing employment declined from 0.44% to 0.42%. The decline was particularly severe among the high-technology and medium–high-technology sectors. In those sectors combined indigenous industry's share of EU employment dropped from 0.33% to 0.25%. However, if we use the Forfás *Annual*

Employment Survey data, as discussed above, indigenous industry's share of total EU-15 manufacturing employment held steady at 0.39% in both 2000 and 2006, while its share of EU employment in the high-technology and medium–high-technology industries increased slightly from 0.25% in 2000 to 0.26% in 2006.

Thus, the combination of the two data sets shows again that there were quite significant net transfers of ownership from Irish to foreign during 2000–2006, with these transfers being heavily concentrated among the high-technology and medium–high-technology sectors. In the absence of such net transfers of ownership, there would have been little or no change in the Irish indigenous share of total EU manufacturing employment while the indigenous share of the EU high-technology and medium–high-technology sectors could have increased a little.

Output Trends

Trends in the output of Irish indigenous manufacturing were generally consistent with its employment trends. Thus, there was a marked improvement in output growth in indigenous manufacturing beginning in the late 1980s.

Unfortunately, the data on this are not ideal because there is no output data series for indigenous industry in constant prices, which would show trends in the volume of Irish indigenous industrial production. Instead, published data on the volume of production in "traditional" and "modern" manufacturing have often been seen as proxy measures for data on Irish indigenous and foreign-owned industry respectively, because the "traditional" sectors were predominantly Irish-owned while the "modern" sectors were largely foreign-owned.[5] Before the boom, the volume of production in traditional manufacturing was growing very slowly at just 1.0% p.a. in 1982–1987 but its growth then accelerated to 3.7% p.a. in 1987–1995 (O'Malley 1998).

[5] In the 1980s the "modern" sectors were pharmaceuticals, office & data processing machinery, electrical engineering, instrument engineering and miscellaneous foods, while the "traditional" sectors were all other manufacturing sectors. Following a change in the industry classification system after 1990 (as discussed in Appendix), "modern" and "traditional" industry continued to include the nearest equivalent sectors from the new classification system.

However, traditional manufacturing is by no means perfect as a representative of indigenous manufacturing since about one-third of the output of foreign-owned manufacturing firms was in traditional manufacturing in the early 1990s, while almost 10% of the output of Irish indigenous manufacturing firms was in modern manufacturing.

As an alternative, O'Malley (1998) presented estimates of the output of indigenous manufacturing measured in constant prices in 1985–1995. These estimates were derived by constructing an "indigenous" manufacturing price index, based on the official price indices for each individual manufacturing sector, combined together in accordance with their weighting in Irish indigenous industry. According to these estimates the volume of production in indigenous manufacturing increased by just 0.6% p.a. before the boom in 1985–1987 and then grew at a rate of 4.0% p.a. in 1987–1995. Thus, the acceleration in indigenous output growth according to this estimate was somewhat greater than the acceleration in the growth of "traditional" industry.

Whether one goes by this estimate of 4.0% p.a. growth in 1987–1995, or the figure of 3.7% p.a. for traditional industry, this growth was a good deal slower than the 9.9% p.a. growth rate for all of industry in Ireland in the same period. Nevertheless, it was significantly faster than the growth rate of industry in the OECD, at 2.0% p.a., or the EU, at 1.7% p.a., whereas the growth of Irish indigenous or traditional industry had been weak compared to those countries in the years before the boom (O'Malley 1998).

Table 5.4 uses output data valued at current prices to show Irish indigenous industry's percentage share of the value of EU-15 gross output in each manufacturing sector in 1991, 2000 and 2006. For the most part, the trends in indigenous industry's share of EU manufacturing output were quite similar to the trends seen above in its share of EU manufacturing employment. Irish indigenous industry's share of total EU manufacturing gross output increased from 0.34% in 1991 to 0.4% in 2000 and then declined to 0.37% in 2006.

At the sectoral level, indigenous industry increased its share of EU output in 1991–2000 in all manufacturing sectors apart from textiles & textile products and transport equipment. Initially in 1991, Irish indigenous industry was relatively under-represented in the higher technology sectors compared to the EU. Thus, indigenous industry had a 0.34% share of total manufacturing output in the EU-15 in 1991 but its share of EU-15 output was much lower in chemicals (0.15%), machinery &

Table 5.4 Irish indigenous industry's share of EU-15 manufacturing gross output, by sector, 1991–2006 (%)

NACE Rev.1	*Sector*	*1991*	*2000*	*2006*
15–16	Food, drink & tobacco	1.29	1.44	1.34
17–18	Textiles & textile products	0.17	0.17	0.12
20	Wood & wood products	0.28	0.56	0.80
21–22	Pulp, paper & paper products	0.36	0.49	0.54
24	Chemicals & chemical products	0.15	0.19	0.16
25	Rubber & plastics	0.19	0.35	0.39
26	Non-metallic mineral products	0.40	0.66	0.88
27–28	Metals & metal products	0.13	0.22	0.23
29	Machinery & equipment	0.09	0.17	0.15
30–33	Electrical & optical equipment	0.09	0.28	0.19
34–35	Transport equipment	0.10	0.05	0.04
36, 37, 19, 23	Furniture, miscellaneous, recycling, oil, leather	0.28	0.31	0.18
15–37	Total indigenous manufacturing	0.34	0.40	0.37

Source: ***Census of Industrial Production*** for Irish Indigenous. EU-15 data from EUKLEMS database (euklems.net). Creative Commons Attribution BY 4.0

equipment (0.09%) and electrical & optical equipment (0.09%). That situation changed considerably during 1991–2000. Irish indigenous output was growing particularly fast in the high-technology and medium–high-technology sectors and consequently the indigenous share of EU output rose very rapidly in those sectors. The indigenous share of EU output increased from 0.15% to 0.19% in chemicals, from 0.09 to 0.17% in machinery & equipment, and from 0.09 to 0.28% in electrical & optical equipment.

As regards 2000–2006, Table 5.4 indicates that Irish indigenous industry's share of EU manufacturing output declined from 0.4% to 0.37%, including declines in all the high-technology and medium–high-technology sectors. However, given the general similarity of the employment trends and output trends, it can be assumed that, as in the case of employment, these declines in share of output probably reflected net transfers from Irish to foreign ownership rather than real weaknesses involving relatively declining businesses.

To conclude on output trends in Irish indigenous industry, these trends were generally consistent with the employment trends in a number of important respects. There was an acceleration in growth starting in the late 1980s, following significant weakness before then. The growth in Irish indigenous industry from the late 1980s onwards was distinctly slower than in foreign-owned industry in Ireland. Nevertheless, the growth in indigenous industry was fast growth by international standards, after being slow by international standards before the boom. There was a marked shift in the sectoral composition of Irish indigenous industry away from the lower technology sectors and towards the higher technology sectors, and this shift was relatively strong by international standards as shown by rapidly rising shares of EU employment and output in the higher technology sectors.

From about 2000 onwards the growth of indigenous industry weakened a good deal and its shares of EU employment and output declined, particularly in the higher technology sectors. However, much of this weakness was caused by net transfers of ownership of companies from Irish to foreign ownership. In the absence of such net transfers of ownership, the Irish indigenous share of EU manufacturing would probably have held up quite well while the indigenous share of the EU high-technology and medium–high-technology sectors could have increased a little.

Exports and Net Foreign Earnings

Regular official data on the exports of Irish-owned manufacturing first became available in the CIP in 1986. However, some earlier survey data on new foreign-owned grant-aided industry make it possible to estimate that exports of industries other than new foreign-owned grant-aided industry amounted to about 26% of their gross output in 1973 and about 27% in 1976 (O'Malley 1989, Table 6.5; 1998). These industries (other than new foreign-owned grant-aided industry) consisted very largely of Irish indigenous firms together with quite a small minority of older foreign-owned firms. Another estimate by Foley (1987) indicated that Irish-owned indigenous industry exported about 31% of its output in 1984.

Against that background, the first official CIP data on indigenous exports showed that indigenous manufacturing exported 26.6% of its gross output in 1986, which was about the same as in 1973 and 1976 but apparently somewhat lower than in 1984. At any rate, it seems reasonably clear that there can have been little or no increase in the export-orientation of indigenous industry over the period 1973–1986.

In contrast to that previous experience, exports as a percentage of the output of indigenous manufacturing began to increase immediately after 1986 rising from 26.6% in 1986 to 33.4% by 1990.

In 1986–1990, the value of indigenous manufacturing exports (in current Irish pounds) increased by 12.2% p.a., which was slightly higher than the growth rate of 11.9% p.a. for exports from foreign-owned industry in Ireland. Indigenous manufacturing exports grew relatively fast in that period compared with other countries. Measured in terms of current US dollars, the growth rates of manufacturing exports were 18.3% p.a. for Irish indigenous industry, 15.2% p.a. for the EU-15 and 14.2% p.a. for the OECD.

In the years 1986–1990, the CIP did not show export data by both nationality and sector at the same time. However, it did include data on output by both nationality and sector, so that it is possible to identify the sectors in which the bulk of the output was produced by indigenous firms. It is clear that in nearly all of those sectors, there was an increase in the percentage of output being exported (O'Malley 1998), which suggests that there was probably an increase in export-orientation across most of the sectors in indigenous industry.[6]

In 1991, the CIP introduced the new NACE Rev.1 system for classifying industries so that there was a discontinuity in the data series between 1990 and 1991. In the period 1991–2000, the growth of indigenous manufacturing exports was less impressive than in 1986–1990 in several respects. The value of indigenous manufacturing exports grew by just 5.0% p.a. in 1991–2000 measured in current Irish pounds, and this was much slower than the growth rate of 20.7% p.a. for exports from foreign-owned manufacturing firms in Ireland. Furthermore, there was no increase in the export orientation of indigenous manufacturing in 1991–2000 since 34.8% of its output was exported in 1991 declining a little to 33.2% in 2000. In addition, indigenous industry's share of the EU's manufacturing exports declined substantially from 0.407% in 1991 to 0.309% in 2000 (see Table 5.5).

[6] It is noticeable that in 1986–1990 there was particularly rapid growth in the exports of the dairy products sector, which was an important source of indigenous manufacturing exports. This might be seen as problematic because there is room for doubt about the accuracy of the data on exports of dairy products, and this raises the question of whether total indigenous manufacturing exports really grew as fast as they appeared to. This issue is discussed in Appendix where it is concluded that the growth of total indigenous manufacturing exports was not significantly weaker than it appeared to be.

Table 5.5 Irish indigenous industry's share of EU-13 manufacturing exports, by sector, 1991–2000 (%)

NACE Rev.1	*Sector*	*1991*	*2000*
15–16	Food, drink & tobacco	2.967	2.220
17–18	Textiles & textile products	0.252	0.162
20	Wood & wood products	0.304	0.238
21–22	Pulp, paper & paper products	0.319	0.313
24	Chemicals & chemical products	0.158	0.144
26	Non-metallic mineral products	0.553	0.485
27–28	Metals & metal products	0.217	0.212
29	Machinery & equipment	0.077	0.139
30–33	Electrical & optical equipment	0.117	0.219
19, 23, 25, 34–35, 36–37	Other manufacturing	0.150	0.112
15–37	Total indigenous manufacturing	0.407	0.309
17–37	Total non-food	0.170	0.171

Note "EU-13" in this table means the 15 EU member states prior to May 2004 except Ireland and Luxembourg
Source Adapted from O'Malley (2004, Table A11)

This export performance by indigenous industry was undoubtedly poorer than in 1986–1990, although the absence of any increase in export-orientation was not necessarily a clear sign of weakness given the context of the 1990s. Since there was exceptionally fast economic growth in Ireland and hence exceptionally fast growth of domestic demand, it was possible for the domestic sales of many indigenous firms to grow unusually rapidly. Consequently, it was not necessarily a clear indication of export weakness if their exports grew no faster than their domestic sales.

The large loss in share of EU exports was a more telling indication of export weakness. The weakness here related to some sectors more than others, and it was partly structural in nature, in the sense of being a result of a very unfavourable sectoral composition. Thus, at the start of the period indigenous industrial exports were relatively highly concentrated in sectors that had relatively slow growth for all countries' exports during the period. As a result, 56% of the total loss in share of EU exports occurred because of the unfavourable sectoral composition of indigenous industrial exports, while the remaining 44% of the loss in export market share occurred because individual indigenous sectors had declining shares of EU exports of their type of products.[7]

Much of the loss in export market share related to the food, drink & tobacco sector, which was a relatively large component of Irish indigenous industry. This sector suffered from a slow-growth environment since the growth of all countries' exports of food, drink & tobacco products was exceptionally slow, while the Irish indigenous sector also had a substantial loss of export market share as shown in Table 5.5. If we leave that sector aside, Irish indigenous industry's share of EU exports in other manufacturing sectors was quite mixed. In non-food manufacturing as a whole, the export share increased marginally, from 0.17% in 1991 to 0.171% in 2000, as shown in the last row of Table 5.5. It was probably a considerable improvement over previous experience before the boom for the exports of this broad group of indigenous industries to keep up with the growth of EU exports, particularly since the 1990s was a time when EU exports were growing rapidly.[8]

It is also of interest to note that, as in the case of employment and output, there was relatively strong growth of exports from indigenous firms in the high-technology and medium–high-technology sectors, after starting from a position of being under-represented in those sectors. In Table 5.5 those higher technology sectors are represented by electrical & optical equipment, machinery & equipment, and chemicals & chemical products. Although chemicals & chemical products had some loss in EU export market share in 1991–2000, the other sectors mentioned had large increases in their export market share. Taking all these higher technology sectors as a group, indigenous industry had a relatively low share of EU exports of their products at just 0.116% in 1991 but its share of EU exports then increased to 0.175% by 2000. This group of sectors also increased a good deal in importance in terms of its share of total indigenous manufacturing exports. Its share grew from 11.3% of the total in 1991 to 25.4% by 2000.

After 2000 the growth of indigenous manufacturing exports slowed down, from 5.0% p.a. in 1991–2000 to 3.4% p.a. in 2000–2007, measured in current values. At the same time, the growth of exports from

[7] Calculated from data presented in O'Malley (2004, Table A12).

[8] The volume of exports from the EU-15 grew by 6.7% p.a. in 1991-2000, compared to 4.6% p.a. in 1981-90 or 3.2% p.a. in 2001–2005 (*European Economy, Statistical Annex*).

foreign-owned manufacturing firms in Ireland slowed down far more dramatically from 20.7% p.a. in 1991–2000 to 3.6% p.a. in 2000–2007. Thus, exports from the indigenous and foreign-owned groups grew at almost the same rate in 2000–2007. There was only a small increase in the export-orientation of indigenous manufacturing as the proportion of its output being exported rose from 33.2% in 2000 to 34.9% in 2007. This export performance by indigenous manufacturing looked relatively weak by international standards since its share of EU-27 manufacturing exports declined from 0.28% in 2000 to 0.239% in 2007.[9]

It was noted above that in the 1990s the growth of indigenous manufacturing exports was held back by an unfavourable sectoral composition, but that was not the case to any significant extent in 2000–2007 (O'Malley 2013). However, their growth was restrained by the substantial net transfers of ownership of companies from Irish to foreign ownership in the period after 2000. As was pointed out above when discussing trends in employment, these transfers of ownership were very largely concentrated among the high-technology and medium–high-technology sectors. These sectors of indigenous manufacturing were a good deal more highly export-oriented than most other sectors, exporting 48% of their output in 2000 compared with just 30% for the rest of indigenous manufacturing. Consequently, transfers of ownership which primarily affected these higher technology sectors probably had a substantial negative influence on indigenous export trends.

Although it is not possible to present precise figures on this, it seems safe to make two qualitative statements here. First, indigenous manufacturing exports would have grown faster than exports from foreign-owned manufacturing in Ireland in the period after 2000 if there had been no net transfers of ownership. Second, most of the loss in indigenous industry's share of EU exports in that period can be attributed to transfers of ownership rather than to companies actually losing market share.

As was discussed in Chapter 4, it is useful to look deeper than the figures on exports to examine trends in "net foreign earnings"—meaning the value of exports minus the value of imported inputs contained in the exports minus profit outflows that arise from the production of

[9] The figures quoted here for shares of EU exports refer to the EU-27—a wider group of countries than the EU-13 referred to in Table 5.5. Ireland's share of EU-27 exports was naturally somewhat smaller than its share of EU-13. All Irish exports data cited in this paragraph are from the CIP while EU-27 data are from the Eurostat website.

the exports. Among Irish indigenous companies, net foreign earnings have generally amounted to a substantially higher proportion of the value of exports than they have in the case of foreign-owned companies. This is so partly because (a) indigenous companies have tended to be more concentrated in the sectors where net foreign earnings are a relatively high proportion of exports, and partly because (b) within each individual sector, indigenous companies have generally had higher net foreign earnings as a proportion of exports than their foreign-owned counterparts.

To illustrate the first point (a), at the broad macro-sectoral level in 2005, we estimate that net foreign earnings as a percentage of exports were highest in agriculture at 82%, lower in market services at 62% and lowest in manufacturing at 30%.[10] In this context, indigenous producers accounted for virtually 100% of agricultural exports, 19% of services exports and just 8% of manufacturing exports. At a more disaggregated sectoral level within manufacturing there was a similar pattern. Some sectors had relatively high net foreign earnings as a percentage of exports, such as non-metallic mineral products at 78% and food, drink & tobacco at 58%, while others had particularly low net foreign earnings as a percentage of exports, such as metal & engineering products at 26% and chemical products at 20%. In this context indigenous producers accounted for 55% of exports in non-metallic mineral products and 29% of exports in food, drink & tobacco, compared to just over 4% of exports in metal & engineering products and just over 1% in chemical products.

Table 5.6 illustrates point (b) above—that, within each individual sector, indigenous companies generally had higher net foreign earnings as a proportion of exports than their foreign-owned counterparts. The estimated figures were higher for indigenous companies than for foreign-owned companies in every sector listed in the table. This was partly because there was generally an outflow of profits from the foreign-owned companies in each sector, but not from the indigenous companies. In addition, foreign-owned companies in each sector tended to import a

[10] The procedure used to estimate net foreign earnings by sector was outlined in Appendix in Chapter 4. See Appendix for an outline of how that procedure was extended in this chapter to estimate the net foreign earnings of indigenous and foreign-owned companies in different sectors.

higher proportion of their purchased inputs, whereas indigenous companies in the same sector were more likely to source a higher proportion of their inputs from suppliers in Ireland.

The bottom row of Table 5.6 shows the aggregate results of these influences in 2005. Net foreign earnings amounted to a much higher proportion of the value of exports in indigenous companies than in foreign-owned companies. Specifically, net foreign earnings amounted to an estimated 87% of the value of exports of indigenous companies in all manufacturing and market services, compared to just 34% for all foreign-owned companies.

Table 5.6 also shows that net foreign earnings were a higher proportion of the value of exports in services than in manufacturing, with figures

Table 5.6 Estimated net foreign earnings as a percentage of exports, Irish indigenous and foreign-owned by sector, 2005

	Irish indigenous	*Foreign-owned*	*Total*
Agriculture, forestry & fishing	82	n.a	82
Food, beverages & tobacco	89	45	58
Textiles, clothing, leather products	61	45	51
Chemical products	58	19	20
Rubber & plastics	73	65	69
Non-metallic mineral products	91	61	78
Metal products, engineering & electronics	66	24	26
Vehicles, other transport equipment	68	54	56
Other industry	47	26	27
Total manufacturing	78	26	30
Market services	94	55	62
All sectors	87	34	41

Notes
"Net foreign earnings" here means the value of a sector's exports minus the value of the imported inputs that are used in producing the exports minus the profit outflows that arise from the production of the exports
"Metal Products, Engineering & Electronics" here include metal products, agricultural & industrial machinery, office machinery & computers, other electrical and electronic products, and medical, precision & optical instruments
Source Derived primarily from Central Statistics Office (CSO) data, including input–output tables, the balance of international payments, the Census of Industrial Production, and the Annual Services Inquiry, as well as data from Forfas, Annual Business Survey of Economic Impact. See Appendix for further details. Creative Commons Attribution BY 4.0

of 62% for total market services and 30% for total manufacturing. Consequently, net foreign earnings were a particularly high proportion of the value of exports in indigenous market services, at 94%, while the figure for foreign-owned manufacturing was particularly low at 26%.

Since net foreign earnings were generally a higher proportion of exports in indigenous companies than in foreign-owned companies, indigenous companies were generally responsible for a larger share of Ireland's net foreign earnings than their share of Ireland's exports. In that sense, indigenous companies were generally more important for the economy than their share of exports would suggest. Similarly, since net foreign earnings were a higher proportion of exports in services than in manufacturing, service exports were more important for the economy than their share of total exports would suggest.

Table 5.7 shows that in 2000 Irish indigenous manufacturing companies accounted for 7.0% of total exports, whereas they accounted for 14.5% of total net foreign earnings. In the same year, Irish indigenous producers in all sectors combined accounted for 12.0% of total exports compared to 27.5% of total net foreign earnings. A similar point applies to each sector in each year shown in Table 5.7—Irish producers always accounted for a larger share of net foreign earnings than their share of exports.

As regards trends over time, it is clear in Table 5.7 that foreign-owned companies increased their share of both exports and net foreign earnings over the total period of the boom from the mid-1980s to 2007, with their share of exports rising from about 70% to 87% while their share of net foreign earnings rose from about 56% to 70%. Within this long period, however, there were differences between shorter periods, so that the trend in indigenous companies was relatively strong in the late 1980s and the 2000s while the 1990s was the time when growth was clearly faster among foreign-owned companies.

It was already noted above that the value of indigenous manufacturing exports increased at a slightly faster rate than the growth of exports from foreign-owned industry in Ireland in 1986–1990. Since indigenous manufacturing accounted for almost 30% of total net foreign earnings in 1985, and almost 40% of net foreign earnings from manufacturing, its rapid export growth at that time made an important contribution to transforming the 1980s recession into an economic boom.

Later, between 2000 and 2007, indigenous companies increased their share of total exports from 12.0% to 13.4% and they increased their share

Table 5.7 Percentage distribution of exports and estimated net foreign earnings, Irish indigenous and foreign-owned, 1985, 2000 and 2007

	Exports 1985	*Exports 2000*	*Exports 2007*	*Net foreign earnings 1985*	*Net foreign earnings 2000*	*Net foreign earn-ings 2007*
Irish indigenous						
Agriculture	3.5	0.8	0.6	5.4	2.0	1.3
Manufacturing	20.3	7.0	6.0	29.2	14.5	12.1
Services	6.3*	4.2	6.8	9.5*	11.1	17.0
Total Irish	30.0	12.0	13.4	44.2	27.5	30.4
Foreign-owned						
Agriculture	0.0	0.0	0.0	0.0	0.0	0.0
Manufacturing	63.8	73.8	56.5	46.3	49.1	26.8
Services	6.3*	14.2	30.1	9.5*	23.3	42.8
Total foreign	70.1	88.0	86.6	55.8	72.5	69.6
All						
Agriculture	3.5	0.8	0.6	5.4	2.0	1.3
Manufacturing	84.1	80.8	62.5	75.5	63.6	38.9
Services	12.5	18.4	36.9	19.1	34.4	59.8
Grand total	100.0	100.0	100.0	100.0	100.0	100.0

Notes
"Net foreign earnings" here means the value of a sector's exports minus the value of the imported inputs that are used in producing the exports minus the profit outflows that arise from production of the exports
* As regards services in 1985, the total comes from officially published data, but the indigenous/foreign breakdown here comes from a crude assumption of a 50:50 divide, in the absence of useful data on this point
Source Derived primarily from Central Statistics Office (CSO) data, including input–output tables, the balance of international payments, the Census of Industrial Production, and the Annual Services Inquiry, as well as data from Forfas, Annual Business Survey of Economic Impact. See Appendix for further details. Creative Commons Attribution BY 4.0

of net foreign earnings from 27.5% to 30.4%. This primarily reflected trends in manufacturing as the trends in both exports and net foreign earnings were a good deal weaker in foreign-owned manufacturing than in indigenous manufacturing at that time. In the services sector, the growth of exports and net foreign earnings was rapid in both indigenous and foreign-owned companies, so both groups participated in the rising importance of services in total exports and total net foreign earnings.

R&D and Innovation

It was noted above that during much of the boom the sectoral composition of Irish indigenous industry was changing, moving away from the lower technology sectors and towards the higher technology sectors. This shift was relatively strong by international standards in the 1990s, although it ceased in the last phase of the boom largely because of foreign takeovers of Irish companies in the higher technology sectors.

This shift towards the higher technology sectors is not necessarily conclusive evidence that there was a move into genuinely higher technology activities because the higher technology sectors would include some niches where companies were making relatively simple products with mature technologies. Therefore, it is relevant to ask whether there was any supporting evidence of technological upgrading in Irish indigenous industry—in the form of more research & development (R&D) and a high rate of innovation.

To take the question of R&D first, at the start of the boom a relatively small amount of R&D was being performed in Ireland compared to many other countries. In 1986, gross expenditure on research & development (GERD) amounted to just 1.0% of GNP in Ireland,[11] whereas the corresponding figures for most other OECD countries were between 1.4 and 2.7%.[12] The Irish figure rose considerably from 1.0 to 1.43% by 1998 and remained at that level in 2004, although that was still relatively low compared to 1.85% for the EU and 2.24% for the OECD.[13]

GERD data refer to all R&D performed in a country, including in higher education, government research organisations, etc., as well as in businesses, whereas business expenditure on research & development (BERD) is a focused measure of R&D in businesses. In most developed economies, BERD accounts for a substantial majority of GERD, but BERD was so limited in Ireland at the start of the boom that it accounted for only about half of GERD and 0.5% of GNP in 1986 (Eolas 1990). BERD then increased relatively fast so that it accounted for 65–70% of

[11] Eolas (1990) for GERD as % of GDP, adjusted to GERD as % of GNP using GDP and GNP data from Department of Finance, *Budgetary and Economic Statistics*, December 2013.

[12] National Board for Science and Technology, *Irish Science and Technology Statistics*, 1986.

[13] Forfas, *Research and Development in Ireland 2005—At a Glance.*

GERD in the late 1990s and 2000s. BERD as a percentage of GNP also rose quite fast from 0.5% in 1986 to between 0.95 and 1.05% in the late 1990s and early 2000s. The Irish figure then was quite close to, but still below, the EU level which ranged between 1.06 and 1.17%. The Irish figure was further below the OECD level which was generally close to 1.5%.[14]

To focus more specifically on Irish indigenous industry, indigenous companies accounted for less than half of BERD throughout the boom, but that partly reflected the fact that their output and sales were lower than those of foreign-owned firms in Ireland. If we look at BERD intensity, BERD as a percentage of gross output was 0.5% in indigenous manufacturing at the start of the boom in 1988, and that was just a little lower than the figure of 0.6% for foreign-owned manufacturing.[15] BERD intensity in indigenous manufacturing increased substantially to 1.1% of gross output by 1997, while there was also a similar increase in foreign-owned manufacturing, to 1.2% of gross output. The figure for indigenous industry declined later to 0.75% by 2003, while BERD intensity in foreign-owned firms declined more sharply to 0.65% in 2003, almost the same level as in 1988.[16]

Even at the peak level in the late 1990s, BERD intensity in both indigenous and foreign-owned firms was low compared with the OECD. Thus, the 1997 BERD intensity figures of 1.1% in Irish indigenous manufacturing and 1.2% in foreign-owned manufacturing in Ireland were both a good deal lower than the OECD figure of 2.4%. However, the reasons for this were quite different in indigenous and foreign-owned industries.

In indigenous industry, overall BERD intensity was relatively low because of the sectoral composition of indigenous industry—being relatively highly concentrated in sectors that generally had low R&D intensity in most countries, and relatively less concentrated in the sectors which generally had the highest R&D intensity. When viewed sector by sector,

[14] Forfas, *Research and Development in Ireland 2005—At a Glance*, and Forfas, 2007, *Research & Development Performance in the Business Sector, Ireland 2005/6*. Dublin: Forfas.

[15] R&D data from Eolas (1990); gross output data from *Census of Industrial Production*.

[16] Forfas, *Survey of Research and Development in the Business Sector 1997* for 1997. Forfas, *Business Expenditure on Research and Development (BERD) Ireland 2003/4*, for 2003.

Irish indigenous firms did not have systematically lower R&D intensity than OECD firms in the same sectors. Thus, Table 5.8 shows that in 1997 Irish indigenous companies had higher R&D intensity than the OECD in 8 out of 14 manufacturing sectors, including electrical & electronic equipment—a high-tech sector, and machinery & equipment—a medium–high-tech sector. Irish indigenous companies also had almost the same R&D intensity as the OECD in medical & technical instruments—another high-tech sector.[17]

In contrast, foreign-owned industry in Ireland was particularly highly concentrated in the sectors that generally had high R&D intensity in most countries, but for the most part foreign-owned firms in Ireland tended to have systematically lower R&D intensity than OECD firms operating in the same sectors as themselves. Thus, Table 5.8 shows that in 1997 foreign companies in Ireland had lower R&D intensity than the OECD in 11 out of 14 manufacturing sectors. In most of the high-technology and medium–high-technology sectors, R&D intensity in the foreign companies in Ireland was much less than the level seen in the OECD. It was possible for them to prosper in this way, despite their lower R&D intensity, because they could benefit from the R&D performed by other branches of the same MNCs in other countries.

When R&D intensity declined later in the 2000s in both Irish indigenous and foreign-owned industries, the reasons for this were again quite different in indigenous and foreign industries. In foreign-owned industry, the main reason was because of the decline of the electronics industry, which was already mentioned above. In 1997 the electrical & electronic equipment sector accounted for 49% of all R&D in foreign-owned firms, so trends in that sector had a great influence on total R&D in foreign firms. Between 1997 and 2003, the sector's share of the total output of foreign-owned industry declined significantly and its R&D intensity dropped from 1.7% of gross output to 0.7%. It seems that cutting R&D activity was an aspect of a broader reduction of electronics production.

In Irish indigenous industry, the decline in R&D intensity, from 1.1% of gross output in 1997 to 0.75% in 2003, was less severe than in foreign-owned industry. When viewed sector by sector, there was no general

[17] The classification of sectors as "high-tech", "low-tech", etc. is generally done in accordance with each sector's R&D intensity in a group of developed economies. Consequently, the OECD's R&D intensity figures shown in columns 2 and 5 of Table 5.8 are a good guide to the relative standing of the different sectors in terms of such a classification.

Table 5.8 BERD intensity (BERD as % of gross output), by nationality of ownership and manufacturing sector, compared to the OECD, 1997

	Irish indigenous R&D intensity	*OECD R&D intensity*	*Irish intensity as % of OECD intensity*	*Foreign-owned R&D intensity*	*OECD R&D intensity*	*Foreign-owned intensity as % of OECD intensity*
Food, drink & tobacco	0.5	0.3	167	0.5	0.3	167
Textiles & clothing	1.9	0.3	633	0.5	0.3	167
Wood & wood products	0.7	0.2	350	1.4	0.2	700
Paper, printing & publishing	0.3	0.4	75	0.0	0.4	0
Chemicals (less pharmaceuticals)	0.8	3.2	25	0.4	3.2	13
Pharmaceuticals	4.0	11.5	35	5.1	11.5	44
Rubber & plastic products	1.7	1.2	142	0.8	1.2	67
Non-metallic mineral products	1.1	0.8	138	0.7	0.8	88
Metals & metal products	1.3	0.7	186	0.2	0.7	29
Machinery & equipment	2.4	2.1	114	1.2	2.1	57
Electrical & electronic equipment	6.4	5.6	114	1.7	5.6	30

	Irish indigenous R&D intensity	*OECD R&D intensity*	*Irish intensity as % of OECD intensity*	*Foreign-owned R&D intensity*	*OECD R&D intensity*	*Foreign-owned intensity as % of OECD intensity*
Medical & technical instruments	6.7	7.0	96	2.0	7.0	29
Transport equipment	1.8	4.5	40	2.8	4.5	62
Other manufacturing	0.5	1.0	50	0.2	1.0	20
Total manufacturing	1.1	2.4	46	1.2	2.4	50

Source Forfas. 1999. *Survey of Research and Development in the Business Sector 1997*. Dublin: Forfas

pattern of decline in R&D intensity across most of the R&D intensive indigenous sectors, and there was also no single one of them that experienced a very sharp decline in R&D intensity comparable that seen in foreign-owned electronics. Rather, the main cause of the overall decline in indigenous R&D intensity was the generally declining share of the most R&D intensive sectors in total indigenous manufacturing output. As was discussed above in connection with Tables 5.2, 5.3 and 5.4, the high-technology and medium–high-technology sectors tended to constitute a declining portion of indigenous manufacturing in the early 2000s, largely because of foreign takeovers of indigenous companies in these sectors. Since these sectors were far more R&D intensive than total indigenous manufacturing, their declining share of total indigenous manufacturing output had the effect of reducing the total R&D intensity of indigenous manufacturing.[18]

In order to be of real benefit for companies and industries, business expenditure on R&D has to lead to innovation, which in turn can be expected to result in commercial or economic benefits such as increases in productivity, sales, profitability and employment. In the Irish context, there is good evidence that R&D did in fact tend to have a significant positive influence on innovation. Hewitt-Dundas and Roper (2008) found that in 2003–2005 there were "strong positive R&D effects on both product and process innovation as well as innovation success". Thus, they found that having in-house R&D significantly increased the probability that a plant would engage in product innovation and process innovation, while it also increased the share of plants' sales accounted for by new and improved products.

Using a different and independent set of data for 2004–2006, Doran et al. (2012/2013) again found that having in-house R&D significantly increased the probability that plants would engage in product innovation, and they found that this effect was almost twice as strong for Irish indigenous businesses as for foreign-owned businesses. They also found that having in-house R&D significantly increased the likelihood that Irish indigenous plants would engage in process innovation, although this

[18] Data for 1997 and 2003 in the foregoing paragraphs are from the sources mentioned in footnote 15. R&D data published for later years such as 2005 and 2007 are not suitable for our purposes here, because they do not make distinctions by nationality and sector in a way that would allow us to derive R&D intensity figures for indigenous and foreign-owned industry.

effect was not significant in foreign-owned companies. Thus, the influence of in-house R&D activity on innovation was generally more important for Irish indigenous plants than for foreign-owned plants, presumably because a good deal of the innovation that occurred in the foreign-owned plants was coming from R&D performed in other branches of the same MNC located in other countries.

Levels of innovation activity in Ireland were quite high compared to other European countries in the 1990s. Data from the Community Innovation Survey 1 (CIS1), collected in 1993, indicate that Ireland ranked highest among a group of ten European countries in terms of the percentage of establishments that had introduced a technologically changed product or process during the previous three years. When ranked in terms of the percentage of innovating plants' sales derived from innovative products, Ireland was in the middle of the group of ten countries. In a later survey carried out in 1997, CIS2, Ireland ranked highest among a group of fifteen European countries in terms of the percentage of firms introducing innovative products and also ranked highest in terms of the percentage of firms introducing innovative processes. In that 1997 survey Ireland ranked somewhat higher than previously, at fourth out of fifteen countries, in terms of innovative products as a percentage of sales (O'Malley et al. 2008, Table 5.1).

These findings refer to all manufacturing plants in Ireland, including Irish indigenous and foreign-owned plants. A different series of surveys, the Irish Innovation Panel surveys, found that Irish indigenous plants were generally less likely than foreign-owned plants to be product or process innovators (Hewitt-Dundas and Roper 2008, Table 2). However, since the proportion of indigenous plants who were innovators was just 3 or 4 percentage points below the overall national figures for Ireland in the late 1990s (Hewitt-Dundas and Roper 2008, Tables 1 and 2), Irish indigenous industry still ranked quite highly by European standards.

As regards trends in innovation over time, the pattern in Irish indigenous industry looks broadly consistent with the trend in R&D intensity in the 1990s and early 2000s, although the innovation figures did not change by large amounts. For example, the proportion of indigenous plants that were product innovators increased from 57.8% in 1991–1993 to 61.8% in 1997–1999 and then declined to 53.6% in 2000–2002. Also, the proportion of indigenous plants that were process innovators increased from 51.3% in 1994–1996 to 61.7% in 1997–1999 and then declined to 51.3% in 2000–2002 (Hewitt-Dundas and Roper 2008, Table 2).

In order to be of real economic significance, R&D and innovation must have beneficial consequences for output, productivity, employment, etc. There is good evidence that such consequences did occur in Ireland in the 1990s and early 2000s.

Roper and Love (2004) used the proportion of a plant's sales that was derived from innovative products as an indicator of a plant's innovation success, and they found that there was a strong positive link between product innovation success and business growth. The effects of product innovation on productivity were negative in the short-term due to temporary disruption but then the longer term effects on productivity were positive. The benefit of process innovation for productivity was more immediate and enduring.

Kearns and Ruane (1998) found that technological activity in plants was an important determinant of their probability of survival. Looking at Irish indigenous manufacturing plants that existed in 1986, they found that technologically active plants had a higher probability of surviving until 1996 than comparable plants that were less technologically active. This was true for several different variables that were used to represent "technological activity", including the scale of R&D, R&D intensity and sales of innovative products developed within the plant. Kearns and Ruane (1999) found that foreign-owned plants that undertook R&D in Ireland were more likely to survive in Ireland for longer than those that did not undertake R&D. The R&D performers also had lower rates of job loss and their jobs lasted for longer than among those that did not undertake R&D.

As was outlined in Chapter 2, the state's industrial policy began in the mid-1980s to put a somewhat greater emphasis on the aim of developing Irish indigenous industry. Part of that effort was the introduction of enhanced measures to support technological development in indigenous companies. Consequently, the share of the industrial policy budget going to science and technology measures increased from 11% in 1985 to 21% in 1992.

Given that background, it is worth noting here that Roper and Love (2004) found evidence that grant support for product innovation was a statistically significant and positive influence on innovation success. They found that there was a significant policy effect working through specific grants for R&D and innovation and through stimulating investment. Similarly, Hewitt-Dundas and Roper (2008, 2010) found that state support was important in increasing the probability that plants would be engaging in product and process innovation as well as having success with their innovations.

To sum up on R&D and innovation, there was a substantial increase in R&D intensity in Irish indigenous manufacturing between the start of the boom and the late 1990s, which helps to confirm that there was a genuine shift into higher technology activities. By the late 1990s, R&D intensity in individual indigenous manufacturing sectors was generally comparable to the corresponding sectors in the OECD, including the higher technology sectors, while the relatively low overall R&D intensity of indigenous manufacturing was a result of its sectoral composition. When indigenous R&D intensity declined after the late 1990s, that was mainly an effect of foreign takeovers of indigenous companies in the higher technology sectors. The evidence on innovation levels and innovation trends is broadly consistent with this account of R&D levels and trends.

There is also evidence that confirms the expectations that R&D should lead to innovation while both R&D and innovation should lead to economic effects such as faster growth, higher productivity and better employment prospects. Finally, the state's industrial policy provided important assistance which supported R&D and innovation.

Company Size

As was outlined in Sect. 2.2 in Chapter 2, the industrial policy changes that were introduced during the 1980s aimed to develop larger and stronger Irish indigenous firms by adopting a somewhat more selective approach. It was intended to focus state support and incentives more on building larger Irish companies that would be able to export more successfully by developing greater competitive advantages in areas such as scale of production, technological capabilities and export marketing.

This policy objective arose in the 1980s at a time when a major long-term decline had been occurring among the larger Irish indigenous companies in the more internationally traded activities. The larger companies were generally engaged in activities in which there were significant economies of scale—hence their relatively large size by Irish standards. But they were generally not large enough to match larger and longer established foreign competitors in a free trade environment. At the same time as many larger firms were declining, growth was occurring among small firms. The small firms were generally engaged in activities in which economies of scale were not important and most of them were limited to serving the Irish market.

In Table 5.9, the first column shows this process of fragmentation or deconcentration during 1973–1987. In a context of declining total indigenous manufacturing employment, the employment decline was very rapid in the relatively large establishments employing over 200 people, the decline was slower in the middle size establishments employing 50–199, and employment increased in the smallest establishments.

This pattern changed in the early years of the boom, 1987–1990, as seen in the second column of Table 5.9. Total indigenous manufacturing employment started to grow but the smallest size class contributed very little to this growth while instead the middle size class grew by most. The decline of the largest size class did not stop but it did slow down a good deal. This did not amount to a clear-cut reversal of the long-established trend of fragmentation, but it was a distinct change from that previous trend.

Subsequently, in 1991–2001, total indigenous manufacturing employment grew quite fast and all the size classes grew at much the same rate. Thus, there was a definite end to the previous process of fragmentation. While the largest size class did not grow any faster than the other size classes, it did grow quite fast just by growing at close to the average rate, and the number of indigenous establishments employing over 200 increased from 61 to 74 while the number employing over 500 increased from 12 to 16.

Table 5.9 Average annual percentage employment change in Irish indigenous manufacturing, by size class of establishments, 1973–2001

Employment size	*1973–1987*	*1987–1990*	*1991–2001*
Less than 50	1.2	0.3	1.4
50–199	−1.9	2.7	1.6
200 and over	−6.3	−1.5	1.3
Total	−2.2	0.7	1.5

Source O'Malley et al. (1992, Chapter 2), for columns 1 and 2. *Census of Industrial Production – Census of Industrial Local Units*, 1991 and 2001, for column 3

In the final phase of the boom, in 2001–2007, there was some re-emergence of the fragmentation trend, as seen in Table 5.10, although the contrast between decline in the largest size class and growth in the smallest size class was much less marked than in 1973–1987.[19] It seems quite possible that the fragmentation trend in 2001–2007 was partly a reflection of takeovers of indigenous companies in the higher-tech sectors by foreign companies, which were discussed above, since the indigenous companies that attracted the attention of foreign buyers would probably have tended to be relatively successful and hence probably larger than average.

A notable aspect of the development of Irish indigenous companies was the fact that, relative to the overall size of indigenous industry in Ireland, there was extensive development of Irish MNCs operating successfully in other countries. This feature was already visible in the 1980s before the boom began (O'Malley 1989, Chapter 6) and it increased a good deal over the next two decades. By 2010, Irish MNCs in all sectors employed 249,000 people in other countries, with 75,000 of these being in affiliates of Irish manufacturing companies.[20] Compared to 101,000 employed in indigenous manufacturing in Ireland in 2010, this seems like a large number.

Table 5.10 Average annual percentage employment change in Irish indigenous manufacturing, by size class of enterprises, 2001–2007

Employment Size	*2001–2007*
Less than 50	0.6
50–199	−1.7
200 and over	−2.0
Total	−0.8

Source: Census of Industrial Production – Census of Industrial Enterprises, 2001 and 2007. Creative Commons Attribution BY 4.0

[19] The data in Tables 5.9 and 5.10 are not strictly comparable since Table 5.9 refers to individual establishments or plants while Table 5.10 refers to enterprises. In most cases these amount to the same thing, but some enterprises own more than one establishment. Data on enterprises would be most relevant for the discussion here since some advantages of large size can arise at the level of the enterprise rather than the establishment, in areas such as R&D, marketing or finance, but there are no published enterprise data by size and nationality of ownership covering the 1980s and 1990s.

[20] CSO, 2012, *Business in Ireland 2010*. Dublin: Stationery Office.

While many indigenous manufacturing companies had foreign subsidiaries by then, the bulk of the employment was in the overseas branches of just the top ten or so. Forfas (2001) observed that most of the largest manufacturing companies concerned were in traditional industrial sectors such as construction materials, paper, packaging & printing, and agribusiness. They tended to be dominant home market players, often in non-traded sectors, and they used their existing strong positions in terms of expertise and finance in the domestic market in order to develop overseas. It is noticeable that most of their expansion overseas took the form of acquiring existing foreign companies in their own or related lines of business, rather than establishing new greenfield operations.

This type of growth produced some prominent companies that were clearly great successes in business terms, but it is unlikely that this growth had a commensurate impact on Ireland's economic development. Such growth probably had some benefits for the home economy, such as more employment in higher value-added functions, and additional income coming from the flow of profits back to Ireland with consequent benefits for tax revenue and employment, etc. (Forfas 2007). However, such benefits could hardly compare to the effects of a similar amount of growth occurring in Ireland.

The extensive growth of Irish MNCs does at least show that Ireland was reasonably well endowed with the entrepreneurial ability and management skills required to build large and internationally successful companies. Therefore, if the development of indigenous manufacturing in Ireland remained unsatisfactory, this was not due to an absence of business ability and skills but was more an effect of the constraints confronting indigenous industrial companies in a late-industrialising country such as Ireland (as discussed in Sect. 2.2 in Chapter 2).

5.2 Growth and Development of Indigenous Market Services

Output, Exports and Net Foreign Earnings

The services sector accounted for a large part of total output and employment long before the boom, but traditionally it was not seen as a significant source of exports because most of the more traditional services had to be provided locally for local customers. There were always some exceptional services which could be exported such as transport services, tourism and some financial services but in the mid-1980s, just before the boom began, these exports were relatively small in Ireland compared to manufacturing exports.

In 1985, services accounted for 39% of total output but only 12% of total exports. Just 10% of services output was exported while 62% of manufacturing output was exported. This picture changed substantially over the next two decades as technological and organisational changes resulted in services becoming a growing part of international trade in Ireland and in the wider world. By 2005 services still accounted for 39% of output in Ireland, but the proportion of their output that was exported had increased greatly and they accounted for 33% of Ireland's exports.[21]

During the period 1985–2005, the value of services exports increased by €40 billion, from €2 billion in 1985 to €42 billion in 2005. Over the same period, the value of total exports from Ireland increased by €114 billion, so services accounted for 35% of the total increase in exports.

Net foreign earnings were generally a higher percentage of the value of exports in services than in manufacturing, largely because imported material inputs were generally a smaller proportion of the value of exports in services than in manufacturing. Consequently, the services sector accounted for a greater share of total net foreign earnings than its share of exports. By 2005, services accounted for 50% of net foreign earnings according to our estimates,[22] and services had accounted for 56% of the total increase in net foreign earnings since 1985.

Given the key role of exports, and especially net foreign earnings, in driving overall economic growth in Ireland, the services sector clearly played a very important part in the boom. Unfortunately, however, the data on services are generally not as comprehensive or as detailed as the available data on manufacturing, and there is a particular scarcity of data on services distinguishing between Irish indigenous and foreign-owned firms.

The CSO's *Annual Services Inquiry* (ASI) did not include data on services by nationality of ownership until 2001. The data by nationality that it began to publish in 2001 included turnover, gross value-added and employment—but no data on exports—and then exports by nationality

[21] Output and export data from CSO, *Input-Output Tables for 1985*. Dublin: Stationery Office; and CSO, *Supply and Use and Input-Output Tables for Ireland: 2005*. Dublin: Stationery Office.

[22] The derivation of our estimates is outlined in Appendix.

of ownership was first included in 2008. The data concerned referred to service enterprises with 20 or more persons engaged and did not include financial services and insurance.

The ASI data show that the services sector was mostly Irish-owned in 2001–2007. Although the Irish indigenous part of the sector grew quite fast during that period, its share of the sector's employment and turnover was declining as the foreign-owned part of the sector was growing even more rapidly. Irish indigenous firms accounted for 79% of the sector's employment in 2001 declining to 73% by 2007, while they accounted for 65% of the sector's turnover in 2001 declining to 56% in 2007.[23]

Irish indigenous firms had a much smaller share of services exports than their share of employment or turnover. When the ASI published data on exports by nationality of ownership in 2008, Irish indigenous firms accounted for 22.7% of non-financial services exports. Our own estimate for 2007 indicates that indigenous firms accounted for 18.5% of all services exports, including financial services.[24]

Net foreign earnings were generally a higher percentage of the value of exports in Irish indigenous services than in foreign-owned services. Consequently, although indigenous companies accounted for about 18.5% of total services exports in 2007, their share of total net foreign earnings in services was a good deal higher at an estimated 28.4%.

As a result, in terms of net foreign earnings, indigenous services were making a quite important contribution to the overall economy in 2007. As was seen in Table 5.7, indigenous services accounted for about 17% of all net foreign earnings, compared to 12.1% for indigenous manufacturing, 1.3% for agriculture, and a total of 30.4% for all indigenous firms.

As regards trends over time, we have reasonably good estimates for 2000 as well as 2007. These estimates indicate that indigenous services exports and net foreign earnings grew faster than total exports and total net foreign earnings from all sectors during that period, increasing their

[23] The ASI data quoted here did not include the many small services firms with less than 20 persons engaged, which would have been very largely Irish-owned. Consequently, the indigenous share of the whole sector would have been somewhat larger than the ASI data suggest.

[24] The difference between these two figures is very largely because our own estimate includes financial services while the ASI figure does not, given that in our estimates indigenous companies had a smaller share of financial services exports than their share of other services exports.

share of total exports from 4.2% to 6.8% and increasing their share of total net foreign earnings from 11.1% to 17.0% (Table 5.7). Furthermore, indigenous services exports were growing faster than total commercial services exports from the EU-27 in 2000–2007, increasing their share of this total from 0.65% to 1.06%.[25] At the same time, however, exports and net foreign earnings from indigenous services were growing more slowly than exports and net foreign earnings from foreign-owned services in Ireland.

Taking a longer view over the whole period of the boom, it is known that services accounted for 12.5% of all exports in 1985, as was seen in Table 5.7, but we do not have any adequate estimate of how much of that came from indigenous or foreign-owned companies. In Table 5.7, a simple assumption is made that half came from indigenous companies and half came from foreign-owned companies, but this is just a technical assumption that is not based on evidence and consequently it could be wrong by a wide margin.

However, services exports were so limited in 1985 that, even if there is a high degree of inaccuracy in breaking down this small amount between indigenous and foreign companies, it is still possible to make some valid remarks on long-term trends. Thus, using the estimates underlying Table 5.7, we can say that the increase in the current value of exports in 1985–2007 was roughly four and a half or five times greater in foreign-owned services than in indigenous services. In a similar vein, we can conclude that the increase in the current value of net foreign earnings in 1985–2007 was about two and a half or three times greater in foreign-owned services than in indigenous services. These observations are valid regardless of whether indigenous companies accounted for as little as one-quarter or as much as three-quarters of services exports in 1985.

Although the long-term growth of exports from Irish indigenous services looks rather weak when compared with foreign-owned services in Ireland, it was actually quite strong when compared with wider international experience. The broader context here is that the growth of total services exports from Ireland was much faster than in most other countries. Loungani et al. (2017, Table 2) found that Ireland was the 32nd largest exporter of services in the world in 1980, rising to 30th in 1990,

[25] The EU-27 data on exports of commercial services come from the WTO. "Commercial" services here means all services except services from the public sector.

22nd in 2000 and 14th in 2010. They also reported that Ireland's services exports increased from $1.4 billion in 1980 to $89.1 billion in 2010 (valued in current US dollars), which means that they grew by 14.8% p.a. Much of this was due to the growth of exports from foreign-owned services in Ireland, but indigenous growth was also significant. If we take it that Irish indigenous companies accounted for no more than 90% of services exports in 1980 and at least 17% of the figure for 2010,[26] the value of their exports increased by at least 8.6% p.a. in 1980–2010. For comparison, the corresponding growth rates for the largest services exporters in the world were USA 8.6% p.a., UK 6.9% p.a., Germany 6.8% p.a., France 5.2% p.a. and Japan 6.6% p.a.

As regards the composition of services exports from Ireland, it was noted in Chapter 4 that at the start of the boom they consisted largely of transport services (41% of total services exports) and lodging & catering (23%), with smaller contributions coming from a wide variety of other services.[27] We have no data on this distinguishing between indigenous and foreign-owned companies, but it seems likely that the transport and lodging & catering services were mostly indigenous. In the case of transport services, there were a few prominent Irish companies involved in international transport in 1985—Aer Lingus, B&I line and Aer Rianta—which were large enough on their own to have accounted for a substantial majority of Ireland's exports of transport services if we assume that about 35% or more of their sales were exports.[28]

At the end of the boom, when we have data on services exports by nationality of ownership, the data show that exports of transport services were predominantly indigenous as Irish-owned companies accounted for 82% of all exports of transport services—including air, water and land transport as well as warehousing and support services for transport.[29]

[26] Our estimate for 2007 was 18.5% as mentioned above. We cannot apply exactly the same method to derive an estimate for 2010 because of changes in data availability for services but, allowing for the fact that the share of foreign-owned companies in services turnover continued to rise, we estimate that the Irish indigenous share of services exports was about 17.7% by 2010.

[27] Derived from CSO, *Input-Output Tables for 1985.*

[28] "Top 500 Companies", *Irish Business*, January 1987. There were also foreign-owned companies providing international transport services into and out of Ireland, but if their services were not based in Ireland they would not have been counted as part of the Irish economy or exports.

[29] Derived from Lawless and Studnicka (2017, Tables 30 and 32).

These transport services were still a substantial component of all indigenous services exports at the end of the boom, although their share of the total was probably lower than it had been in the 1980s. Table 5.11 shows the sectoral composition of Irish indigenous services exports in the period 2008–2012, based on data from the *Annual Services Inquiry*. The four transport categories in the table together accounted for 33% of the total.[30]

Two other types of services made up most of the remainder—(1) software, with about 27% of the total, and (2) a range of professional, scientific and technical services with about 26% of the total. Software services are in the first item in Table 5.11, which includes the publishing of software (as well as publishing of books etc.), together with computer programming, consultancy and related activities. The range of professional, scientific and technical services in Table 5.11 includes scientific research & development, legal & accounting activities, head office activities and management consultancy, and architectural & engineering activities.

There are two significant omissions from Table 5.11, financial services & insurance as well as accommodation & food services. Financial services & insurance are left out because the data in Table 5.11 come from the *Annual Services Inquiry* (ASI) which did not cover that sector. Accommodation & food services are largely absent from the table because the ASI is a survey of companies, and companies in that type of business are often not able to report how much of their sales were exports—meaning how much of their sales were to customers who are normally resident in another country—since they provide their services in Ireland to customers who come to them in Ireland. Hence the CSO needs to use separate surveys of foreign residents at airports and ferry ports to collect the data it requires on export tourism expenditure for the balance of payments, national accounts, input–output tables, etc. (Lawless and Studnicka 2017, Chapter 3).

Our own estimates (derived as explained in Appendix) of the value of indigenous financial services & insurance exports indicate that they

[30] Table 5.11 shows exports of air transport services at €472.5 million, whereas the turnover of the largest Irish airline, Ryanair, was far larger than this, at €2,942 million in the year to March 2009. The disparity between these two figures reflects the fact that many of Ryanair's services were based outside Ireland and could not be counted as part of Ireland's economy or exports.

Table 5.11 Irish indigenous services exports by sector, 2008–2012

NACE 2	*Sector*	*Services exports (€ million)*	*Share of total (%)*
58 and 62	Publishing activities and computer programming	792.0	26.6
51	Air transport	472.5	15.9
72	Scientific research and development	322.9	10.8
69	Legal and accounting activities	269.0	9.0
52	Warehousing and support for transport	222.8	7.5
50	Water transport	186.7	6.3
77	Rental and leasing activities	158.1	5.3
70	Head office activities; management consultancy	101.7	3.4
49	Land transport and transport via pipelines	101.2	3.4
71	Architectural and engineering activities	77.6	2.6
53	Postal and courier activities	65.9	2.2
63	Information service activities	31.2	1.0
	Other sectors	175.4	5.9
	Total	2977.0	100.0

Note Lawless and Studnicka (2017) found that companies that export services often export some goods as well. The data here refer to their exports of services only, after excluding their goods exports

Source Adapted from Lawless and Studnicka (2017, Table 30). Based on data from the *Annual Services Inquiry*. Lawless, Martina, and Zuzanna Studnicka. 2017. *Services Exports and Exporters of Services*. Dublin: ESRI, Department of Jobs Enterprise and Innovation, and Enterprise Ireland. Creative Commons Attribution BY 4.0

accounted for about 18% of all indigenous services exports in 2005 and 2007. As regards accommodation and food services, the input–output table for 2005 indicates that exports of hotel & restaurant services were worth a similar amount to exports of transport services. We do not have an indigenous/foreign breakdown of the exports of hotel & restaurant services, but available data indicate that they were predominantly indigenous,[31] so it seems possible that the indigenous component was broadly comparable in value to indigenous exports of transport services.

Combining these observations with Table 5.11, it seems that the overall composition of indigenous services exports at the end of the boom was approximately as follows: transport services 20%, hotels & restaurants 20%, financial services & insurance 18%, software 17%, professional, scientific & technical services 16%, and others 9%. Obviously, these figures cannot be regarded as precise, particularly in the case of hotels & restaurants and, to a lesser extent, financial services & insurance.

Whereas the role of transport services and hotel & restaurant services represented elements of continuity with the past situation before the boom, the prominence in indigenous services exports of software, financial services and the other professional, scientific and technical services were newer developments which largely emerged, or at least grew rapidly from small beginnings, during the boom.

These newer types of exports were much the same as the types of indigenous service activities that received a good deal of attention and assistance from state development agencies such as Forbairt or Enterprise Ireland since the 1980s, on the grounds that they had good potential to develop exports unlike many other services. As a consequence of the interest of these development agencies, surveys such as the *Annual Employment Survey*, the *Annual Business Survey of Economic Impact* and the regular surveys of business R&D (BERD), which were conducted by or for the agencies, generally covered a group of selected service activities in addition to all of manufacturing. This group of selected services was sometimes called "internationally traded services", sometimes "software and other services" or sometimes "information, communication and other services", when presenting results of the surveys concerned. The categories of services within this group included computer programming, consultancy & related activities; other IT & computer services;

[31] In the ASI for 2005, the turnover of hotels & restaurants combined with retail and repair of motor vehicles was 91% indigenous and 9% foreign owned. At the same time, hotels & restaurants accounted for 70% of the combination of hotels & restaurants and retail and repair of motor vehicles, measured in terms of GVA. If the 9% of the two sectors combined that was foreign owned was all in hotels & restaurants, it would have amounted to about 9 out of 70, or 13%, of hotels & restaurants. Hence about 87% or more of the hotels & restaurants sector was indigenous, so that most exports of hotels & restaurants were probably indigenous.

some elements of financial services; business services; education; and other services.

The surveys mentioned above indicate that these services tended to be relatively highly skilled. Thus, their pay levels were relatively high, with average payroll costs per employee generally being 20–30% higher than in indigenous manufacturing in 2000–2007.[32]

In addition, the surveys of R&D show that Irish indigenous companies in these services were particularly R&D intensive. In 2003 indigenous companies in this group of services spent €131 million on conducting R&D, which amounted to 44% of all indigenous expenditure on R&D in manufacturing and this group of services combined.[33] For comparison, in the same year this group of services accounted for just 17% of sales and 19% of employment in indigenous companies in manufacturing and this group of services combined.[34] Expenditure on R&D had grown very rapidly in these indigenous services, by 26.5% p.a. in 1993–2001, valued in current prices, compared to 8.0% p.a. in indigenous manufacturing and 10.0% p.a. in foreign-owned manufacturing in Ireland.[35]

These points concerning R&D are especially relevant to the software industry. In 1993–2001, R&D expenditure in indigenous "software & computer related services" increased by 35% p.a., and by 2001 it accounted for more than three-quarters of indigenous R&D in the group of selected services. The remainder of this section looks at the indigenous software industry in a little more detail.

The Irish Indigenous Software Industry

Some of the earliest software firms in Ireland began in the 1970s and more started in the early 1980s, but the substantial expansion of the industry really began in the mid-1980s as major foreign software MNCs

[32] Forfas, *Annual Business Survey of Economic Impact—2008*, Appendix, Table B6.

[33] Forfas, 2005, *Business Expenditure on Research and Development (BERD) Ireland 2003/4*, Table 3.1.

[34] Derived from Forfas, *Annual Business Survey of Economic Impact—2008*, Appendix, Tables B1 and B2.

[35] Derived from Forfas, 2003, *Business Expenditure on Research and Development (BERD), 2001*, Tables 3.2 and 3.3.

started up in Ireland while the indigenous branch of the industry also grew quickly. In 1986, there were only about 1,800 people employed in the industry, with about 1,200 being in Irish indigenous firms and about 600 in foreign-owned firms. By 1991, employment in the industry was 7,800, rising to about 24,900 by 1999, so that employment grew by 15.6% p.a. in 1991–1999 (O'Malley and O'Gorman 2001; Crone 2002).

Throughout the 1990s, about half of employment in the industry was in indigenous firms and about half was in foreign-owned firms. Employment in indigenous companies grew by 16.8% p.a. in 1991–1999. The rate of growth of sales revenue in the indigenous industry was extremely high in 1991–1999 at 29.4% p.a., while the growth rate of indigenous exports was even higher at 37.3% p.a. The indigenous branch of the industry was becoming increasingly export-oriented, with exports rising from 40.7% of sales in 1991 to 62.0% by 1999. By 1995, 80% of indigenous software companies were exporting to some extent (O'Malley and O'Gorman 2001; Crone 2002).

The late 1980s and the 1990s was a period when software was a relatively fast-growing industry in other countries too. However, the sales and exports of the Irish indigenous software industry were growing a good deal faster than the international market for software, so the industry was gaining market share (O'Malley and O'Gorman 2001).

It was noted in Sect. 5.1 that there was also relatively strong growth in the indigenous branches of the high-technology manufacturing sectors at this time. However, indigenous development in the software sector was on a different scale. Indigenous companies accounted for only small minorities of employment in the high-tech manufacturing sectors, whereas they accounted for half the employment in the software sector. Indigenous employment of over 9,000 in software by 1997 was far more than the 4,900 in the indigenous computers, pharmaceuticals and instrument engineering sectors combined (O'Malley and O'Gorman 2001).

In the period after about 2000, the growth of the indigenous software industry slowed down a good deal, although its growth did continue at a more modest pace. The data on the industry that are available for the 2000s are not precisely comparable to the earlier data quoted above for the 1990s, since the 1990s data originally came from the National Software Directorate whereas the available data for the 2000s come from the *Annual Employment Survey* and the *Annual Business Survey of Economic*

Impact. Nevertheless, it is evident that the indigenous software industry grew a good deal more slowly in the 2000s.

In 2002–2007, employment in Irish indigenous "computer programming, consultancy and related activities" increased by 1.3% p.a., which was a little faster than indigenous manufacturing but slower than some other indigenous services.[36] In 2000–2007, sales of the same sector increased by 5.2% p.a. while its exports grew by 6.3% p.a., in current values.[37] Again, this was somewhat faster than indigenous manufacturing but slower than some other indigenous services.

It was found in Sect. 5.1 that a significant cause of growth slowing down at this time in the indigenous branches of the high-technology manufacturing sectors was because many of the Irish companies concerned were being taken over by foreign-owned companies and consequently disappearing from the indigenous ranks. There is evidence that a similar trend was beginning to have a substantial effect in the software sector in the late 1990s.

In 1998 and 1999, industry data from the National Software Directorate made a three-way distinction between Irish-owned, foreign-owned and "takeover" companies—"takeover" companies being those that were originally Irish-owned and then subsequently acquired by foreign owners. The number of takeover companies was quite small at just 11 in 1998 and 12 in 1999 compared to over 600 Irish-owned firms. However, the takeover companies were relatively large and highly export-oriented, so that their employment amounted to 19% of employment in Irish-owned companies in both 1998 and 1999, their sales amounted to 20% of sales of Irish-owned companies in 1998 and 17% in 1999, while their exports amounted to 28% of exports of Irish-owned companies in 1998 and 23% in 1999 (Crone 2002, Table 1).

Unfortunately, data are not available to follow this through into later years. However, it is relevant to note that Crone (2013) presented brief profiles of eight of the most prominent indigenous software companies to have been established in the period between the mid-1990s and 2001/2002, and he mentioned that five of the eight had been acquired by foreign-owned companies by October 2009.

[36] Forfás, *Annual Employment Survey 2011*, Table A5.

[37] Forfás, *Annual Business Survey of Economic Impact 2008*, Tables B1 and B3.

When Irish firms were taken over by foreign firms they dropped out of the "Irish indigenous" category, which weakened the trend in statistics for that category. That, in itself, was not necessarily always a bad thing for the Irish economy, since it was possible that the new parent company might aim to promote the continuing growth and development of the Irish subsidiary in Ireland. However, it was somewhat more likely that the new parent company would be focused essentially on promoting its own growth by gaining access to the Irish subsidiary's technology, marketing or other assets. In that case, growth or even maintenance of activity in the Irish subsidiary could become at best a secondary consideration that would not receive much support.

Ó Riain (2004, p. 123) quoted journalist John Sterne's analysis of eighteen takeovers (domestic and international) in the Irish IT industry in the late 1980s:

> IT acquisitions in this country, with just a couple of exceptions, have meant job losses rather than gains and reductions, not increases, in the functions and responsibilities of organisations here. Every so often, though, an agreement is struck which builds on what has gone before, strengthening instead of weakening the country's technology base. (*Irish Computer*, March 1992)

As noted above, the growth of the indigenous branch of the software industry in the late 1980s and 1990s occurred alongside the rapid growth of the foreign-owned branch of the industry. There were some major differences between the two branches. Much of the foreign-owned branch consisted of large companies which were engaged in large-scale production of software packages or products for mass markets. Typically, these were US MNCs which initially developed their products in the USA. They adapted or "localised" their products in Ireland to make them suitable for many different markets in Europe and elsewhere, and then produced and exported them. Since many of these were leading companies in the world software industry—such as Microsoft, Oracle and Lotus—Ireland became the second largest exporter of software in the world in the 1990s.

Irish indigenous companies in the software sector were generally much smaller and their activities were different. It is helpful to make a distinction between software products and software services. Software product companies developed a software programme which could be copied many times and sold to many customers, whereas software services were provided uniquely to each customer as required, rather than involving repeated selling of copies of a standardised product. Such software services could include bespoke (or once-off, customised) development of programmes for individual customers, system integration, consultancy and technical training. The main foreign-owned software companies in Ireland were predominantly focused on products, whereas indigenous companies had significant involvement in both products and services.

In addition, the indigenous companies' products were generally more specialised and more focused on narrow niche markets compared to the major foreign-owned companies, so their products were sold in much smaller quantities. For example, indigenous companies' products aimed to address the specific requirements of different types of customers in financial services, dairy processing, distribution, drinks, chemicals and many other sectors.

It seems that the indigenous software industry was engaged equally in products and services in the 1990s (O'Malley and O'Gorman 2001; Crone 2002), although it is difficult to be precise about this since many firms were involved in both to some extent. Indeed, since many of the industry's products were specialised for a limited range of customers, selling such products often required the companies concerned to provide some related services, such as an element of additional bespoke development, installation, training and after-sales support.

Another difference between indigenous and foreign-owned firms was that foreign-owned companies had much higher sales and exports per employee than indigenous companies. Although indigenous companies accounted for close to half the industry's employment, they accounted for less than 20% of sales and 15% of exports in the late 1990s (Crone 2002). However, this did not mean that indigenous companies had exceptionally low sales and productivity per employee, since it was the foreign-owned companies in Ireland that were unusual in having such extremely high sales per employee. This arose because much of the value embedded in the output of those companies was generated, not by their subsidiaries and employees in Ireland, but elsewhere in the value chain by the R&D and other activities in other parts of the same MNCs (O'Malley and O'Gorman 2001).

As regards the size of indigenous software companies, in 1991 they employed an average of 13.1 people, rising to 14.7 by 1998. In 1991, there were 14 companies, or 4.8% of the total number of indigenous companies, that employed over 50, and they accounted for 33% of total employment in the indigenous software industry. By 1998, the number of companies employing over 50 increased to 34, or 5.4% of the total, and they accounted for 43% of total employment.[38] Thus there was an increase in company size, but at the same time, there was nothing on the scale of the largest companies in the USA or Western Europe where some software companies employed thousands.

This did not necessarily have to be a major problem for indigenous software companies if much of the market continued to be quite segmented and if the Irish companies were appropriately specialised in selected segments. O'Malley and O'Gorman (2001) made the point that even in the USA there was a large number of successful small companies and the size structure of much of the software industry was similar to the indigenous industry in Ireland, with only the top few per cent of US companies being far larger than any of the Irish companies. However, small size did present a substantial barrier to competing in significant areas of the market which were dominated by large firms.

The software industry was one of the more successful stories in Irish indigenous growth during the boom and this success was explained by several favourable influences in combination.[39] First, a suitably qualified and high-quality labour force was available for the industry at a time when shortages of relevant skills occurred quite commonly in other countries. The education system in Ireland was turning out graduates in computer science and software engineering at a rate that was relatively high compared with most other OECD countries. Initially, much of the motivation for rapidly increasing the supply of computing graduates was to take advantage of the perceived opportunity to attract foreign software MNCs to Ireland if the right type of skills were made available, but it soon emerged that indigenous software companies were also capable of benefiting from the skills concerned. In addition to the formal education system, the skills of the labour force were further developed by staff acquiring specialised expertise on the job and by companies' staff development activities.

Demand conditions in the Irish market were also helpful for the development of many indigenous companies because they were often selling

[38] Derived from O'Malley and O'Gorman (2001, Table 1) and Crone (2002, Table 5).

[39] This paragraph and the following two paragraphs draw mainly from O'Malley and O'Gorman (2001) and Crone (2002).

to relatively successful and sophisticated companies in Ireland in sectors such as pharmaceuticals, chemicals, drinks, dairy products and financial services. In many cases the customers concerned were foreign-owned MNCs. Irish software companies often found that their interactions with such local customers were beneficial for the development of their business and helped to prepare them for export success.

In addition, there were a number of industries in Ireland that were somewhat related to the indigenous software industry and had a helpful influence of some importance. One significant type was industries that helped to develop and improve the pool of labour skills which the indigenous software industry could draw on, such as the foreign-owned software, computer hardware and telecommunications equipment industries. Such industries constituted a relatively large concentration of information technology activities in a small economy. Another type of related industry was those in which indigenous software entrepreneurs had previously worked and gained relevant experience. These naturally included other indigenous software companies, as well as other indigenous and foreign-owned companies in information technology activities.

It can be seen from these remarks that indigenous software companies were benefiting in several different ways from being part of a type of cluster or agglomeration of similar or related industries (O'Malley and O'Gorman 2001; Crone 2002, 2013).

The state also played an important part in assisting the development of the industry. A fundamental aspect of this was the role of the education system as mentioned above, while software was also one of the selected service sectors that were eligible for support under industrial policy measures. O'Malley and O'Gorman (2001) found that four-fifths of the indigenous software companies who they interviewed had received financial assistance under such measures, and just over half of those said that it had been important or very important for their company's development. Most of their interviewees had also received non-financial assistance, such as marketing information and assistance with developing management skills and business planning. About one-third of their interviewees said that state development agencies had influenced their strategy or goals, mostly by encouraging and assisting them to focus on developing software products for export markets.

Crone (2002) made a number of similar points about the role of state assistance, commenting that "in the late 1980s and early and mid-1990s, when there was no significant private venture capital industry in

Ireland, the State agencies were the dominant external supplier of finance to indigenous software firms". He noted that these agencies offered both grant aid and equity investment, and provided softer forms of assistance with marketing, management development and training, while the state also created a specialised set of supporting institutions for the industry.

Ó Riain (2004) presented an extensive analysis of the role of state assistance in promoting the indigenous software industry. This included quantitative data and analysis on the extent and actual effectiveness of financial support, as well as more qualitative analysis of the way in which the relevant state institutions worked.

He noted that the state agencies did not try to direct particular firms to take very specific steps such as developing specified technologies or markets. However, they did influence firms' decisions indirectly—"primarily by attempting to create specific kinds of firms: those that are oriented toward learning, R&D, and 'high-value-added' competition" (Ó Riain 2004, p. 91). The agencies focused on encouraging firms to develop software products for export markets—because products were easier to export than services and because the small size of the Irish market made exporting essential. To influence firms towards software products for export, the agencies were more receptive to such firms when they applied for grants, and they focused some state supports on the problems of product exporting (p. 97). Furthermore,

> state grant-giving practices ... promoted a general company development program including marketing, management development, training, and R&D. The precise form this took was flexible, depending on the company, but the state agencies required that such efforts at company development take place. (O Riain 2004, p. 100)

Seen in terms of "carrot and stick" policy measures, this type of policy was all carrot with little or no stick, but the carrots were often offered subject to conditions requiring the recipients to act in ways that would contribute to long-term economic development.

Finally, the question arises why the growth of the indigenous software sector was a good deal stronger than the growth of the indigenous branches of the high-tech manufacturing sectors (although indigenous growth in those other sectors was also relatively fast except by comparison with the software industry). One important reason was probably because of differences in the structure of these industries internationally, since the other industries concerned tended to be more highly concentrated in relatively large firms, offering fewer opportunities for new or small firms. By comparison, the software industry presented lower entry barriers and it offered more significant scope for new or small firms to develop in specialised niches serving segmented markets.

Also, the rapid growth of FDI in Ireland probably had a greater positive influence on indigenous firms in the software industry than on those in the other sectors. Foreign MNCs in a range of different sectors helped to generate sophisticated and rapidly growing domestic demand for indigenous software, no doubt to a greater extent than the demand generated by foreign MNCs for products from indigenous firms in high-tech manufacturing sectors. In addition, foreign MNCs—in the software sector as well as other sectors—were employing people with software programming skills and helping to strengthen the high-level skills of the software workforce through on-the-job experience in R&D and through further training. The scale of this effect was probably greater in software than in the high-tech manufacturing sectors, as indicated by the fact that software firms accounted for a highly disproportionate share of total R&D in all foreign MNCs.[40]

5.3 The Indigenous Contribution to the Boom

This section considers to what extent Irish indigenous companies contributed to causing the boom.

In view of the importance of exports—and especially net foreign earnings—as determinants of economic growth, an obvious way to look at this is to consider how much did indigenous companies contribute to the growth of exports and net foreign earnings. In that regard, the indigenous contribution over the whole course of the boom looks considerably less than the contribution of foreign-owned companies. Between 1985 and 2007, the current value of exports from Irish indigenous companies increased by an estimated 7.5% p.a. compared to 12.6% p.a. for foreign-owned companies. Net foreign earnings are more important than exports as determinants of economic growth, and the difference between

[40] R&D expenditure by foreign-owned firms in the software industry accounted for 23% of total R&D expenditure by foreign-owned firms in Ireland in 1993, although the software industry accounted for only about 5% of total employment in foreign-owned industry (O'Malley and O'Gorman 2001).

indigenous and foreign-owned companies was smaller but still significant when measured in terms of net foreign earnings. The current value of net foreign earnings for indigenous companies grew by an estimated 7.4% p.a. in 1985–2007 compared to 10.4% p.a. for foreign-owned companies.

Table 5.7 shows how the balance between indigenous and foreign-owned companies changed as a result of these different growth rates. Indigenous companies accounted for about 30.0% of exports in 1985, declining to about 13.4% in 2007. At the same time indigenous companies accounted for an estimated 44.2% of net foreign earnings in 1985, declining to about 30.4% in 2007. Thus, the indigenous contribution to net foreign earnings remained much greater than it appeared to be in terms of exports, but the indigenous share of net foreign earnings was declining due to faster growth among foreign-owned firms.

In two respects, however, the indigenous contribution to the boom looks more significant than these numbers suggest—first concerning the timing and, second, concerning the degree of *change* or improvement in performance compared to the period before the boom.

As regards timing, it is noticeable that the indigenous contribution was relatively important in the late 1980s and in the 2000s whereas the foreign-owned contribution was very dominant in the 1990s. Thus, the indigenous contribution was influential at the time when the economy was pulling out of the lengthy recession of the 1980s and embarking on a prolonged period of rapid growth, and it was influential again later in maintaining a relatively high rate of growth well into the 2000s.

This point concerning the late 1980s was seen in Sect. 5.1 above where it was shown that Irish indigenous manufacturing exports grew a little faster than exports from foreign-owned manufacturing in 1986–1990, while they also grew significantly faster than manufacturing exports from the EU and the OECD. This was important at that time since indigenous companies accounted for almost 40% of manufacturing net foreign earnings (Table 5.7). There is no adequate indigenous/foreign breakdown of exports from the services sector in the 1980s, but services exports were relatively small then.

In 2000–2007, indigenous exports and net foreign earnings grew faster than foreign-owned exports and net foreign earnings, as seen in Table 5.7. That was a period when there was a very marked deterioration in trends in foreign-owned manufacturing, particularly in electronics, so that the contributions of indigenous companies and foreign-owned services were essential for sustaining a relatively high rate of economic growth.

The other way that the contribution of Irish indigenous companies looks significant is when one considers what was it that *changed*, compared to the period before the boom, resulting in a substantial rise in the rate of economic growth. Fast growth among foreign-owned firms was clearly a very prominent feature of the boom, but the increase in growth rates compared to earlier trends was greater among indigenous firms.

O'Malley (1998) examined this issue in terms of employment trends in the periods 1980–1988 and 1988–1996. He found that employment in foreign-owned manufacturing declined by 0.9% p.a. in 1980–1988 and this improved to growth of 2.3% p.a. in 1988–1996—an increase by 3.2 percentage points. In indigenous manufacturing, employment declined by 3.2% p.a. in 1980–1988 and this improved to growth of 0.8% p.a. in 1988–1996—an increase by 4.0 percentage points. Thus, the rate of growth in 1988–1996 was higher in foreign-owned industry than in indigenous industry, but the increase in growth compared to the period before the boom was greater in indigenous industry. Consequently, by 1996, employment in indigenous industry was 33,100 higher than it would have been under a continuation of the 1980–1988 trends, while employment in foreign-owned industry was 22,400 higher than it would have been under a continuation of the earlier trends.

It is not possible to do the same sort of calculations for exports because the necessary data on exports by nationality of ownership are not available for years before 1986, but there must have been a somewhat similar effect with respect to exports. It is evident that the value of exports from foreign-owned industries was already growing fast before the boom because sectors that were predominantly foreign-owned (measured in terms of output) had fast growth of exports at that time, whereas other sectors had much slower export growth. For example, O'Malley and Scott (1987) identified a group of export categories that came from predominantly foreign-owned industry sectors. The value of those exports was growing more than twice as fast as other industrial exports in 1980–1986. Consequently, when Irish indigenous manufacturing exports then accelerated to the extent that they were growing slightly faster than exports from foreign-owned manufacturing in 1986–1990, this was a major change from trends before the boom. It means that the change in the performance of indigenous exports was probably the key change that started the boom in the late 1980s.

5.4 The Role of Industrial Policy

As was outlined towards the end of Sect. 2.2 in Chapter 2, a series of changes were made in industrial policy beginning in the mid-1980s, often with the intention of providing more focused and effective assistance for the development of Irish indigenous industry (including selected internationally tradeable services). There is a certain amount of evidence indicating that such policy measures were quite effective in significant respects, at least for some time, although the findings of this chapter have shown that ultimately the overall outcome for indigenous development was no more than a partial or qualified success. This section first outlines some of the evidence that policy measures were effective and then considers why the overall outcome was not satisfactory.

O'Malley et al. (1992, Chapter 3) examined employment trends in the period up to 1990 in existing industrial companies (i.e., leaving aside new start-ups) that were assisted by grants under industrial policy measures, and they compared those trends with trends in non-assisted industrial companies. They found that the grant-assisted companies consistently had much stronger employment trends than the non-assisted companies—for example growth of 5.7% p.a. for those awarded grants in 1987 compared to −1.8% p.a. for non-assisted companies, or 11.5% p.a. for those awarded grants in 1988 compared to −1.1% p.a. for non-assisted companies. They also cited survey evidence from the Department of Industry and Commerce (1990, Chapter 11) showing that most of the companies who received grants for investments said that the support received was a major factor in their investment decision. Thus, they concluded that it was probable that state financial support usually had a beneficial effect in producing growth.

O'Malley et al. (1992, Chapter 3) noted that it was a stated aim of policy after the mid-1980s to focus attention more selectively on building on existing relatively promising companies, rather than spreading assistance too thinly among large numbers of small firms. As evidence that increasing selectivity was applied in practice, they found that the cohorts of existing firms that were awarded grants declined in size each year between 1984 and 1990. Those that received grant approval in 1984 employed 25,900 whereas those receiving grant approval in 1990 employed 13,200.

At the same time, the employment trends improved very substantially over time in each succeeding cohort of grant-assisted existing companies, e.g., growth rates in the period up to 1990 at 2.3% p.a. for the 1985 cohort, 5.7% p.a. for the 1987 cohort and 11.5% p.a. for the 1988 cohort. O'Malley et al. (1992) considered whether this improvement over time could have been caused by the increasingly favourable economic environment during this period, or whether it could have been an automatic effect of applying increasing selectivity over time.

As regards the increasingly favourable economic environment, they noted that there was also improving growth over the same period in non-assisted firms, and this presumably was an effect of the strengthening economic environment. However, the improvement was far greater in the case of grant-assisted firms, so much of the improvement in their performance could not be explained simply by the economic environment.

As regards the possibility that the improving growth in grant-assisted firms might have been an automatic effect of applying increasing selectivity in grant assistance over time, they noted that increasing selectivity would be expected to result in better average growth *rates* among grant-assisted companies by means of weeding out less promising grant applicants. However, increasing selectivity per se could not have resulted in rising *absolute* employment increases in succeeding cohorts, especially when succeeding cohorts of grant-assisted firms were declining in size each year. But, in fact, there were rising absolute employment increases in succeeding cohorts of grant-assisted firms, from net increases of 1,300 or less per year for the 1984 and 1985 cohorts to between 3,200 and 3,700 per year for the 1988, 1989 and 1990 cohorts—despite the declining size of cohorts and declining expenditure on grants. Thus, they concluded that grants were not only awarded more selectively by refraining from aiding weaker firms but they were also awarded to the more promising firms in the context of industrial policy measures which were becoming increasingly effective.

O'Malley et al. (1992, Chapter 3) also noted that it was an aim of industrial policy after the mid-1980s to focus attention more on supporting development of Irish indigenous companies. They found that the pattern of rising absolute employment increases in succeeding cohorts of grant-assisted companies was most pronounced in indigenous companies. Employment increases per year in the period up to 1990 rose from less than 500 for the 1984 and 1985 cohorts of grant-assisted indigenous firms to between 1,700 and 2,100 for the 1988, 1989 and 1990 cohorts. The corresponding rise in foreign-owned industry was smaller—from 800 or less to between 1,200 and 1,600. Again, this was consistent with stated policy goals and suggested that the policy was effective.

Further evidence that policy measures were effective was already discussed above in the section on "R&D and Innovation". Studies were quoted there which found that policy measures had positive influences on R&D and innovation success.

In addition, the section above on the "Irish Indigenous Software Industry" referred to studies which found that industrial policy measures made a significant contribution to the development of that sector. A *Sunday Business Post* report in 2003 on 62 indigenous technology start-ups featured the same theme:

> If you ask their bosses about Enterprise Ireland's cash-funding policies, they are unanimous in swearing that the money has made a big difference. ... Even though most of the entrepreneurs admit that the money is by far the most important thing they rely on from the state agency, they stress that it is not the only element: ... "They have excellent contacts all over the place." ... "They have knowledgeable local resources in virtually every part of the world."[41]

Some reports on industrial policy measures, including some reports from the Industry Evaluation Unit, paid attention to the issues of deadweight and displacement. In this context, displacement means the degree to which output from an assisted firm displaces output from another existing firm. Deadweight means the degree to which increased output or employment in an assisted firm would have happened anyway in the absence of assistance under policy measures.[42] Lenihan (2003/2004) and Lenihan et al. (2005) drew together the findings of literature on this issue in Irish industrial policy, concluding that estimates of displacement were generally low, from usually around 3 or 4% up to 12%. Estimates of deadweight were a good deal higher, mostly at around 45–60%.

To be clear, a level of deadweight at, say, 50% means that half of the expansion seen in assisted firms was attributable to the assistance in the sense that it would not have happened without the assistance. The other

[41] Adrian Weckler, "60 Tech Start-Ups" in supplement on "Computers in Business", *Sunday Business Post*, October 2003.

[42] Lenihan et al. (2005) noted that the term deadweight can have a different meaning in some other areas of economics.

half would have happened anyway, without assistance. Consequently, the policy measure concerned did have real positive effects, but those effects might potentially have been achieved at less cost if it was possible to identify in advance some of the assistance that was going to be unnecessary. Although a level of deadweight at around 50% may seem high, the positive effects of industrial policy measures were probably still crucial in generating the growth seen in indigenous industry.

For example, employment increases between 1988 and 1989 in new and expanding indigenous manufacturing firms amounted to 11.5% of 1988 indigenous employment. At the same time, employment reductions in declining or closing indigenous firms amounted to 9.8% of 1988 indigenous employment (*Census of Industrial Production 1989*, Table 5). Consequently, there was net employment growth of 1.7%. The same source also indicates that assisted firms accounted for a large majority of the increases, although the data on this are incomplete. If we take it that at least 60% of the increases came from assisted firms, their increases amounted to at least 6.9% of 1988 employment. If the level of deadweight was 50%, about half of that 6.9% would have gone ahead without assistance but the other half would not have gone ahead without assistance. Consequently, if there had been no assistance under industrial policy measures, total increases would have been about 8.1% of 1988 employment rather than 11.5%, so that employment reductions at 9.8% of 1988 employment would have outweighed the increases resulting in net decline by about 1.7%.

If we take the example of 1994–1995, when growth was a good deal stronger, a similar calculation indicates that actual indigenous manufacturing employment growth of 5.3% would have been only 1.2% in the absence of assistance under industrial policy measures.

It can be concluded that policy measures were quite effective and had substantial results in some significant respects. However, earlier findings of this chapter showed that ultimately the overall outcome for indigenous development was not very satisfactory. Specifically, the trends in indigenous manufacturing looked strong at first in the late 1980s, including exports. Then in the 1990s export trends continued to be good in the high-tech and medium–high-tech sectors, but overall indigenous manufacturing exports looked relatively weak by international comparisons. In the 2000s, export trends also became weaker in the high-tech and medium–high-tech sectors. In indigenous services, the trends mostly remained better for longer and exports continued to grow relatively fast by EU standards. However, when we focused on the software industry, there were signs of growth slowing down a good deal in the 2000s after an earlier period of extremely rapid growth.

In general, it seems that the industrial policy system had considerable success in promoting the growth of small and medium-sized firms particularly in the high-tech and medium–high-tech sectors, and in enhancing R&D and innovation. But such success continued only up to a certain point. Few of the companies concerned in the higher-tech sectors became large, and the more prominent ones often became takeover targets for foreign MNCs, so that the overall growth momentum tended to weaken over time.

In order to achieve more lasting and sustainable success in indigenous development, it would have been necessary for industrial development agencies to invest much more substantially in developing the scale and capabilities of some promising companies. For example, equity investment in companies by the agencies was generally limited to a 10% share, but that would have needed to be a good deal larger in selected cases. A related problem was that agencies had no way of preventing foreign takeovers and there needed to be a way of deterring that trend, whether by having larger shareholdings or by some other means.

Before concluding this section on industrial policy, it should be mentioned that a commonly stated goal of policy in the 1990s and later was to develop clusters of linked and related industries, with a view to enhancing competitiveness and growth. In the context of Ireland, this issue often involved both foreign-owned and Irish indigenous industries, and the relations between those two groups. This issue is not discussed in the present chapter as it will be more convenient to consider it in the next chapter on foreign-owned companies in Ireland.

5.5 Conclusion

Against a background of prolonged weakness before the boom, there was a substantial improvement in the growth and development of indigenous manufacturing in the late 1980s. Its performance became more uneven later, with some strong points as well as some weak points which grew more evident over time. In indigenous services, the trends mostly remained better for longer, as exports continued to grow relatively fast by EU standards up to the end of the boom.

Industrial policy was partly responsible for the improvement that occurred, since a series of changes were made in policy for indigenous companies beginning in the mid-1980s and the new policy measures were quite effective in some significant respects. However, the overall outcome for indigenous development was ultimately not very satisfactory. There was considerable success in promoting growth of small and medium-size firms particularly in the high-tech and medium–high-tech sectors, and in enhancing R&D and innovation. But the success did not continue beyond a certain point. Few of the companies concerned in the higher-tech sectors became large and many of the most prominent ones were taken over by foreign MNEs, so the growth momentum tended to fade over time.

The indigenous contribution to growth over the whole course of the boom was a good deal less than the contribution of foreign-owned companies, when assessed in terms of growth of exports and net foreign earnings. Consequently, indigenous companies' share of exports declined from about 30.0% in 1985 to about 13.4% in 2007, while their share of net foreign earnings declined from about 44.2% in 1985 to about 30.4% in 2007. Thus, the indigenous contribution to net foreign earnings remained much greater than it appeared to be in terms of exports, but the indigenous share of net foreign earnings was declining due to faster growth among foreign-owned firms.

The indigenous contribution to the boom was particularly significant at certain times. It was relatively important in the late 1980s and in the 2000s, whereas the foreign-owned contribution was very dominant in the 1990s. Thus, the indigenous contribution was influential at the time when the economy was pulling out of the lengthy recession of the 1980s and embarking on a prolonged period of rapid growth, and it was also influential again later in maintaining a relatively high rate of growth well into the 2000s.

In fact, the improvement in performance in indigenous industry in the late 1980s was probably the most important change that got the boom started at that time. The value of exports from foreign-owned industries was already growing fast before the boom, whereas the trend in indigenous exports was much weaker. Consequently, when indigenous manufacturing export growth then accelerated to more than match the growth of exports from foreign-owned industry, that was a major turnaround that changed the trajectory of the economy.

Appendix: Data and Estimates for This Chapter

Table 5.1

In Table 5.1 the data for 1993, 2000 and 2006 come from the *Census of Industrial Production* (CIP). There was a break in the CIP data series between 1990 and 1991 because of a change in the industry classification system from NACE 70 in 1990 to NACE REV.1 in 1991. This involved virtually no change in the definition of total manufacturing employment, but as explained in O'Malley (1998), it did apparently increase the Irish indigenous share of the total by about 1.6 percentage points, to judge from the 1990–1991 trend in the IDA/Forfás Employment Survey. Therefore, the shares of Irish indigenous and foreign-owned companies in total CIP manufacturing employment in 1988 were adjusted by this amount to obtain the 1988 figures in Table 5.1, in order to produce consistency between the 1988 and 1993 figures in Table 5.1. Since the CIP did not include data distinguishing firms by nationality of ownership in the early 1980s, the figures for 1980 in Table 5.1 were derived by applying the 1980–1988 change in indigenous and foreign-owned manufacturing employment from the IDA/Forfás Employment Survey to the 1988 figures in Table 5.1.

There was another change in the industry classification system in the CIP from NACE REV.1 in 2001 to NACE REV.1.1 in 2002. This involved virtually no change in the definition of total manufacturing employment and it also involved virtually no alteration to the Irish indigenous share of the total, to judge from the 2001–2002 trend in the Forfás Employment Survey. Therefore, the CIP data for 2006 were used in Table 5.1 without requiring any adjustment to produce consistency with the data before 2001.

The CIP expanded its coverage somewhat in 2007 compared with 2006 which led to a discontinuity in the series. Since the expanded coverage brought in more relatively small firms, these additional firms were probably mostly indigenous, giving an artificial boost to apparent indigenous growth in 2006–2007. Consequently, the figures in Table 5.1 (and Fig. 5.1) finish in 2006 rather than 2007.

Figure 5.1

In Fig. 5.1, the CIP figures for 1988–1990 were adjusted in the same way as the 1988 figure in Table 5.1, for the reasons outlined above with respect to Table 5.1. Figure 5.1 terminates with 2006 rather than 2007 for the reason mentioned above concerning Table 5.1.

Table 5.2

The change in the industry classification system in the CIP from NACE REV.1 in 2001 to NACE REV.1.1 in 2002 resulted in no visible difference for manufacturing sectors at the NACE 2-digit level which is presented in Table 5.2. Therefore, the CIP data for 2006 were used in Table 5.2 without requiring any adjustment to produce consistency with the data before 2001.

Dairy Products Exports in 1986–1990

It was mentioned in footnote 6, in the "Exports and Net Foreign Earnings" part of Sect. 5.1, that in 1986–1990 there was particularly rapid growth in the exports of the dairy products sector. This sector was largely Irish-owned and it accounted for about one-fifth of all indigenous manufacturing exports. Unfortunately, there is room for doubt about the accuracy of the data on exports of dairy products. The doubt arises because the Central Statistics Office warned that one should be cautious about using export data on the food industries because respondents to the CIP might vary in the extent to which they interpreted sales into EC Intervention and to An Bord Bainne as exports. The reason why their interpretation could vary was because products sold by producers to EC Intervention or to An Bord Bainne were being sold to a purchaser in Ireland who would be expected to sell them on later to export markets. Since dairy products exports were quite an important component of total indigenous manufacturing exports, this doubt about data on dairy products exports raises the question of whether total indigenous manufacturing exports really grew as fast as they appeared to in 1986–1990.

While it is not possible to give a very precise answer to this question, it is worth bearing in mind that the data on the total output of dairy products should be just as reliable as any other data. The only reason why the export data might be inaccurate is because of possible flaws in the allocation of the output data between exports and domestic sales. Such inaccuracies could result in a false appearance of rapid export growth during a particular period if there were a large increase in misallocation of output data towards exports during that period.

Given this situation, it is significant that the output of dairy products really did grow very rapidly in 1986–1990, by 19.1% p.a. measured in current Irish pounds. The growth rate of exports of dairy products, at 21.6% p.a., was not a great deal higher. Thus, even if there had been no increase in the proportion of output being reported as exported, the rate of growth of exports would still have been high. Just in case the faster growth of exports reflected an increased misallocation of output data to exports, we can consider what would have been the outcome if dairy product exports had grown at only the same rate as dairy product output (i.e., export growth at 19.1% p.a. instead of 21.6% p.a.), so that the percentage of output being exported remained unchanged at 56.6% in both 1986 and 1990. In that event, total indigenous manufacturing exports would have grown by about 11.4% p.a.[43] measured in current Irish pounds, instead of the recorded rate of 12.2% p.a. This would still have been close to the 11.9% p.a. growth rate of exports from foreign-owned industry in Ireland. Under the same assumption, total indigenous manufacturing exports would have grown by about 17.5% p.a. valued in current US dollars, which would still have been faster than the growth of exports from the EU-15 at 15.2% p.a. or the OECD at 14.2% p.a.

It is mathematically possible that the true rate of growth of dairy product exports was even lower than the rate of growth of output, so that domestic sales grew faster than exports, but that seems highly unlikely in reality. It is difficult to see how the rapid growth of sales of food items such as dairy products could have been led by particularly rapid growth of sales into a mature domestic market that had no population growth at that time. It is far more likely that rapid growth of sales of such food products had to be led by rapid growth of sales into new or expanding export markets.

[43] This estimate cannot be precise because it is not known exactly what proportion of dairy products exports came from indigenous firms or what proportion of total indigenous manufacturing exports were accounted for by dairy products. Therefore, this estimate simply assumes that all dairy products exports were indigenous, which is not strictly correct but is probably not far from the truth since it is known that 84–89% of output of dairy products came from indigenous firms in 1986–1990.

Net Foreign Earnings

Appendix in Chapter 4 explains the procedure used to derive estimates of net foreign earnings for each sector—with "net foreign earnings" being defined as the value of the sector's exports minus the value of the imported inputs that are contained in the exports, minus the profit outflows that arise from production of the exports. This section outlines how that procedure was extended for this chapter to estimate the net foreign earnings of indigenous and foreign-owned companies in each sector.

As explained in Appendix in Chapter 4, the sectoral export data were taken from the official input–output tables for the year concerned, while the input–output tables also provided the data that were used for each sector's imported inputs. For this chapter, those numbers had to be broken down into exports of Irish indigenous companies and foreign-owned companies, and imported inputs used by the Irish indigenous companies and foreign-owned companies. Appendix in Chapter 4 also outlined how each sector's profit outflows were estimated. Since the outflows were of relevance only for foreign-owned companies, those numbers were used unchanged when estimating net foreign earnings of foreign-owned companies for this chapter.

To break export data down into indigenous and foreign components, the general principle, in the case of manufacturing sectors, was to use data from the *Census of Industrial Production* (CIP) on exports by sector and nationality. The export data for each sector from the input–output tables were divided into indigenous and foreign components in proportion to the indigenous and foreign shares of the sector's exports in the CIP.

While that was a general principle, and it could be applied for some sectors in some years, there were also some sectors in some years where the necessary data on exports by sector and nationality were not available in the CIP. In those cases, CIP data from the closest year that had the necessary data were used to calculate exports as a percentage of gross output for the sector and nationality concerned. Then those percentages were applied to gross output data for the relevant sector and nationality in the year required.

In the case of 2007, no input–output tables were published for that year. The estimates of indigenous and foreign manufacturing exports for 2007 were derived by applying the growth seen in those two categories in the CIP in 2005–2007 to the estimates derived for 2005 as outlined above.

The method used to break export data down into indigenous and foreign components in the case of services was mostly analogous to the method for manufacturing, with the *Annual Services Inquiry* (ASI) taking the place of the CIP. Since the ASI had no data by nationality of ownership before the 2000s, we did not attempt to make estimates of services exports by nationality before that time.

The ASI had no data on exports by nationality of ownership before 2008, although it did have data on turnover by nationality for earlier years in the 2000s. Therefore, we used data on exports as a percentage of turnover by sector and nationality from 2008, and then applied those percentages to turnover data by sector and nationality from earlier in the 2000s, in order to obtain the required export estimates for earlier in the 2000s. This meant that we were assuming that about the same percentage of output was exported in 2000 and 2005 as in 2008. To give some assurance that this was a reasonable assumption, it can be noted that the Annual Business Survey of Economic Impact (ABSEI) indicates that exports generally were a stable percentage of sales in 2000–2008 in the selected internationally traded services covered in that survey, at 38–42% for indigenous companies and 92–94% for foreign-owned companies.

The ASI did not cover financial services and insurance. Instead, we used some figures from Accenture (2010) on exports from Enterprise Ireland client companies (i.e., Irish-owned companies) in financial services, and on the scale of employment in international financial service activities in the main Irish banks. Together with export growth trends in Enterprise Ireland client companies from the ABSEI, this enabled us to estimate that indigenous companies accounted for about 10–11% of the financial services exports in the input–output tables for 2000 and 2005. With additional guidance from export growth trends in the Balance of Payments, our estimate for 2007 was similar. The estimates for this sector would be less reliable than for other service sectors.

As regards imported inputs, Appendix in Chapter 4 already explained how the value of imported inputs that were contained in each sector's exports was derived from input–output tables. For this chapter, those numbers had to be broken down into imported inputs contained in Irish indigenous companies' exports and imported inputs contained in foreign-owned companies' exports.

For that purpose, data from the ABSEI on sales and imported inputs, by sector and nationality, were used to calculate imported inputs as a percentage of sales for each sector by nationality of ownership. Then those percentage figures were applied to the estimates of exports by sector and nationality, derived as outlined above, to obtain estimates of imported inputs contained in exports, by sector and nationality. Finally, the data that were derived directly from the input–output tables on imported inputs contained in exports, by sector, were divided into indigenous and foreign components in proportion to the indigenous and foreign shares of our estimated imported inputs contained in exports by sector derived using the ABSEI data.

An exception was made in the case of financial services because it was found that there was a particularly low representation of foreign-owned financial services companies in the ABSEI. Instead, since our export estimates had indicated that foreign-owned companies accounted for almost 90% of all financial services exports, we simply took it that imported inputs as a percentage of all financial services output derived from the input–output tables were sufficiently representative of foreign-owned financial services companies. As indigenous financial services companies were quite well represented in the ABSEI, we used the same method for them as for all other sectors.

For 1985, the data used to estimate imported inputs by nationality for the manufacturing sector were taken from an earlier forerunner of the ABSEI called the Irish Economy Expenditures Survey. Results of that survey were reported in Industrial Development Authority. (1985). *The Irish Economy Expenditures of the Irish Manufacturing Sector*. Dublin: IDA, and the results relevant to our purpose here were reported in O'Malley (1989, Table 7.3).

References

Accenture. 2010. *The IFSC: The International Financial Services Sector in Ireland*. Dublin: Financial Services Ireland, IBEC.

Crone, Mike. 2002. The Irish Indigenous Software Industry: Explaining the Development of a Knowledge-Intensive Industry Cluster in a Less Favoured Region. 42nd Congress of the European Regional Science Association, Dortmund.

Crone, Mike. 2013. New Venture Internationalisation and the Cluster Life Cycle: Insights from Ireland's Indigenous Software Industry. In *The Changing Geography of International Business*, ed. Gary Cook and Jennifer Johns. Basingstoke: Palgrave.

Department of Industry and Commerce. 1990. *Review of Industrial Performance 1990*. Dublin: Stationery Office.

Doran, Justin, Declan Jordan, and Eoin O'Leary. 2012/2013. Effects of R&D Spending on Innovation by Irish and Foreign-Owned Businesses. *Journal of the Statistical and Social Inquiry Society of Ireland* XLII: 15–41.

Eolas. 1990, November. Irish Research and Development Statistical Tables.

Foley, Anthony. 1987. Indigenous Exports: Aspects of Firm and Sectoral Performance. Paper Presented to the Industrial Studies Association, Dublin.

Forfas. 2001. *Statement on Outward Direct Investment*. Dublin: Forfas.

Forfas. 2007. *Forfas Statement on Outward Direct Investment*. Dublin: Forfas.

Hewitt-Dundas, Nola, and Stephen Roper. 2008, Summer. Ireland's Innovation Performance: 1991 to 2005. In *Quarterly Economic Commentary*, ed. Alan Barrett, Ide Kearney, and Martin O'Brien. Dublin: Economic and Social Research Institute.

Hewitt-Dundas, Nola, and Stephen Roper. 2010. Output Additionality of Public Support for Innovation: Evidence for Irish Manufacturing Plants. *European Planning Studies* 18 (1): 107–122.

Jacobson, David, and Eoin O'Malley. 2018. Indigenous Industrialisation. In *Upsetting the Apple Cart: Tax-Based Industrial Policy in Ireland and Europe*, ed. David Jacobson. Dublin: Glasnevin Publishing.

Kearns, Allan, and Frances Ruane. 1998. The Post-Entry Performance of Irish Plants: Does a Plant's Technological Activity Matter? Trinity Economic Papers Series, Technical Paper No. 98/20, Dublin.

Kearns, Allan, and Frances Ruane. 1999. The Tangible Contribution of R&D Spending Foreign-Owned Plants to a Host Region: A Plant Level Study of the Irish Manufacturing Sector (1980–1996). Trinity Economic Papers Series, Technical Paper No. 99/7, Dublin.

Lawless, Martina, and Zuzanna Studnicka. 2017. *Services Exports and Exporters of Services*. Dublin: ESRI, Department of Jobs Enterprise and Innovation, and Enterprise Ireland.

Lenihan, Helena. 2003/2004. Modelling the Factors Associated with Deadweight and Displacement: An Example of Irish Industrial Policy Evaluation. *Journal of the Statistical and Social Inquiry Society of Ireland* XXXIII: 40–82.

Lenihan, Helena, Mark Hart, and Stephen Roper. 2005, Summer. Developing an Evaluative Framework for Industrial Policy in Ireland: Fulfilling the Audit Trail or an Aid to Policy Development? In *Quarterly Economic Commentary*, ed. Daniel McCoy, David Duffy, Adele Bergin, Shane Garrett, and Yvonne McCarthy. Dublin: Economic and Social Research Institute.

Loungani, Prakash, Saurabh Mishra, Chris Papageorgiou, and Ke Wang. 2017. *World Trade in Services: Evidence from a New Dataset*. IMF Working Paper No. 17/77.

O'Malley, Eoin. 1989. *Industry and Economic Development: The Challenge for the Latecomer*. Dublin: Gill and Macmillan.

O'Malley, Eoin. 1998, April. The Revival of Irish Indigenous Industry 1987–1997. In *Quarterly Economic Commentary*, ed. T.J. Baker, David Duffy, and Fergal Shortall. Dublin: Economic and Social Research Institute.

O'Malley, Eoin. 2004, Winter. Competitive Performance in Irish Industry. In *Quarterly Economic Commentary*, ed. Daniel McCoy, David Duffy, Adele Bergin, Shane Garrett, and Yvonne McCarthy. Dublin: Economic and Social Research Institute.

O'Malley, Eoin. 2013. Ireland's Competitive Performance. In *The Nuts and Bolts of Innovation: New Perspectives on Irish Industrial Policy*, ed. David Jacobson. Dublin: Glasnevin Publishing.

O'Malley, Eoin, and Colm O'Gorman. 2001. Competitive Advantage in the Irish Indigenous Software Industry and the Role of Inward Foreign Direct Investment. *European Planning Studies* 9 (3): 303–321.

O'Malley, Eoin, and Sue Scott. 1987. Determinants of Profit Outflows from Ireland. In *Medium-Term Review: 1987–1992*, ed. J. Bradley, J. Fitz Gerald, and R.A. Storey. Dublin: The Economic and Social Research Institute.

O'Malley, Eoin, Kieran A. Kennedy, and Rory O'Donnell. 1992. The Impact of the Industrial Development Agencies. Report to the Industrial Policy Review Group. Stationery Office, Dublin.

O'Malley, Eoin, Nola Hewitt-Dundas, and Stephen Roper. 2008. High Growth and Innovation with Low R&D: Ireland. In *Small Country Innovation Systems: Globalization, Change and Policy in Asia and Europe*, ed. Charles Edquist and Leif Hommen. Cheltenham: Edward Elgar.

Ó Riain, Seán. 2004. *The Politics of High-Tech Growth: Developmental Network States in the Global Economy*. Cambridge: Cambridge University Press.

Roper, Stephen, and James H. Love. 2004. Innovation Success and Business Performance: An All-Island Analysis. Report to InterTradeIreland (Quoted in O'Malley, Hewitt-Dundas and Roper, 2008).

Open Access This chapter is licensed under the terms of the Creative Commons Attribution 4.0 International License (http://creativecommons.org/licenses/by/4.0/), which permits use, sharing, adaptation, distribution and reproduction in any medium or format, as long as you give appropriate credit to the original author(s) and the source, provide a link to the Creative Commons license and indicate if changes were made.

The images or other third party material in this chapter are included in the chapter's Creative Commons license, unless indicated otherwise in a credit line to the material. If material is not included in the chapter's Creative Commons license and your intended use is not permitted by statutory regulation or exceeds the permitted use, you will need to obtain permission directly from the copyright holder.

CHAPTER 6

Foreign-Owned Companies

Foreign-owned companies were already prominent in the Irish economy before the boom started in the late 1980s. A large amount of foreign direct investment (FDI) had come into Ireland—particularly into export-oriented manufacturing—over the previous thirty years or so. This previous history was outlined in Chapter 2, where it was mentioned that, by 1987, foreign firms accounted for 43% of manufacturing employment, 52% of manufacturing output and 74% of manufactured exports (*Census of Industrial Production*, 1987). It was also mentioned in Chapter 2 that the contribution of such FDI to Ireland's growth appeared to have weakened during the 1980s compared to the 1960s and 1970s.

This chapter examines the role of foreign-owned companies in the boom years beginning in the late 1980s. Section 6.1 briefly presents some basic data on the growth and sectoral composition of foreign-owned industry. Section 6.2 discusses the nature and characteristics of FDI in Ireland, Sect. 6.3 considers what motivated foreign companies to invest in Ireland, and Sect. 6.4 considers various effects or impacts of FDI on the Irish economy.

© The Author(s) 2024

E. O'Malley, *Ireland's Long Economic Boom*, Palgrave Studies in Economic History, https://doi.org/10.1007/978-3-031-53070-8_6

6.1 Growth and Composition of Foreign-Owned Companies

Employment in foreign-owned manufacturing gradually declined in the period before the boom, but it then grew very rapidly in the period up to 2000, before declining again in the final phase of the boom after 2000. The rates of growth in foreign-owned manufacturing employment were −0.9% p.a. in 1980–1988, 3.8% p.a. in 1988–2000, and −2.6% p.a. in 2000–2006. Foreign-owned companies accounted for 43% of manufacturing employment in 1988, and this increased to 48% by 2000 and then remained at 48% in 2006 (see Table 5.1 in Chapter 5).

Foreign-owned companies also increased their share of manufacturing gross output, from 52% in 1987 to 79% by 2001 and 80% in 2006. At the same time, their share of manufacturing exports rose from 74% in 1987 to 91% in 2001 and 92% in 2006. Throughout this period, a high percentage of the output of foreign-owned manufacturing firms was exported, with 85% being exported in 1987 and 93% in 2006.

Table 6.1 shows employment by sector in foreign-owned and Irish indigenous manufacturing in 2000. Compared to the indigenous industry, foreign-owned companies were more highly concentrated in pharmaceutical products, other chemicals, office machinery & computers, electrical machinery & apparatus, communication equipment, technical instruments and transport equipment. This means that foreign companies were far more concentrated in the sectors that are conventionally defined as high-technology and medium–high-technology sectors.[1] This group of sectors accounted for 64% of employment, 74% of gross output and 76% of exports in foreign-owned manufacturing in Ireland in 2000.

In addition, it should be mentioned that foreign-owned companies were also major producers and exporters of software products, another high-technology activity, which was contained within the broader "printing & publishing" sector (NACE 22). The exports of software products from foreign-owned companies probably amounted to about another 10% of total foreign-owned manufacturing exports, so that about 86% of the exports of foreign-owned manufacturing came from high-tech or medium–high-tech sectors.

[1] Section 5.1 in Chapter 5 briefly outlines how sectors are classified as high-tech, medium–high tech etc.

Table 6.1 Employment in foreign-owned and Irish indigenous manufacturing, 2000

NACE Rev.1 code	*Sector*	*Foreign employment*	*Percent*	*Indigenous employment*	*Percent*
15–16	Food, drink & tobacco	13,170	10.7	34,932	26.3
17–18	Textiles & textile products	3,546	2.9	6,719	5.1
20	Wood & wood products	1,111	0.9	5,138	3.9
21	Pulp, paper & paper products	898	0.7	4,030	3.0
22	Printing & publishing	6,559	5.3	12,329	9.3
244	Pharmaceutical products	6,986	5.7	1,587	1.2
24 less 244	Other chemicals	10,888	8.9	3,737	2.8
25	Rubber & plastics	3,951	3.2	6,895	5.2
26	Non-metallic mineral products	1,584	1.3	9,582	7.2
27–28	Metals & metal products	3,554	2.9	13,330	10.0
29	Machinery & equipment	6,436	5.2	7,960	6.0
30	Office machinery & computers	18,303	14.9	2,420	1.8
31	Electrical machinery & apparatus	9,438	7.7	5,703	4.3
32–33	Communication equipment, technical instruments	28,120	22.9	4,983	3.8
34–35	Transport equipment	5,365	4.4	4,245	3.2
36, 37, 23, 19	Furniture, miscellaneous, recycling, oil, leather	3,069	2.5	9,076	6.8
15–37	Total manufacturing	122,978	100.0	132,666	100.0

Source: *Census of Industrial Production 2000*. Creative Commons Attribution BY 4.0

During the period before 2000, the growth of exports from foreign-owned manufacturing was the main driver of the growth of total exports from Ireland, as foreign-owned manufacturing firms increased their share of all exports from 64% to 74% between 1985 and 2000 (see Table 5.7). Within that trend, it was the high-tech and medium–high-tech sectors mentioned above that were largely responsible for the growth of foreign-owned manufacturing exports.

Subsequently, in 2000–2007, export growth from foreign-owned manufacturing firms slowed down dramatically and their share of all exports fell from 74% to 57%, while services exports became increasingly important (Table 5.7). That weaker trend after 2000 in foreign manufacturing was largely an effect of a much weaker trend in electronic products, while export growth remained stronger in chemicals, software, etc.

Net foreign earnings were a relatively low proportion of the value of exports in foreign-owned manufacturing, particularly in the more high-tech sectors, as was noted already in Chapter 5. Consequently, when foreign-owned manufacturing increased its share of total exports from 64% to 74% between 1985 and 2000, its share of total net foreign earnings increased from just 46% to 49%. Thus, its contribution to the economy and to growth was certainly important, but it was not as dominant as it appeared to be when seen in terms of exports.

When foreign-owned manufacturing's share of total exports then declined from 74% in 2000 to 57% by 2007, its share of total net foreign earnings declined from 49% to 27% (Table 5.7), while the contribution of services increased rapidly.

The data that are available on the services sector are generally not as detailed as the data on manufacturing, and there is a particular scarcity of data distinguishing between Irish indigenous and foreign-owned services. Nevertheless, it is evident that foreign-owned companies were heavily involved in the growth of services exports. It was seen in Chapter 5 that foreign-owned companies increased their exports of services about five times faster than the growth of services exports from Irish indigenous companies in 1985–2007, and they accounted for about 77% of services exports in 2000, rising to 82% by 2007. Meanwhile, foreign-owned companies had a much smaller share of services employment and turnover. They accounted for just 21% of services employment in 2001, rising to 27% by 2007, while their share of services turnover was 35% in 2001, rising to 44% by 2007.

Foreign-owned services exports were worth much less than 10% of all exports in 1985, but they accounted for 14% of all exports by 2000, rising to 30% by 2007.

As regards sectoral composition, we can take it that sectoral data on total services exports must give quite a good indication of the composition of foreign-owned services exports, because foreign companies accounted for the bulk of services exports and most of their growth. The fastest growth in services exports during the boom occurred in computer services, business services, insurance and financial services. They became the dominant category of services exports and they accounted for 86% of total services exports by the end of the boom (see Chapter 4).

Net foreign earnings amounted to about 55% of the value of exports in foreign-owned services, which was a low figure compared to about 94% in Irish indigenous services but was much higher than the figure of 26% in foreign-owned manufacturing (Table 5.6). The result was that foreign-owned services accounted for a greater share of all net foreign earnings than their share of all exports. Consequently, when their share of total exports increased from 14% in 2000 to 30% in 2007, their share of all net foreign earnings increased from 23% to 43%.

Finally, when foreign-owned manufacturing and services are combined together, their share of total net foreign earnings increased from about 56% in 1985 to 73% in 2000 and then declined a little to 70% in 2007 (Table 5.7). By that criterion, foreign companies made a major contribution to economic growth over the full period of the boom. However, as Chapter 5 concluded, the indigenous contribution to the boom was relatively important in the late 1980s and again in the 2000s, whereas the foreign-owned contribution was very dominant in the 1990s.

6.2 The Nature and Characteristics of FDI in Ireland

It was noted in Chapter 2 that much of the FDI that came to Ireland before the boom had a good deal in common with the type of mobile industry that was able to move to less-developed or newly industrialising countries. At first, in the 1960s, this meant technologically mature and often labour-intensive products such as clothing, footwear, textiles, plastic products, light engineering, etc. Subsequently, from about the late 1960s, FDI in Ireland increasingly involved newer, more technologically advanced products, such as electrical and electronic products, machinery, pharmaceuticals, and medical instruments and equipment. These were mostly products of high-technology or medium–high-technology industries, but it was sometimes observed that there was still some parallel here with the type of mobile industry that was able to go to newly industrialising countries. This was because many of these industries in Ireland involved only certain stages of production which were not the most demanding on local technological inputs, skills and high-quality suppliers.

In a major review of industrial policy in the early 1980s, the Telesis Consultancy Group (1982) highlighted such characteristics of these industries. They reported that nearly all of the foreign-owned electrical and electronic firms that they surveyed were "manufacturing satellites, performing partial steps in the manufacturing process. Skill development and linkages in Ireland have been limited". On mechanical engineering firms, they said that they "consist mainly of sub-assembly and assembly shops of the sort commonly found in newly industrialising countries … of the 34 shops surveyed about half had only one or two skilled blue-collar workers and one or two engineers". They also remarked that, in general, foreign-owned firms in Ireland, with few exceptions, "do not embody the key competitive activities of the businesses in which they participate; do not employ significant numbers of skilled workers; and are not significantly integrated into traded and skilled sub-supply industries in Ireland".

While there were similarities here to the type of mobile industry that was able to go to newly industrialising countries at that time, the industries going to Ireland did include some more highly skilled activities, even if they usually lacked the key business functions of the firm. Thus, in the early 1980s, 60% of employees in the electronics industry in Ireland were unskilled, non-craft production workers, compared with over 90% in the electronics industries in Singapore and Hong Kong. At the same time, the figure of 60% for Ireland was a good deal higher than the figures of 34–39% for the UK, USA and Denmark (O'Brien 1985, Table 6.10). The electronics industry in Ireland also undertook far less R&D in relation to sales than the industries in the USA or UK (O'Brien 1985).

As regards the motivation for export-oriented FDI in Ireland, at first the main attractions were tax concessions, grants and relatively low-wage costs compared to more advanced industrial countries, as was outlined in Chapter 2. After Ireland joined the EEC in 1973, there was the additional important attraction of assured access to the large EEC market, which was a major draw for growing numbers of companies from the

USA. The basic objective of many of the foreign investors after that time was to establish a factory somewhere within the EEC (and later the EC or EU) to produce for European markets, and then they selected Ireland as suitable for that purpose. Consequently, Ireland's main competitors in attracting such industries were usually Western European countries rather than developing countries with much lower wages. Other influences in attracting FDI to Ireland were the effective work of the Industrial Development Authority (IDA), and the work of the Irish education system in producing a good supply of graduates with the types of skills that were required for rapidly growing industries such as electronics, pharmaceuticals and software. The fact that the Irish labour force is English-speaking was also an attraction for many overseas investors, particularly those from the USA.

By the mid-1980s and subsequently, official policy statements concerning foreign-owned industry in Ireland tended to say that policy would aim to attract and develop a higher quality of FDI—meaning higher skill levels, more key business functions such as R&D and marketing, and more extensive purchasing linkages within the country (e.g., *Industrial Policy* 1984, pp. 7, 12). The report of the Industrial Policy Review Group (1992, p. 67), also known as the Culliton report, said that "far greater integration of foreign industry into the Irish economy is needed in terms of linkages with other industrial firms and the undertaking of important management functions in relation to investment, marketing and R&D". The objective of this approach was to make companies more integrated or embedded in the Irish economy so that their presence in Ireland would be enduring, to make higher pay levels more sustainable, and to increase companies' contribution to Ireland's value-added and net foreign earnings. During the boom, some progress was made towards these goals in certain respects, although there was less evidence of progress in other respects and significant setbacks sometimes occurred.

Purchasing Linkages

Before the boom began, it was already an aim of industrial policy to increase the purchasing linkages that foreign-owned MNCs had with the Irish economy. A policy measure called the National Linkage Programme was introduced in 1985 to strengthen linkages between foreign MNCs and suppliers in Ireland by enhancing the technical and business competence of suppliers in cooperation with MNC customers (Crowley 1996). This type of policy was primarily focused on MNCs in manufacturing and their purchases of material inputs. For some time, there was evidence that the foreign manufacturing firms were purchasing an increasing proportion of their material inputs in Ireland, but that trend levelled off before very long.

Foreign-owned non-food manufacturing companies purchased about 15% of their material inputs in Ireland in 1986 and this rose to about 21% in the early 1990s, but then it stayed at around that level during most of the 1990s (O'Sullivan 2000). By 2000, foreign non-food manufacturing companies were purchasing 18% of their material inputs in Ireland, and this declined to 11% in 2005 and 10% in 2006.[2] Thus over the whole two decades, there was no progress on linkages when measured in terms of the proportion of materials purchased in Ireland by foreign manufacturing companies, despite the advance seen in the early years.

The decline after 2000 in the percentage of material inputs purchased in Ireland was particularly marked in computers, electronic & optical products, although it also occurred to a lesser extent in the rest of non-food manufacturing. In computers, electronic & optical products, 17% of material inputs was purchased in Ireland in 2000 and this fell to 5% by 2006. Meanwhile, in the rest of non-food manufacturing the corresponding decline was from 21% to 15%.[3]

Van Egeraat and Jacobson (2004) documented this declining trend in the computer hardware industry, noting that suppliers of the relevant material inputs in Ireland experienced increasing competition in the late 1990s from low-wage economies, particularly those in the Far East. This was then compounded by the exodus of the personal computer assemblers from Ireland, which disrupted local market conditions for sub-supply companies that had grown up to supply them with some of their input requirements. Van Egeraat and Jacobson (2004) also noted that the data on purchasing linkages cited above tended to overestimate the extent of local sourcing in the computer industry, partly because the data included expenditure on items that were bought from local turnkey supply-chain-managers but were manufactured in other regions.

[2] Forfas, 2008, *Annual Business Survey of Economic Impact—Appendix*. Dublin: Forfas.

[3] Ibid.

R&D

As regards R&D, it was already noted in Chapter 5 that business expenditure on R&D (BERD) intensity increased rapidly in manufacturing between 1988 and 1997. BERD intensity in Irish indigenous manufacturing rose from 0.5% of gross output to 1.1% during that period, while there was a similar increase in foreign-owned manufacturing from 0.6 to 1.2% of gross output. However, these figures declined later in 1997–2003, to 0.75% in the case of indigenous industry and to 0.65% in foreign-owned industry. By 2003 the figure for foreign-owned industry was back to nearly the same level as in 1988.[4]

Even at the peak level in the late 1990s, BERD intensity was low compared with the OECD. It was particularly noticeable that foreign-owned industry in Ireland was highly concentrated in the sectors that generally had high R&D intensity in most OECD countries, but for the most part foreign-owned firms in Ireland had substantially lower R&D intensity than OECD firms operating in the same sectors as themselves (see Table 5.8 in Chapter 5). It was possible for them to function in this way because they could benefit from the R&D performed by other branches of the same MNCs in other countries.

When R&D intensity declined after the late 1990s, the main reason for this in the foreign-owned industry was because of the decline of the electronics industry. In 1997 the electrical & electronic equipment sector accounted for half of all R&D in foreign-owned firms, so trends in that sector had a strong effect on total R&D trends in foreign-owned firms. Between 1997 and 2003, the sector's share of the total output of foreign-owned industry declined while its R&D intensity dropped by more than half, from 1.7% of gross output to 0.7%. It seems that cutting R&D activity was one aspect of a broader declining trend in electronics production in Ireland.

Meanwhile, R&D intensity also declined in the same period in the other major R&D performing sectors in foreign-owned industry, but the

[4] Forfas, *Survey of Research and Development in the Business Sector 1997*, for 1997. Forfas, *Business Expenditure on Research and Development (BERD) Ireland 2003/4*, for 2003.

decline there was much less marked than in electrical & electronic equipment. R&D intensity was reduced from 2.0% to 1.9% in medical and technical instruments and from 5.1% to 3.7% in pharmaceuticals.[5]

Such trends in R&D probably did have real economic effects in Ireland. For example, as was noted in Sect. 5.1 in Chapter 5, Kearns and Ruane (1999) found that foreign-owned plants that undertook R&D in Ireland were more likely to survive in Ireland for longer than those that did not undertake R&D. The R&D performers also had lower rates of job loss and their jobs lasted for longer than among those that did not undertake R&D.

Van Egeraat and Barry (2009) provided insights into the type of R&D conducted by foreign-owned MNCs in the pharmaceutical industry in Ireland. They reported that the value chain in the pharmaceutical industry worldwide included three main types of R&D, as well as manufacturing, sales and marketing, etc. The three main types of R&D were discovery, product development, and process R&D. Discovery included research into the causes of diseases and the identification of compounds that have a pharmacological effect. Product development included the further development of these compounds, and notably their testing in pre-clinical and clinical trials. Process R&D involved the development of safe and efficient manufacturing processes.

Van Egeraat and Barry (2009) also reported that discovery and clinical trials were generally considered to be high value-added activities, while process R&D—along with sales and marketing—was regarded as medium-level, and manufacturing was often seen as lower value-added. They found that Ireland's relative role in discovery remained very limited and clinical trial activities remained under-represented in Ireland, whereas process R&D had increased substantially.

Thus, the growth of process R&D represented an increase in the level of value creation in the sector during the boom period, as compared with manufacturing. However, much of the industry's highest value-added R&D was still under-represented in Ireland.

As regards innovation capabilities, it was shown in Chapter 5 that levels of innovation activity in Ireland were quite high compared to other European countries in the 1990s, with foreign-owned plants generally reporting somewhat higher levels than Irish indigenous plants. However,

[5] Derived from the sources mentioned in footnote 2.

since many of the innovations in foreign-owned plants could have been sourced from other parts of the same MNCs in other countries, such innovation data for Ireland do not tell us a great deal about the capabilities within the foreign-owned plants in Ireland in the field of innovation.

Decision-Making Autonomy

Hewitt-Dundas et al. (2002) presented survey findings on decision-making autonomy in relation to a range of different management issues in large foreign-owned MNC plants in Ireland in 2000. They also presented some additional findings on sales and marketing and on R&D.

They found that a large majority of plants (71–92%) had full autonomy on a number of operational-type issues—selecting suppliers, selecting subcontractors, awarding service contracts and staff training. A smaller majority (56–59%) had full autonomy in recruiting senior staff and setting wage/salary levels. At the same time, a significant minority of plants (21–33%) had full autonomy on a range of more strategic issues—design of products/packaging, setting product prices, purchasing production machinery, determining market territory served and sales promotion activities. Major capital investment was the only area in which very few plants (7%) had full autonomy.

As regards sales and marketing, Hewitt-Dundas et al. (2002) found that 39% of the large MNC plants had no need for a sales and marketing function because all their sales went to other group sites. In addition, a further 21% had no sales function and 16% had no marketing function because sales and marketing was done for them elsewhere in the group. On the other hand, 18% of the plants had full responsibility for sales and marketing in relation to the products they manufactured, while 21% were partly responsible for sales and 26% were partly responsible for marketing.

Hewitt-Dundas et al. (2002) also presented findings on R&D activity in the large foreign-owned MNC plants. They found that 53% of the plants had an R&D department, with 3% of total employment hours being in R&D. The type of R&D work was weighted more towards development, upgrading and adaptation of products, rather than pure research on new product technologies.

In the absence of comparable data from the 1980s, it is difficult to say with certainty whether the findings of Hewitt-Dundas et al. (2002) amounted to progress compared with the situation at the start of the boom. However, it appears to represent some advance from the situation described above in the quotes from the Telesis report, since by 2000 there was at least a substantial minority of large MNC plants that could not be described in terms such as "manufacturing satellites" or "assembly shops".

Pay Levels

Pay levels in foreign-owned firms have sometimes been used as an indicator of the level of skills employed by those companies. The evidence in that respect shows that foreign-owned firms had relatively high and rising pay levels throughout the boom.

In manufacturing, average wages and salaries per head in foreign-owned companies were 16% higher than in Irish indigenous companies in 1986, 24% higher in 2000 and 36% higher in 2007.[6] Average pay per head increased by 6.7% p.a. in foreign-owned manufacturing in 1986–2007, in current values, compared with 5.9% p.a. in Irish indigenous manufacturing. For comparison, the value of GNP per person at work increased by 6.0% p.a. in the same period.

Comparable data for the services sector are available only for the period beginning in 2001. In services, average wages and salaries per head were 28% higher in foreign-owned companies than in indigenous companies in 2001, and 18% higher in 2007.[7] In this case, average pay per head increased more slowly in foreign than in Irish companies, although the pay level remained a good deal higher in the foreign firms. The rate of increase was 4.2% p.a. in foreign-owned services in 2001–2007, in current values, compared with 5.7% p.a. in Irish indigenous services.

To the extent that pay levels indicate skill levels, the data suggest that foreign-owned companies had relatively high and rising skill levels, especially in manufacturing. However, there is some room for doubt whether their pay levels truly reflected skill levels. This is mainly because the foreign-owned companies were mostly very profitable, their labour costs were usually quite low relative to the value of their sales, and they were often producing goods or services that were not particularly price-sensitive. Consequently, many of them would have been able to pay relatively well for any given skill level if they chose to do so, for example

[6] Derived from *Census of Industrial Production*.

[7] Derived from *Annual Services Inquiry*.

to facilitate recruitment of new staff, retention of employees, or good industrial relations.

However, pay levels in foreign-owned companies were at least consistent with the idea that they had relatively high skill levels compared with Irish indigenous companies and their skill levels were generally rising.

Sector Studies

A number of reports on individual sectors shed more light on the issue of stages of production and skill levels within foreign-owned MNC plants in Ireland.

Van Egeraat and Jacobson (2004) reported that the computer hardware manufacturers who had operations in Ireland and Scotland generally kept their computer development facilities concentrated in their own home country. Their operations in Europe typically included a range of other functions such as sales and marketing, customer service, technical support and regional headquarters, but these were not necessarily in Ireland or Scotland. Their European headquarters and sales and marketing headquarters were usually located in core European regions rather than in Ireland or Scotland.

At least until the early 1990s, Ireland and Scotland were acting as a "semi-periphery" of Europe, attracting the more factor-cost-sensitive parts of the production chain, including the system assembly plants. Then in the second half of the 1990s, rising wage rates in Ireland and Scotland, combined with the opening up of Eastern European economies as locations for FDI, caused computer assembly activity to shift to Eastern Europe.

Thus, in this case, the more factor-cost-sensitive and lower-skill parts of the industry could not prosper indefinitely in Ireland, and they eventually succumbed to competition from lower-cost locations. Van Egeraat and Jacobson (2004) concluded that IDA Ireland responded appropriately for the most part in seeking to attract other functions within the industry to Ireland, such as system development, software development, sales and technical support call centres, shared services and regional headquarters. By the early 2000s, progress along these lines was partly offsetting the very substantial loss of manufacturing activity.

Van Egeraat and Barry (2009) examined the pharmaceutical industry in Ireland, focusing particularly on Ireland's changing role in manufacturing and in R&D in that industry. Their main conclusions on R&D

were outlined earlier in this section, under the heading of R&D. To recap, they found that Ireland's relative role in the highest value-added types of R&D—discovery and product development—had remained quite limited. However, process R&D had increased substantially in Ireland and, although this was not the highest value-added type of R&D, it did represent an increase in the level of value creation in the sector in Ireland during the boom period.

As regards manufacturing in the pharmaceutical sector, Van Egeraat and Barry (2009) found that Ireland's involvement shifted in the direction of relatively higher value-generating activities during the boom. Specifically, they noted that pharmaceutical manufacturing included the manufacture of active ingredients (the drug substance), drug formulations (the tablet, capsule or injection material), and the material inputs into those items. They found that in Ireland very little growth occurred in the relatively low value-generating activity of basic chemical inputs. Instead, employment growth occurred mainly in drug formulation and the higher value-generating active ingredients sub-sector.

Taking account of both R&D and manufacturing, they concluded that "although the picture is complex and differentiated, the level of value creation in the Irish pharmaceutical industry has increased substantially over the Celtic Tiger era."

Best et al. (2010) recognised that as the growth of high-tech industry in Ireland was driven primarily by foreign-owned MNCs, the sustainability of that growth had remained a basis for debate. They developed a new database that aimed to provide a deeper understanding of technological activities, technological change and technology management capabilities. They then carried out two case studies: (1) an examination of the emergence, growth, dynamics and capabilities of the medical technology sector in Ireland; (2) an assessment of the future of the renewable energy sector in Ireland, examining its potential and the barriers facing it.

In the medical technology sector, they found that the industry had evolved from low value-added branch plant manufacturing to upgraded product development and world-class manufacturing capabilities. They concluded that the capabilities were in place to allow a transition to a new business model based on endogenous development. In the renewable energy sector, they found that there was potential for an emerging industrial cluster operating at the intersection of two or more existing technology-based clusters.

Overall, Best et al. (2010) concluded that, from a capabilities perspective, Ireland had assimilated technological, manufacturing and managerial capabilities from MNCs which could be mobilised and enhanced as potential drivers of economic growth.

Conclusion

Some of the trends examined here did not show much sign of progress towards the desired objectives. This was true of the overall trends in material purchasing linkages and R&D intensity, although both had looked quite promising for some time in the earlier stages of the boom.

On the other hand, there were indications of progress in some other respects. There appeared to be advances in autonomy in decision-making including in marketing. There were indications of rising skill levels and more advanced activities in sectors such as pharmaceuticals and medical instruments & equipment. After a period of very negative trends in manufacturing of computers around the end of the 1990s, there were also subsequent moves into more skilled activities. At the same time, pay trends in foreign-owned MNCs were consistent with the idea that skill levels were relatively high and rising.

Thus, the trends were quite uneven and mixed. The overall effect was probably to make the FDI sector more skilled, more embedded in the Irish economy because of greater reliance on skills, and more capable of sustaining higher pay levels. At the same time, such effects must have been weaker than they would have been with higher levels of R&D intensity and purchasing linkages.

6.3 Motivations for Investing in Ireland

This section considers the question why foreign-owned MNCs decided to undertake direct investment in Ireland and, more specifically, why their investment in Ireland increased very substantially during the boom. This issue was already mentioned briefly earlier in this chapter, referring to factors such as tax concessions, grants, relatively low-wage costs, access to large European markets and the education system. These and related matters are examined in more detail here.

Since the expansion of export-oriented FDI in Ireland began in the 1950s, a number of studies have attempted to identify the reasons why the companies concerned chose to invest in Ireland. Two relatively early examples in the 1960s, Donaldson (1965) and the Survey of Grant-Aided Industry (1967), both highlighted the importance of four main attractions for foreign investors. These were tax concessions, government grants, market access and labour. At the time, the main tax concession was export profit tax relief (EPTR) which meant that there was no corporation tax on profits of manufacturing industry arising from export sales. "Market access" at the time primarily meant free access to the UK market, and the attraction of labour in Ireland lay in both its availability (at a time of full employment in many developed economies) and its relatively low cost compared to more developed economies.

About fifteen years later, a survey report commissioned and published by the Allied Irish Bank (1981) presented rather similar findings. The survey first asked foreign-owned companies in Ireland what had been the key criteria for them when they were evaluating which country to invest in. The most common response referred to the financial package of grant and tax incentives. Other very common responses referred to labour (specifically production costs, availability of labour, and availability of skilled/competent labour), and to market access (specifically location/access to market, and membership of EC). When the companies were then asked what was the most important reason for their decision to locate in Ireland, the most common response was grant and tax incentives with particular emphasis on tax incentives. After that, the most common responses again referred to labour and to market access.

Of course, an important change by 1981 compared to the mid-1960s was that Ireland had become a member of the European Community (EC), so that the market access mentioned by the respondent companies in 1981 referred primarily to the EC market. In fact, two-thirds of them regarded a site within the EC as an important attraction for them since their main markets were in Europe.[8]

Nearly two decades later, when the boom was in full swing, further investigations in this area highlighted the importance of somewhat similar factors in attracting foreign investment. Hannigan (1998, 2000) presented the findings of survey research on foreign-owned companies that had located in Ireland. Hannigan's key conclusion was that Ireland's corporate tax regime was the single most important factor attracting

[8] From a related article in *Allied Irish Bank Review*, April 1981 (cited by O'Malley 1989, p. 170).

multinationals to the country.[9] Subsequently, Hannigan reiterated this point, while noting that the quality workforce was also crucial.[10]

At around the same time, Gunnigle and McGuire (2001) had a particular interest in labour issues in their research on factors influencing US multinationals in Ireland, but they noted first that "for most organisations the critical factor positively influencing the final decision in Ireland's favour was its low rate of corporation tax". They also found that an EU location and government grants were often important influences on location decisions, as well as labour availability and quality.

The Increase in FDI During the Boom

The record of export-oriented FDI in Ireland goes back to the 1950s, but the contribution of FDI to Ireland's economic growth appeared to weaken during most of the 1980s compared to the 1960s and 1970s, as was noted in Sect. 6.1. However, FDI then accelerated again and made a major contribution to economic growth during the boom. Thus, total employment in foreign-owned manufacturing companies grew strongly after 1988. Inflows of FDI from the USA into Ireland grew particularly fast at that time, both because US FDI inflows into the EU increased sharply and because Ireland's share of these inflows also increased substantially (Barry et al. 1999b, Figures 3.8 and 3.10; Barry 2005, Figure 3).

This raises the question what caused this acceleration during the period of the boom? One aspect that needs to be examined in answering this is to consider whether there were significant enhancements to Ireland's existing key attractions for FDI—namely in the areas of tax concessions, grants, market access and labour.

As regards the government's financial package of grants to encourage investment, there were no significant changes in these measures that would account for the rise in FDI. In fact, the attractiveness of Ireland's grants may have been reduced after the mid-1980s by a somewhat increased emphasis on obtaining better value for the state's expenditure by tightening grant spending relative to employment generated.

[9] Kevin Hannigan, "Irish Economy Has Developed Its Own Momentum", *The Irish Times*, 13 November 1998.

[10] "Multinationals Integral to Economy's Success", *The Irish Times*, 19 April 1999.

In the area of tax concessions, there have been some changes over the years since the 1950s but, for the most part, these would not be linked to the surge in FDI that began in the late 1980s. The original main tax concession since the 1950s was export profit tax relief, as noted above. This was supplemented by other tax measures including double taxation agreements with a range of countries, and favourable depreciation allowances which varied over time and by region.

In 1978 the government announced that EPTR would be replaced by a new low rate of corporation tax of just 10% for all profits (i.e., including profits arising from domestic sales as well as from exports), to apply to manufacturing as well as selected internationally traded services from 1981 onwards.[11] This change was motivated by pressure from the EEC against discrimination in favour of exports contained in EPTR.

After that, there were no substantial changes concerning the key tax concessions for most sectors throughout the 1980s and most of the 1990s. Thus, consideration of timing indicates that the boom was not created primarily by major new tax concessions, since the main tax concessions for most sectors were largely in place and quite stable long before the boom.

In the late 1990s, the government began to move gradually towards a new standard corporation tax rate of 12.5% for *all* sectors in the economy. The tax rate applicable to sectors other than manufacturing and the selected internationally traded services had been 40%, and this was reduced to 32% in 1998 and finally to 12.5% by 2003. This move to 12.5% for all sectors in 2003 meant there was a small increase from 10% for manufacturing and the selected internationally traded services, as well as a much larger decrease in the rate for other sectors. This change is of little significance in explaining the surge of FDI in the boom years, because of its timing, because its effect on most internationally trading activities was slightly unfavourable, and because the sectors that gained the most from it were generally not the major recipients of FDI. Incidentally, the introduction of the new standard rate of 12.5% was again a response to the view of the EU, which considered that there was an unacceptable pro-trade bias inherent in the previous two-tier tax system.

It is necessary to mention one further point concerning tax concessions, which was relevant for explaining a particular part of the increase in

[11] Full EPTR would continue to apply for another decade to existing firms which qualified for it before 1981.

FDI during the boom. This was the government's decision to extend the scope of the tax concession regime after 1987 to approved international financial services provided to non-residents from the new International Financial Services Centre (IFSC) in Dublin. The tax concession regime had already applied throughout the 1980s to selected internationally traded services such as software and other computer-related services, R&D, engineering, architectural and other services, but these did not include financial services before 1987.

Financial services exports from Ireland grew rapidly after that, with most of the growth coming from new FDI. It is clear from the timing that the new tax concession was a major reason for this growth. Consequently, that new tax concession can be counted as a major cause of this specific part of the country's boom in FDI. However, this was an untypical and relatively minor part of the overall boom. Honohan (2001) noted that employment in the IFSC grew rapidly from a start-up in 1987 to 11,000 by 2001, which was one-quarter of total financial sector employment, but at the same time, it was less than 1% of total employment in the economy. The growth in exports of financial and insurance services looked impressive, from just 0.4% of all exports in 1985 to 4.4% by 2000,[12] with most of these exports in 2000 resulting from FDI. However, despite the impressive growth, this was clearly a minor part of the overall boom.

As regards the role of market access as an attraction for FDI, there was an obvious enhancement to this attraction when the EU's single European market was introduced. Prior to the single European market, there was already free trade between EU member states in the sense of an absence of tariffs and quotas on such trade, but it was commonly observed that there were significant remaining non-tariff barriers which acted as impediments to genuine free trade. Such non-tariff barriers included administrative formalities and delays at national borders, different technical standards and requirements in different countries, and preferential public sector purchasing from each country's own national suppliers.

The objective of the single European market programme was to achieve full integration of the individual markets of the member states into one EU market, by implementing a series of measures to remove the non-tariff barriers over the eight years up to 1992. It was expected that this would have the effect of increasing trade between member states

[12] CSO, *Input-Output Tables for* 1985; and CSO, *2000 Supply and Use and Input-Output Tables*.

with resulting gains in efficiency. It was also expected that it would attract more FDI into the EU from external sources, because of the increased attraction of producing and selling in such a large integrated market.

In fact, there was quite a dramatic increase in flows of US FDI into the EU in the late 1980s as mentioned above, and the US Department of Commerce *Survey of Current Business* (March 1991) attributed much of this to the single European market programme. Consequently, it can be concluded that improved market access in the single EU market was a significant cause of the surge in FDI coming into Ireland. In addition, however, Ireland's share of the US FDI inflows into the EU also increased dramatically in the early 1990s (Barry et al. 1999a, 1999b), and this would have to be explained by other factors that were more specific to Ireland.

As regards the role of Ireland's labour supply as an attraction for FDI, the Irish education system was already quite well equipped, before the late 1980s, to provide the type of technical graduates that would be required by incoming FDI. It also had a feature that was somewhat unusual compared to other EU countries—namely regular interaction and dialogue between third-level education and the industrial policy system, with the aim of adjusting the supply of technical graduates from the education system in response to the changing employment opportunities and requirements in growing industries (Barry 2005).

This feature was already in place by the early 1980s. It meant that, as the opportunities emerged in the late 1980s to attract substantially more FDI in the high-tech sectors, the Irish education system was able to respond and adapt to the latest requirements of such industries more rapidly and flexibly than most other EU countries. In this way, the attraction of Ireland's labour supply for FDI could be continually renewed, and probably increased relative to some other countries which adapted more slowly. Thus, it became noticeable during the boom that some other countries tended to experience shortages of graduates with the relevant skills more than Ireland did.

Apart from conditions in Ireland that could help to attract FDI, there was also a major new trend in the international economy which was increasing the supply of FDI that was potentially available for Ireland. This new trend, which occurred mainly in the USA, was the emergence and very rapid growth of new industries based on new technologies—especially computers, telecommunications equipment and related hardware, as well as software. Later, the development of the internet led to further strong growth. In addition, there was also very rapid growth and development of some longer established high-tech industries, including pharmaceuticals and medical instruments & equipment.

All of these were recognised and targeted relatively early by Ireland's IDA as potential sources of new FDI for Ireland. Mac Sharry and White (2000, Chapter 15) noted that the IDA was continuously monitoring trends in the market. It developed a "rifle-shot" rather than a "scatter-gun" approach when seeking foreign investment, which involved identifying not only the sectors but also the companies that could operate well in Ireland and could bring economic benefits to the country. As a result of frequent interaction with the market, the IDA was regularly adjusting its targeting of sectors and companies, so that it was well aware of the potential offered by the fast-growing high-tech industries.

In view of the points outlined above concerning reasons for the surge in FDI in Ireland during the boom, it may be concluded that the major new developments that initiated the surge occurred outside Ireland. At the same time, however, policies and other conditions in Ireland were exceptionally well suited to taking advantage of the available opportunities, and adapting flexibly so as to secure substantial inflows of FDI.

The emergence and rapid growth of high-tech industries, together with the EU's single European market programme, ensured that there was going to be a substantial increase in the supply of FDI looking for locations to settle in within the EU. Ireland was already a relatively attractive location for FDI, with a disproportionate share of FDI in the EU compared to its small size. Consequently, Ireland was always likely to receive a sizeable share of the new incoming FDI. As it turned out, however, its share of the inflow increased substantially. This was not because of significant new policy measures in Ireland, except in the case of new tax concessions for financial services. Rather, it was mainly because existing practices in Ireland were very well suited to attracting the type of industries that predominated in the rising wave of FDI.

In particular, Ireland's concessions on corporation profit tax were well suited to attracting companies that were exceptionally profitable—such as much of the new wave of fast-growing high-tech industries. Thus, Telesis (1982, Chapter 6) had already found in the early 1980s that, compared to a selection of other EU countries and regions, Ireland's package of financial incentives for industrial projects was particularly well geared to attracting companies that were highly profitable, as well as being of medium capital-intensity. They also observed that companies of this type accounted for almost all the projects sought by Ireland.[13]

The role of the IDA, and the interaction between it and the third-level education system, were two other aspects of existing practice in Ireland that were well suited to attracting FDI by new fast-growing high-tech companies. As outlined above, they enabled Ireland to be unusually responsive and adaptable to newly emerging and rapidly changing opportunities.

Finally, another point concerning motivations for FDI in Ireland was emphasised by Barry and Bradley (1997). It is possible that MNCs, when searching for a new overseas location, focus particularly on areas that their competitors have already explored and found to be satisfactory. If so, the inflow of FDI in a given sector may develop self-sustaining characteristics once a critical mass of firms has been established in that sector.

The Increase in Services FDI

Before concluding on motivations for FDI in Ireland, a few points should be mentioned about services FDI specifically.

Services accounted for a rather small share of both FDI and exports during most of the boom, until around the end of the 1990s (see Fig. 4.3). They amounted to less than one-fifth of total exports throughout that period, but their share of exports then rose very rapidly to about 45% by 2007.

Although it might appear that something must have happened to cause a sudden acceleration in services exports and FDI, that was not actually what happened. Services exports, which mostly came from FDI as was seen in Sect. 6.1, had been growing fast throughout the boom, but they were not very prominent for quite a long time because they were starting from a small initial base and because manufacturing exports were also growing fast. Services exports then became much more prominent quite suddenly because manufacturing exports stopped growing (see Sects. 6.1 and 6.2) while services exports carried on growing fast.

[13] Stewart (2013) noted that international evidence showed that tax concessions were not usually the most important factor in attracting FDI in most countries. But he also recognised that they could have been very influential in Ireland if Ireland was attracting the type of companies for which low tax was particularly important, provided that low tax rates were accompanied by other elements of an accommodating tax regime.

For the most part, the motivations for FDI in services were similar to those already outlined above, although the aircraft leasing sector presents a somewhat distinctive case. Ireland became a major centre of aircraft leasing during the boom, and it was commonly reported some years later that about half of the world's leased commercial aircraft were managed from Ireland (Osborne-Kinch et al. 2017). This meant that about one-quarter of all commercial aircraft in the world were leased aircraft that were managed from Ireland, since about half of the world's commercial aircraft were leased.

Most of the companies involved in the sector in Ireland were foreign-owned. The tax regime in Ireland was an obvious motivation for their choice of location, meaning not just the low corporate tax rate but also the double tax treaty network and the treatment of depreciation.

At the same time, however, another significant motivation was the presence of people with specialised skills that were relevant to the sector, including financial, legal, operational and technical skills. This pool of skills had developed in Ireland since the 1970s, because of the pioneering role of the Irish-based company Guinness Peat Aviation (GPA), which is credited with having invented aircraft leasing. After GPA collapsed in the early 1990s, the skilled staff were still available to work in the industry for other companies.

One indication of the strength of the skills environment was the fact that universities in Dublin were offering specialised courses that were specifically relevant to the industry, including an MSc degree in aviation finance which was claimed to be the only one in Europe.[14]

Another distinctive type of development occurred in the ICT sector, where foreign-owned service activities often emerged from previously existing manufacturing companies. This happened particularly around the end of the 1990s and early 2000s, when manufacturing activities in the sector were often in decline in Ireland.

Barry and Van Egeraat (2008) noted that, by the late 1990s, Ireland was a major centre of computer hardware production, accounting for 5% of global computer exports and about one-third of personal computer exports sold in Europe. Ireland also accounted for around 6% of global exports of electronic components. However, the sector in Ireland then

[14] Gavin McLoughlin, "Why Is Ireland a Hub for the Global Aircraft Leasing Sector", 17 April 2016, Independent.ie. "Aviation Sector Contributes More Than €4 Billion to Irish Economy", *The Irish Times*, 19 January 2017.

experienced a sharp decline as production was relocated eastwards to Central and Eastern Europe and to China.

Barry and Van Egeraat (2008) reported that some of the industry's former staff found employment in other related manufacturing companies in Ireland, while others moved to employment in more diverse sectors. At the same time, however, some of the former hardware manufacturing companies shifted their Irish operations into higher value-added service activities such as sales, technical support call centres and logistics, thereby generating new service employment.

Grimes (2006) focused particularly on this latter aspect, involving service activities emerging in manufacturing companies. He pointed out that some other types of internationally traded services, such as financial services, were typically carried out by specialist services corporations, and were therefore clearly distinct sectors from manufacturing. In many areas of ICT, however, a strong complementarity continued between manufacturing and services, with many corporations involved in a spectrum of manufacturing and service activities. Grimes examined the cases of a number of leading companies in Ireland—including IBM, HP, Microsoft, Sun Microsystems and Apple—to see how they had evolved over time. He found that "the general trend is for an on-going shift away from hardware manufacturing towards a greater involvement in software, R&D and a range of other support services".

In cases such as these, the companies' motivation for establishing service activities in an Irish location would presumably have been influenced considerably by the fact that they already had premises and staff existing in Ireland, with a good deal of experience of operating in the country.

Conclusion

Since long before the boom, the main reasons why foreign-owned companies decided to invest in Ireland lay in the areas of tax concessions, government grants, market access and labour. The precise nature of these attractions changed somewhat over time.

The surge in FDI that occurred at the time of the boom was not mainly caused by new developments in Ireland relating to matters such as tax concessions, grants or labour. Rather, the major new developments that initiated the surge occurred outside Ireland, particularly the introduction of the single European market programme and the rise of new fast-growing high-tech industries. At the same time, however, existing policies and other conditions in Ireland were exceptionally well suited to taking advantage of the new opportunities as they arose, and to adapting flexibly to secure disproportionately large inflows of FDI.

6.4 Secondary Effects of FDI on the Irish Economy

The direct effect of foreign-owned companies, in terms of employment or production, has been outlined earlier in this chapter. This section examines various secondary effects that FDI had on the Irish economy. This discussion is partly related to some of the matters already covered in Sect. 6.2 on the nature and characteristics of foreign-owned companies in Ireland, but the focus here is different—looking at the effects on the wider economy outside the foreign-owned MNCs rather than the MNC subsidiaries themselves.

The issues that are briefly discussed in this section include effects on the balance of payments, potential adverse effects on indigenous companies, purchasing linkages, enhancement of Irish skills or technology, and development of industry clusters.

Balance of Payments

It was seen in Chapter 5 that foreign-owned companies tended to import much of the inputs that they required and to send large amounts of profits out of the country. With that type of cost structure, the impact of foreign-owned companies on Ireland's balance of payments would have been negative if most of their sales had gone to the Irish domestic market, because the cost of imported inputs, as well as outflows of profits, would have outweighed the value of exports. As it was, however, foreign-owned companies in manufacturing and internationally traded services were generally very highly export-oriented, as outlined above. Consequently, their effect on the balance of payments was generally strongly positive, even though their imported inputs and outflows of profits were very substantial.

Some data and estimates of relevance to this were presented in Tables 5.6 and 5.7 in Chapter 5. Table 5.6 shows that the net foreign earnings of foreign-owned manufacturing (much the same thing as its contribution to the balance of payments) were just 26% of the value of its exports in 2005. This was much lower than the corresponding figure of 78% for indigenous manufacturing. Similarly, the net foreign earnings of foreign-owned services were just 55% of the value of its exports in 2005, which was much lower than the corresponding figure of 94% for indigenous services.

At the same time, however, the value of exports from foreign-owned firms was far greater than the value of exports from indigenous companies. The overall result was that the net foreign earnings of foreign-owned firms amounted to about 70% of total net foreign earnings by the 2000s, compared to about 30% for indigenous companies. The contribution of foreign firms had increased very rapidly so that its share of the total had risen from about 56% in 1985 to about 70% by the 2000s.

This contribution of foreign-owned companies to Ireland's balance of payments, and the pace of its growth, was of fundamental importance for the economy, for the reasons outlined in Sect. 4.2. It was probably the most important impact that FDI had on the economy. The growth performance seen in the economy during much of the boom depended heavily on the contribution of foreign-owned companies to the balance of payments.

Potential Adverse Effects on Indigenous Companies

There are several different ways that FDI could potentially have adverse effects on indigenous companies in the host country. One issue, that has occurred in some other countries, arises when indigenous companies lose market share in their home market because of new competition from foreign companies. In Ireland, however, this was seldom a significant issue because most foreign manufacturing and internationally traded services companies were so highly export-oriented.

Another issue that has arisen in other countries is competition for supplies of local primary products as inputs. Again, this was seldom a significant cause of contention in Ireland because most of the foreign-owned companies that were expanding fast during the boom were not in the business of processing local primary products, and they tended to import most of their material inputs.[15]

[15] There were a few examples of this type of competition, involving competition for supplies of milk, in an earlier period before the boom (O'Malley 1989, Chapter 7), but the sectoral pattern of FDI growth during the boom would have made this less likely.

An issue that did surface at times during the boom was competition for skilled labour. This arose sometimes in the software industry in the 1990s when there was rapid growth occurring in both foreign-owned and indigenous software companies at the same time. However, while some Irish companies were affected by this, it seems to have had no more than a limited impact. The education system was usually able to produce a sufficient, or almost sufficient, number of suitable graduates for the industry (O'Gorman et al. 1997, Chapter 3), and the record of rapid growth in indigenous software (Sect. 5.2) indicates that the problem was generally overcome reasonably successfully.

It was sometimes argued that one way that FDI created difficulties for indigenous industry, with consequent employment losses, was by causing wages to increase too rapidly. The argument was that foreign-owned companies had high and rapidly rising productivity and consequently they could afford to pay wage increases that were excessive for indigenous companies with their slower productivity growth. Barry (1996) argued along these lines. As was already discussed in Chapter 2—referring to the period immediately before the boom—he found that, in 1980–1986, average weekly earnings increased by 12.4% per year in the modern (predominantly foreign-owned) sector while the rate of increase was almost as high at 11.2% per year in the traditional (predominantly Irish-owned) sector. At the same time, he found that the volume of net output per person engaged grew by 11.0% per year in the modern sector but at a far slower rate of 4.9% per year in the traditional sector.

However, when we looked at this (in Chapter 2) solely in terms of *values* for both wages and net output per person, we found that the value of net output per person engaged increased by 14.1% per year in the traditional sector in 1980–1986, which was more than the increase in its average weekly earnings. Meanwhile, the value of net output per person engaged increased at an even higher rate in the modern sector. Thus, wage increases in the traditional sector were low enough to protect and enhance its profitability, while being of even greater benefit to the profitability of the modern sector because of its faster productivity growth.[16]

[16] A point worth bearing in mind here is that price trends were frequently quite different for the output of the modern and traditional sectors, mainly because a large part of the output of the modern sector consisted of computers and other electronic products, the prices of which were often declining due to rapid technological progress.

Barry (1996) also included the early years of the boom, 1986–1992, in his analysis, with similar findings to those for 1980–1986. Again, however, if we look at it solely in terms of values, the value of net output per head in the traditional sector increased faster than the rise in its average weekly earnings in 1986–1992, so its profitability was protected and enhanced.[17]

To conclude this section, the potentially adverse effects of FDI on indigenous companies were generally quite limited during the boom. The relative unimportance of these issues, as compared with some other countries, arose partly because FDI in Ireland mainly involved highly export-oriented greenfield plants which did not have much involvement in competition with local companies. The discussion that follows considers whether the FDI that occurred in Ireland was of significant positive benefit in improving the indigenous potential for development.

Purchasing Linkages

As was discussed in Sect. 6.2 above, it was an aim of industrial policy throughout the boom to increase the purchasing linkages that foreign-owned MNCs had with the Irish economy. Initially, at least, there was a particular focus on MNCs in manufacturing and their purchasing of material inputs. However, although foreign-owned manufacturing MNCs did purchase an increasing proportion of their material inputs in Ireland during the early years of the boom, that trend levelled off during the 1990s followed by a declining trend after 2000. Over the whole two decades, there was no progress on linkages when measured in terms of the percentage of material inputs purchased in Ireland by manufacturing MNCs, despite the advance seen in the early years.

Consequently, a comparison of trends in the volume of output from the modern and traditional sectors could often look different to a comparison of trends in the value of their output.

[17] The precise figures on this could vary depending on how one defines the "modern" and "traditional" sectors in 1992, after a change in the sectoral classification system in 1991, but it would remain true that the value of net output per head increased faster than wages in the traditional sector with any plausible definition.

As regards the effect of purchasing linkages on the indigenous economy, O'Malley (1995, p. 57) estimated that the amount of indigenous manufacturing employment supported by foreign-owned manufacturing's purchasing of industrial products was about 8,200 in 1983, rising to 10,800 in 1990 and 11,200 in 1991. These figures were equivalent to 6.3% of total indigenous manufacturing employment in 1983, rising to about 9.6% in 1990 and 10.0% in 1991. Another way of looking at this is that for every 100 jobs in foreign-owned manufacturing in 1983, there were about 9 people employed in indigenous industry producing the products that foreign industry was purchasing as inputs. This number increased to 12 in 1990 and 13 in 1991.

Thus, foreign-owned industry was a quite important and growing market for indigenous industry, although its scale was not likely to transform the prospects for indigenous industry.

Foreign-owned manufacturing also had an impact on services employment in Ireland through its purchasing of services as inputs. O'Malley (1995, Table 5.3) estimated that, for every 100 jobs in foreign-owned manufacturing in 1983, there were about 40 people employed in the services sector in Ireland providing the services that foreign industry was purchasing as inputs. This number increased slightly to 41 in 1990 and 1991. This meant that about 5% of total services employees were engaged in providing services to foreign-owned manufacturing in 1991.

Those service job numbers related only to those employed directly in providing the service inputs purchased by foreign industry, but O'Malley (1995) also presented estimates of further categories of services employment associated with foreign-owned industry. These included: employment in services purchased as inputs by the service companies supplying the foreign manufacturers; employment in services induced by the spending of employees of the foreign manufacturers; further employment in services induced by the spending of all the service employees already mentioned; and employment in services supported by the re-spending of taxes paid by foreign manufacturers, their employees and all the service employees already mentioned.

The total employment in all such categories of services employment that was arguably supported by foreign-owned manufacturing amounted to about 93 jobs per 100 directly employed in foreign manufacturing in 1983 rising slightly to 95 in 1990 and 94 in 1991. Or to put it another way, this amount of services employment was equivalent to about 12% of total employment in the services sector in 1991.

This type of analysis was not replicated for other years late in the boom. However, the data that are available do not suggest that there were strong trends in the development of purchasing linkages during the boom. Expenditure by foreign-owned manufacturing on Irish materials was worth 11.4% of total sales of foreign-owned manufacturing in 1990, and this declined to 7.6% in 2000 and 3.7% in 2007. Similarly, its expenditure on Irish services declined from 12.2% of the value of its sales in 1990 to 5.6% in 2000 and 4.8% in 2007.[18]

Furthermore, foreign-owned manufacturing bought 21.1% of its material inputs in Ireland in 2000, declining to 10.9% in 2007. It also purchased 34% of its services inputs in Ireland in 2000, declining to 20% in 2007.

These declining trends are not quite as weak as they look, because they would be at least partly an effect of changing sectoral composition within foreign-owned industry, as sectors with the lowest linkages grew relatively fast. Nevertheless, the figures mentioned above would not be consistent with strong growth of linkages.

Comparable data on foreign-owned internationally traded services show somewhat similar trends in the period 2000–2007. Expenditure by foreign-owned internationally traded services on Irish materials was worth 5.8% of its sales in 2000, and this declined to 1.4% in 2007. Similarly, its expenditure on Irish services declined from 28.2% of the value of its sales in 2000 to 14.3% in 2007.[19]

Furthermore, foreign-owned internationally traded services bought 24.5% of its material inputs in Ireland in 2000, declining to 9.5% in 2007. It also purchased 67.9% of its services inputs in Ireland in 2000, declining to 37.1% in 2007.

Of course, these data do not provide quantitative estimates of the impact on the indigenous economy or employment. Nevertheless, it

[18] The sources of the data mentioned here and in the next few paragraphs are O'Malley (1995, Table 5.4) for 1990 figures, and Forfas, *Annual Business Survey of Economic Impact 2008: Appendix*, for 2000 and 2007 figures.

[19] The data mentioned here again come from Forfas, *Annual Business Survey of Economic Impact 2008: Appendix*, for 2000 and 2007 figures. "Internationally traded services" in this context refers to those selected service activities that were eligible for industrial policy supports and tax concessions—such as software and other computer-related services, R&D, engineering and architectural services and selected financial services.

seems reasonable to conclude that there was little sign of strong trends in the development of purchasing linkages during the boom.

Effects on Indigenous Technology and Productivity

It has been found that foreign-owned MNCs could have an influence on their indigenous suppliers' propensity to innovate. Jacobson and Mottiar (1999) presented a case study of the software manual printing industry in Dublin which found that a highly specialised software manual printing sector

> ...came into existence entirely because of the establishment in Ireland of the software MNEs. The production processes, quality control and delivery times have all been determined by the buyer firms. To be a supplier in this industry, high-quality product on the basis of just-in-time delivery was a prerequisite. (Jacobson and Mottiar 1999)

In this case, however, the manual printing firms were eventually left vulnerable when their specialist product became obsolete.

In a study covering all manufacturing sectors, Hewitt-Dundas et al. (2002) found that foreign-owned MNCs in Ireland were a potentially important channel through which world-class knowledge could be transferred to supplier businesses, because the MNCs were more advanced in terms of the use of a range of best-practice management and control systems.

Hewitt-Dundas et al. (2002) also examined the nature and intensity of interactions between MNC customers and their local suppliers that might provide the basis for knowledge transfer. They found that developmental interactions between MNC plants and their suppliers were common. For example, 79% of MNC plants had collaborated with local suppliers on product development, while 58% of MNC plants had assisted local suppliers with quality assurance systems. Most MNC plants also reported that they had enhanced the performance and competitiveness of their local suppliers in various ways, including enhancing their sales, productivity, product quality and service quality.[20]

Ruane and Ugur (2005) aimed to examine whether productivity spillovers from foreign-owned MNCs had increased the productivity of

[20] The foregoing paragraphs draw from O'Malley et al. (2008).

indigenous firms. For this purpose, they used regression analysis on plant-level data for all manufacturing to examine whether productivity in indigenous firms was influenced by the scale of the foreign MNC presence in their own sectors. They found only weak evidence of such an influence.

There appear to be some valid reasons why this result from Ruane and Ugur (2005) could be consistent with the findings of Hewitt-Dundas et al. (2002). For example, perhaps many of the indigenous suppliers to MNCs (e.g., suppliers of packaging, plastic components or metal components) were not in the same sectors as their MNC customers (such as pharmaceuticals, computers or medical equipment), so that the benefits of interactions between them did not show up within individual sectors. Or perhaps the MNCs increased the productivity of the suppliers, but those suppliers did not amount to a sufficiently large proportion of their sector to have a substantial effect on the sector's productivity.

Gorg and Strobl (2003) postulated that foreign-owned MNCs could have positive effects on the life-span or survival rate of indigenous firms through technology spillovers. They found that the scale of the foreign MNC presence in a sector in Ireland had a life-enhancing effect on indigenous firms in the same sector, but only in the high-tech sectors. They did not find such an effect in the low-tech sectors. It seems again that the suggestions made in the paragraph above concerning Ruane and Ugur's findings could also apply to the low-tech sectors in Gorg and Strobl's study.

Development of Clusters or Groups of Related Industries

Much of the discussion about industrial policy in Ireland during the boom years in the 1990s was concerned with the proposition that a successful industrial performance required the development of competitive advantage in clusters of interlinked industries or sectors. This discussion reflected the work of international researchers, particularly Porter (1990). It also influenced the "Culliton report", which recommended that Irish policy should aim to develop groups or clusters of related industries (Industrial Policy Review Group 1992, pp. 73–74).

To examine this issue, the National Economic and Social Council (NESC) commissioned studies of three relatively successful Irish indigenous sectors—the dairy processing industry, the popular music industry and the indigenous software industry. The aim was to consider whether the presence of clusters of related or connected industries had been important in accounting for their degree of success, and how relevant was Porter's model in the Irish context. Reports on these three case studies were later published by NESC (O'Connell et al. 1997; Clancy and Twomey 1997; O'Gorman et al. 1997), and Clancy et al. (2001) drew together and integrated the principal findings.

They found that indigenous companies in the three industries were not participants in fully developed clusters of the same type and scale described by Porter. However, the three industries did benefit to some extent from being part of some form of wider grouping of connected or related companies and industries in Ireland, and from interactions between them. Their most relevant finding for our purpose here was that foreign-owned MNCs had sometimes played a significant role in fostering competitiveness in the selected indigenous sectors:

> For substantial parts of the three industries, the important links with related, supporting or customer industries are with foreign-owned MNEs in Ireland, rather than with Irish indigenous companies. These foreign-owned MNEs can have an important and positive influence on indigenous industry. (Clancy et al. 2001)

For example, many of the companies in the indigenous software industry were often selling to relatively successful and sophisticated companies in Ireland in sectors such as pharmaceuticals, chemicals, drinks, dairy products and financial services. In many cases, the customers concerned were foreign-owned MNCs. Irish software companies often found that their interactions with such local customers were beneficial for the development of their business and helped to prepare them for export success.

In addition, there were a number of industries in Ireland that were somewhat related to the indigenous software industry and had a helpful influence of some importance. One significant type was industries that helped to develop and improve the pool of labour skills which the indigenous software industry could draw on, such as the foreign-owned software, computer hardware and telecommunications equipment industries. Such industries constituted a relatively large concentration of information technology activities in a small economy. Another type of related industry was those in which indigenous software entrepreneurs had previously worked and gained relevant experience. These naturally included other indigenous software companies, as well as other indigenous and foreign-owned companies in information technology activities.

In the case of the Irish dairy processing industry, nearly all the companies interviewed agreed that they had learned from the standards and systems employed by their foreign-owned MNC customers in Ireland—an experience that helped them in international markets.

Jordan and O'Leary (2005) presented findings from a survey of companies—both indigenous and foreign-owned—in three high-tech sectors in Ireland. The companies surveyed were mostly engaged in manufacturing, with some service activities also included. They found that large majorities of the companies in all three sectors had regular to continuous interaction with other group companies, customers and suppliers for the purpose of product or process innovation. They also found that there was a clear tendency for the relevant group companies, customers and suppliers to be located more than one hour and usually more than four hours driving time from the high-tech businesses concerned. They concluded that this implied that such interaction did not occur locally or regionally within Ireland and may have been international. They also noted that the results "suggest the absence of strong interaction for the purpose of promoting innovation" between the high-tech businesses and locally or regionally based concentrations of suppliers, customers, etc.

While Jordan and O'Leary (2005) clearly had a valid point in highlighting the long-distance nature of most of the interactions, this did not mean that there was no such interaction locally or regionally. Their Tables 4 and 6 showed that quite substantial minorities of the companies in the high-tech sectors, especially the indigenous companies, had important local or regional interactions for the purpose of innovation. This could well be consistent with indigenous companies getting some significant benefit from interaction with local branches of foreign MNCs, as reported for a different set of sectors by Clancy et al. (2001).

Taken together, the results reported by Clancy et al. (2001) and Jordan and O'Leary (2005) indicate that there were few if any fully developed industry "clusters" in Ireland of the sort that Porter (1990) had found to be the norm among successful industries in advanced industrial economies. Such clusters would be characterised by continuous beneficial interaction occurring primarily between locally concentrated groups of suppliers, customers and other related industries, as well as supporting institutions and agencies.

At the same time, however, there was a more limited amount of beneficial interaction occurring in Ireland between less extensive groups of companies or industries, in which foreign-owned MNCs sometimes played a significant role in fostering competitiveness among indigenous companies.

Conclusion

To conclude this discussion on the secondary effects of FDI on the Irish economy, the effects concerned were quite uneven and varied. One of them stands out as being strongly positive. The contribution of foreign-owned companies to Ireland's balance of payments was probably the most important impact that FDI had on the economy. The rapid growth of the economy during much of the boom depended heavily on that contribution from foreign-owned companies.

Another positive finding was the scarcity of potentially adverse effects of FDI, which have been known to occur in other countries.

The other secondary effects of FDI were more mixed and less clear-cut. Purchasing linkages were beneficial for some indigenous companies but they did not develop as strongly as might have been expected. There was also evidence of a certain amount of beneficial interaction between foreign-owned and indigenous companies, such as the transfer of technology and management expertise, and the development of labour skills. However the overall effect of this remained somewhat limited.

6.5 Conclusion

To conclude this chapter, foreign-owned companies were already prominent in the Irish economy long before the boom, but their contribution to the country's growth had weakened during the 1980s compared to the 1960s and 1970s. Foreign-owned manufacturing then grew very rapidly during the boom until about 2000, as its share of Ireland's manufacturing employment, output and exports all increased. During that period, the growth of exports from foreign-owned manufacturing was the main driver of the growth of total exports from Ireland. Within that trend, it was the high-tech and medium–high-tech sectors that were largely responsible for the growth of foreign-owned manufacturing exports.

Net foreign earnings were a relatively low proportion of the value of exports in foreign-owned manufacturing, particularly in the more high-tech sectors. Consequently, its contribution to the economy and to growth was certainly important, but it was not as dominant as it appeared to be when seen in terms of exports.

After 2000, the trend in exports of foreign-owned manufacturing weakened a good deal, while the contribution of exports from foreign-owned services increased very rapidly. Net foreign earnings amounted to a relatively high proportion of the value of exports in foreign-owned services compared to foreign-owned manufacturing, so that the rapid growth of such services was important for the growth of the economy.

When foreign-owned manufacturing and services are combined, their share of total net foreign earnings increased from about 56% in 1985 to 73% in 2000 and then declined a little to 70% in 2007. By that criterion, foreign companies made a major contribution to economic growth over the full period of the boom. However, the indigenous contribution to the boom was relatively important in the late 1980s and again in the 2000s, whereas the foreign-owned contribution was very dominant in the 1990s.

As regards the nature and characteristics of foreign-owned companies, their purchasing linkages and R&D intensity did not develop strongly during the boom. On the other hand, there probably were advances in the autonomy of decision-making, while there was firmer evidence of rising skill levels and more advanced activities in some of the most important sectors. Thus, the trends were quite uneven and mixed. The overall effect was probably to make the FDI sector more skilled, more embedded in the Irish economy because of greater reliance on skills, and more capable of sustaining higher pay levels. At the same time, such effects must have been significantly weaker than they would have been with higher levels of R&D intensity and purchasing linkages.

Since long before the boom, the motivation for FDI in Ireland had always lain in the areas of tax concessions, government grants, market access and labour. The precise nature of those attractions changed somewhat over time. The surge in FDI that occurred during the boom was not caused mainly by new developments in Ireland relating to tax concessions, grants or labour. Rather, the major new developments that initiated the surge occurred outside Ireland, particularly the introduction of the single European market programme and the rise of new fast-growing high-tech industries. At the same time, however, existing policies and other conditions in Ireland were exceptionally well suited to taking advantage of the new opportunities as they arose, and to adapting flexibly to secure disproportionately large inflows of FDI.

The contribution of foreign-owned companies to Ireland's balance of payments was probably the most important impact that FDI had on the economy. The rapid growth of the economy during much of the boom depended heavily on the growth of that contribution from foreign-owned companies.

More generally, there was also some evidence of a certain amount of other beneficial effects of foreign-owned companies on the indigenous economy, such as transfer of technology and management expertise, and development of labour skills, although purchasing linkages and R&D intensity were clearly less than had been hoped. The overall effect of this remained somewhat limited.

Reflecting on the state of the foreign-owned industry in Ireland in the late 1990s, O'Sullivan (2000) asked two questions that remained pertinent during the remainder of the boom:

> Are, then, foreign enterprises now embedded to a greater extent than before in the Irish economy? And, as a result, is the economic activity that they are currently generating in Ireland likely to provide the capability base on which the Irish economy can generate higher standards of living over a sustained period of time?

The findings discussed in this chapter suggest that the answer to the first question was yes, but only to a limited degree. Consequently, the second question remained open, without a clear answer.

References

Allied Irish Bank. 1981. *Report on Attitudes of Overseas Companies Towards Investment in Ireland*. Dublin: Allied Irish Bank.

Barry, Frank. 1996. Peripherality in Economic Geography and Modern Growth Theory: Evidence from Ireland's Adjustment to Free Trade. *World Economy* 19 (3): 345–365.

Barry, Frank. 2005, Winter. Future Irish Growth: Opportunities, Catalysts, Constraints. In *Quarterly Economic Commentary*, ed. Alan Barrett, Ide Kearney, Shane Garrett, and Yvonne McCarthy. Dublin: Economic and Social Research Institute.

Barry, Frank, and John Bradley. 1997. FDI and Trade: The Irish Host-Country Experience. *Economic Journal* 107 (445): 1798–1811.

Barry, Frank, and Chris Van Egeraat. 2008, Spring. The Decline of the Computer Hardware Sector: How Ireland Adjusted. In *Quarterly Economic Commentary*, ed. Alan Barrett, Ide Kearney, and Martin O'Brien. Dublin: Economic and Social Research Institute.

Barry, Frank, John Bradley, and Aoife Hannan. 1999a. The European Dimension: The Single Market and the Structural Funds. In *Understanding Ireland's Economic Growth*, ed. Frank Barry, 99–118. London: Macmillan; New York: St Martin's Press.

Barry, Frank, John Bradley, and Eoin O'Malley. 1999b. Indigenous and Foreign Industry: Characteristics and Performance. In *Understanding Ireland's Economic Growth*, ed. Frank Barry, 45–74. London: Macmillan; New York: St Martin's Press.

Best, Michael H., Paul Ryan, Satyasiba Das, Oner Tulum, and Majella Giblin. 2010. Capabilities and Competitiveness: A Methodological Approach for Understanding Irish Economic Transformation. The Lucerna Project Report, CISC, NUI Galway.

Clancy, Paula, and Mary Twomey. 1997. Clusters in Ireland—The Irish Popular Music Industry: An Application of Porter's Cluster Analysis. Research Series Paper No. 2, National Economic and Social Council, Dublin.

Clancy, Paula, Eoin O'Malley, Larry O'Connell, and Chris Van Egeraat. 2001. Industry Clusters in Ireland: An Application of Porter's Model of National Competitive Advantage to Three Sectors. *European Planning Studies* 9 (1): 7–28.

Crowley, Martin. 1996. *National Linkage Programme: Final Evaluation Report*. Dublin: Industry Evaluation Unit.

Donaldson, Loraine. 1965. *Development Planning in Ireland*. New York and London: Praeger.

Gorg, Holger, and Eric Strobl. 2003. Multinational Companies, Technology Spillovers and Plant Survival. *Scandinavian Journal of Economics* 105 (4): 581–595.

Grimes, Seamus. 2006. Ireland's Emergence as a Centre for Internationally Traded Services. *Regional Studies* 40 (9): 1041–1054.

Gunnigle, Patrick, and David Mcguire. 2001. Why Ireland? A Qualitative Review of the Factors Influencing the Location of US Multinationals in Ireland with Particular Reference to the Impact of Labour Issues. *Economic and Social Review* 32 (1): 43–67.

Hannigan, Kevin. 1998, Autumn. The Business Climate for Multinational Corporations in Ireland. Irish Banking Review.

Hannigan, Kevin. 2000. Ireland's Economic Performance: A View from the MNCs. *Irish Business and Administrative Research* 21 (1): 69–84.

Hewitt-Dundas, Nola, Bernadette Andreosso-O'Callaghan, Mike Crone, John Murray, and Stephen Roper. 2002. *Learning from the Best: Knowledge*

Transfers from Multinational Plants in Ireland—A North-South Comparison. Belfast: Northern Ireland Economic Research Centre.

Hohohan, Patrick, 2001. European and International Constraints on Irish Fiscal Policy. Budget Perspectives—Proceedings of a Conference Held on 9 October 2001, Economic and Social Research Institute, Dublin.

Industrial Policy. 1984. Government White Paper. Dublin: Stationery Office.

Industrial Policy Review Group. 1992. *A Time for Change: Industrial Policy for the 1990s.* Dublin: Stationery Office. (Also known as the Culliton report).

Jacobson, David, and Ziene Mottiar. 1999. Globalization and Modes of Interaction in Two Sub-Sectors in Ireland. *European Planning Studies* 7 (4): 429–444.

Jordan, Declan, and Eoin O'Leary. 2005, Summer. The Roles of Interaction and Proximity for Innovation by Irish High-Technology Businesses: Policy Implications. In *Quarterly Economic Commentary*, ed. Danny McCoy, David Duffy, Adele Bergin, Shane Garrett, and Yvonne McCarthy. Dublin: Economic and Social Research Institute.

Kearns, Allan, and Frances Ruane. 1999. The Tangible Contribution of R&D Spending Foreign-Owned Plants to a Host Region: A Plant Level Study of the Irish Manufacturing Sector (1980–1996). Trinity Economic Papers Series, Technical Paper No. 99/7, Dublin.

Mac Sharry, Ray, and Padraic White. 2000. *The Making of the Celtic Tiger: The Inside Story of Ireland's Boom Economy.* Cork and Dublin: Mercier Press.

O'Brien, Ronan. 1985. Technology and Industrial Development: The Irish Electronics Industry in an International Context. In *Perspectives on Irish Industry*, ed. J. Fitzpatrick and J. Kelly. Dublin: Irish Management Institute.

O'Connell, Larry, Chris Van Egeraat, and Pat Enright. 1997. *Clusters in Ireland—The Irish Dairy Processing Industry: An Application of Porter's Cluster Analysis.* Research Series Paper No. 1, National Economic and Social Council, Dublin.

O'Gorman, Colm, Eoin O'Malley, and John Mooney. 1997. *Clusters in Ireland—The Irish Indigenous Software Industry: An Application of Porter's Cluster Analysis.* Research Series Paper No. 3, National Economic and Social Council, Dublin.

O'Malley, Eoin. 1989. *Industry and Economic Development: The Challenge for the Latecomer.* Dublin: Gill and Macmillan.

O'Malley, Eoin. 1995. *An Analysis of Secondary Employment Associated with Manufacturing Industry.* General Research Series paper No. 167, Economic and Social Research Institute, Dublin.

O'Malley, Eoin, Nola Hewitt-Dundas, and Stephen Roper. 2008. High Growth and Innovation with Low R&D: Ireland. In *Small Country Innovation Systems: Globalization, Change and Policy in Asia and Europe*, ed. Charles Edquist and Leif Hommen, 156–193. Cheltenham: Edward Elgar.

Osborne-Kinch, Jenny, Dermot Coates, and Luke Nolan. 2017. The Aircraft Leasing Industry in Ireland: Cross Border Flows and Statistical Treatment. Central Bank of Ireland Quarterly Bulletin, Q1 January.

O'Sullivan, Mary. 2000. The Sustainability of Industrial Development in Ireland. *Regional Studies* 34 (3): 277–290.

Porter, Michael E. 1990. *The Competitive Advantage of Nations*. London: Macmillan.

Ruane, Frances, and Ali Ugur. 2005. Foreign Direct Investment and Productivity Spillovers in Irish Manufacturing Industry: Evidence from Plant Level Panel Data. *International Journal of the Economics of Business* 12 (1): 53–66.

Stewart, Jim, 2013, April 11. Effective Corporate Tax Rates in Ireland: Some Recent Evidence. Paper to Statistical and Social Inquiry Society of Ireland.

Survey of Grant-Aided Industry. 1967. Survey Team's Report to the Industrial Development Authority. Dublin: Stationery Office.

Telesis Consultancy Group. 1982. *A Review of Industrial Policy*. National Economic and Social Council Report No. 64. NESC, Dublin.

Van Egeraat, Chris, and Frank Barry. 2009. The Irish Pharmaceutical Industry Over the Boom Period and Beyond. *Irish Geography* 42 (1): 23–44.

Van Egeraat, Chris, and David Jacobson. 2004. The Rise and Demise of the Irish and Scottish Computer Hardware Industry. *European Planning Studies* 12 (6): 809–834.

Open Access This chapter is licensed under the terms of the Creative Commons Attribution 4.0 International License (http://creativecommons.org/licenses/by/4.0/), which permits use, sharing, adaptation, distribution and reproduction in any medium or format, as long as you give appropriate credit to the original author(s) and the source, provide a link to the Creative Commons license and indicate if changes were made.

The images or other third party material in this chapter are included in the chapter's Creative Commons license, unless indicated otherwise in a credit line to the material. If material is not included in the chapter's Creative Commons license and your intended use is not permitted by statutory regulation or exceeds the permitted use, you will need to obtain permission directly from the copyright holder.

CHAPTER 7

The End of the Boom

7.1 The End of the Boom

The boom came to an end in 2007. GNP, in constant prices, had grown at an average rate of 5.0% p.a. in 2002–2007, but it peaked in 2007 and then declined by 2.9% p.a. over the next four years. Similarly, total employment had grown by 3.6% p.a. in 2002–2007, but it peaked in 2007 and then declined by 3.9% p.a. over the next four years. Thus, the boom was followed by an exceptionally long and deep recession.

Some of the key trends in the economy in the period after 2000 were already discussed above in Chapter 4, towards the end of Sect. 4.2. It was noted there that export growth slowed down very markedly after 2000. This led to quite a common view which held that the sustainable export-led boom that had been occurring in Ireland up to about 2000 really came to an end at around that time because export growth became so much weaker, while economic growth became very dependent on unsustainable factors such as the speculative housing boom.

However, it was shown in Sect. 4.2 that the weakening of export growth after 2000 was not as serious for the economy as it appeared to be.

© The Author(s) 2024
E. O'Malley, *Ireland's Long Economic Boom*, Palgrave Studies in Economic History, https://doi.org/10.1007/978-3-031-53070-8_7

Most of the weakness in exports occurred in a sector where net foreign earnings were a relatively low proportion of the value of exports so the dramatic decline in its exports had only a limited negative impact on the overall trend in net foreign earnings. Meanwhile, there was strong growth in exports of services, including indigenous services, where net foreign earnings were a relatively high proportion of the value of exports, so that the strong growth of these exports had a disproportionately large positive impact on the overall trend in net foreign earnings. The net result was that the sharp decline in the growth rate of the current value of exports, from 14.0% p.a. in 1985–2000 to 5.6% p.a. in 2000–2005, left the growth rate of the current value of net foreign earnings virtually unchanged, at 9.9% p.a. in 1985–2000 and 9.6% p.a. in 2000–2005.

Therefore, the sustainability of the boom was not undermined by the weakening in export trends, at least until about 2005. The growth rate of net foreign earnings, at 9.6% p.a. in 2000–2005, was sufficient to sustain the prevailing growth rate of GNP in that period, at 9.0% p.a. in current prices (Table 4.9). Balance of payments data confirm that view, since the balance of payments current account deficits were small in 2001–2004, being in a range between 0% and 1.2% of GNP and averaging 0.7% of GNP, even though the economy was growing a good deal faster than exports.

However, the final few years of the boom were different. In 2005–2007 the growth of our estimated net foreign earnings slowed right down, to 3.8% p.a. in current values, which was not sufficient to sustain GNP growth which continued at a high rate of 8.1% p.a. in current values. This was reflected in a rise in the current balance of payments deficit from 0.7% of GNP in 2004 to 4.1% in 2005 and 2006 and 6.2% in 2007. This means that, in those years, the economy was growing at an unsustainable rate, which was made feasible only because there was a large inflow of finance from abroad associated with the housing boom that was occurring at the time.

This deceleration in the growth of net foreign earnings in 2005–2007 was primarily a result of a virtual cessation of growth among foreign-owned firms, while the growth trend was much stronger among Irish indigenous companies. The current value of the net foreign earnings of foreign-owned firms increased by an estimated 0.2% p.a. in 2005–2007, while the corresponding figure for indigenous firms was 13.9% p.a. Within the foreign-owned category, the weakness was in manufacturing whereas foreign-owned services carried on growing at about the same rate as Irish indigenous companies.

In foreign-owned manufacturing, the weak trend in the current value of net foreign earnings was caused by a combination of slow growth in the value of exports and a significant reduction in the proportion of the value of exports that was retained in the Irish economy as net foreign earnings. The value of foreign-owned manufacturing exports grew by just 3.8% p.a. in 2005–2007, compared with 14 or 15% for the value of foreign services exports and all Irish indigenous exports. At the same time, the estimated value of net foreign earnings declined from 26% of the value of exports in foreign-owned manufacturing in 2005 to 18% in 2007—not because of a rise in profit outflows, but because the value of imported inputs increased substantially as a proportion of the value of sales.[1]

It is not entirely clear why these trends occurred, but it is probably relevant to note that the value of the US dollar declined by 10% against the euro in 2005–2007. The relevance of this is that many of the exports of foreign-owned manufacturing firms in Ireland would have been priced in US dollars so that the euro value of those exports would have been reduced by the changing exchange rate. Unless there was a similar reduction in the euro prices of the imported inputs purchased by those firms, the value of those inputs would have increased as a proportion of the value of their sales.

It is also possible that the weak trend in net foreign earnings was partly an effect of changing pricing or accounting practices in the MNCs concerned. In addition, the weak growth in exports from foreign-owned manufacturing companies in 2005–2007 could be seen as part of a longer term slowing of growth from them after their earlier surge of exceptionally rapid growth. Whatever the cause of the weakness in their net foreign earnings in 2005–2007, it seems to have been specific to foreign-owned MNCs since Irish indigenous companies were not affected.

If there had not been an extraordinary housing boom going on at the time, with its associated financial inflows, the slowdown in the foreign-owned sector would probably have brought an end to the long boom

[1] These figures are based on our own estimates, derived as explained in Appendices in Chapters 4 and 5. However, the main trends discussed here can be found in the published data on which our estimates are based—in the *Census of Industrial Production* for data on manufacturing exports, and in Forfas, *Annual Business Survey of Economic Impact 2008 (Appendix, Tables C1 to C10)* for data on imported inputs.

in the economy in 2005. Such an end to the boom might have been relatively benign, resulting in nothing worse than a return to lower rates of economic growth. As it was, however, the housing boom and its associated financial inflows kept the boom in the economy going for another couple of years. When the housing boom eventually collapsed, with profound financial consequences, it brought a far more damaging end to the boom in the economy.

A Loss of Competitiveness?

It has often been stated that a significant weakness in the Irish economy in the period after 2000 was a loss of competitiveness. For example, the Department of Finance (2011a) said that the 2000s, until 2008, "saw a steady erosion of Ireland's competitive position with consumer prices, asset prices and wages all increasing at rates over and above our European peers". Similarly, the Department of Finance (2011b) said "from 2000 onwards, the economy began to lose competitiveness. This reflected a combination of factors: a higher nominal exchange rate, a loss of price competitiveness and a loss of cost competitiveness". Other organisations, including the Central Bank of Ireland, the European Central Bank and IBEC (Irish Business and Employers Confederation), expressed similar views at around that time (see O'Malley 2013).

In such views, a country's competitiveness is considered to be determined by trends, relative to other countries, in national indicators of costs, costs per unit and prices. Consequently, a rise in Ireland's costs and prices relative to competing countries is regarded as being in effect the same thing as a loss of competitiveness.

However, competitiveness means the ability of an economy to compete effectively in international markets. Prices and costs such as labour costs may have some influence on the ability to compete but there are also other factors that would have an influence on that ability. Relevant factors include characteristics of the companies in a country such as technology, innovation capabilities, marketing, product quality, customer service, etc. They also include characteristics of the economic and social environment such as education, infrastructure, business services, technical services, financial services, public services, etc. They also include the composition of industries in a country's economy, which would often be changing over time, typically tending to shift away from sectors and products that are particularly price-sensitive and cost-sensitive and moving more towards other sectors and products which are less affected by prices and costs.

It has been commonly recognised that competitiveness is influenced by such a wide range of factors. For example, the Swiss-based World Economic Forum has for many years been publishing an annual Global Competitiveness Report which refers to a very wide range of indicators in assessing countries' competitiveness. In Ireland, the National Competitiveness Council, and the National Competitiveness and Productivity Council, have had a long-standing practice of publishing a listing or "scorecard" that includes many different indicators that are considered to be relevant to competitiveness (see, for example, National Competitiveness Council 2011).

For these reasons, costs and prices, on their own, have important limitations as indicators of competitiveness. They are no more than partial and indirect indicators of competitiveness. They are partial indicators in the sense that they refer to only part of a wider range of influences on competitiveness. And they are indirect indicators in the sense that they measure some factors that may have an influence on competitiveness—not the actual record or performance of a country in competing internationally.

If we look directly at Ireland's performance in competing in international markets, there was not a general loss of competitiveness in the period from 2000 to the end of the boom since Irish exports' share of all countries' exports of industrial products and services combined did not decline significantly over that period. Ireland's share started at 1.37% in 2000 and then increased somewhat to 1.65% in 2002 and 1.63% in 2003, before decreasing a little to 1.49% in 2007, which was still above the level in 2000. Similarly, Irish exports' share of EU countries' exports of industrial products and services combined was 3.18% in 2000 and a little higher at 3.29% in 2007. Within those trends, there was a loss in export market share for industrial products, but this was more than offset by a rise in market share for services (O'Malley 2013).

As was noted above, Ireland's exports grew at a slower rate in the period after 2000 compared to the very fast growth in the years before then. The corresponding trend in terms of export market shares was that a very rapid increase in export market shares during the 1990s (O'Malley 2004) came to an end during 2000–2007. However, this change did not amount to a significant decline in market share since Ireland's market share remained a little higher in 2007 than in 2000. Furthermore, as already noted above, the decline in the growth rate of exports left the growth rate of net foreign earnings virtually unchanged because of the changing composition of exports. Consequently, the sustainability of the boom was not undermined by the weakening in export trends, at least until about 2005.

The Housing Boom

For the reasons discussed above, the boom in the economy continued to be sustainable until about 2005, but the boom would probably have ended in 2005 if there had not been an extraordinary boom going on at the time in building & construction, especially in house building.

The first signs of a housing boom began to emerge in the late 1990s when house building activity and house prices began to rise unusually fast. Home completions, which were generally no higher than 35,000 per year in 1975–1995, began to rise above that level in 1997 and carried on rising to 93,000 by 2006 (Honohan 2010; Whelan 2014). Investment in housing increased from no more than 6% of GNP in 1980–1996 to around 14% of GNP in 2006 (FitzGerald 2012). Employment in construction followed a similar trend. It had usually been in a range between 6 and 8% of total employment from the early 1980s until 1996, but it then increased to 13% by 2007 (Honohan 2010; Whelan 2014).

At the same time, house prices, which had generally increased at about the same rate as the consumer price index in 1976–1996, began a surge in 1997 which brought them by 2007 to a level more than three times higher than the level expected if they had remained in line with the consumer price index (Honohan 2010).

This housing boom was facilitated by Ireland's entry to European Monetary Union (EMU), because EMU precipitated a sharp decline in interest rates in Ireland while also giving Irish banks access to much larger eurozone capital markets. The fall in interest rates began from the start of EMU. In late 1998, Irish nominal interest rates began to fall towards German levels, and Irish real interest rates began to fall from about 3% before EMU to negative levels until the end of the boom (Honohan 2010).

A massive increase in borrowing from eurozone capital markets by Irish resident banks began about five or six years later, in 2004. Until the end of 2003, domestic savings in Ireland had been sufficient to fund the housing boom, but banks in Ireland then borrowed increasing amounts abroad and lent these funds to the Irish property sector. Net indebtedness of Irish banks to the rest of the world rose from just 10% of GDP at the end of 2003 to more than 60% of GDP by early 2008. Since most of the growth in bank lending was for the property sector, 60% of bank assets were in property-related lending by 2006 (Honohan 2010; Kearney 2012).

In the early years of this housing market boom, there was nothing very surprising about it. Because of the boom in the economy, employment and incomes were rising fast, so there was a growing number of people who were able and willing to pay more for more housing. Consequently, it was to be expected that this rising demand for housing would generate substantial rises in output and prices in the housing industry. In addition, Ireland had a relatively small housing stock at the start of the housing boom since it was estimated that Ireland had the smallest housing stock per head in the EU (Whelan 2014). Consequently, a period of accelerated house building would have been needed just to increase the stock of housing towards average EU levels.

There is also reason to believe that house prices were somewhat undervalued in Ireland before the housing boom began. McQuinn and O'Reilly (2008) found that there was generally a reasonably consistent relationship between disposable income levels and interest rates on the one hand and house prices on the other hand, during the period 1980–2005. However, relative to the prices predicted by this relationship, house prices looked under-valued in the years 1993–1997. Consequently, a period of above-average price increases would have been needed to return to the expected price level.

However, although the increases in house building and house prices may not have been excessive at first, it is evident that these trends did become excessive later. The amount of new housing being built in the later stages of the housing boom was running well ahead of effective demand from the population for living accommodation, so that 15% of the housing stock was vacant by 2006, with only 3% being holiday homes (Honohan 2010).

As regards house price trends becoming excessive, Honohan (2010) remarked that, long before it peaked, the rise in prices looked unsustainable to most commentators. McQuinn and O'Reilly (2008) found that, from 2003 onwards, house prices rose faster than would have been expected according to their formerly predictable relationship with incomes and interest rates. Since many would argue that the interest rates that applied across the eurozone were too low for the booming Irish economy, this implies that house prices were already excessive before

2003. Kelly (2007) argued that, by 2007, house prices in Ireland had risen so much that they could fall by 40–60% over a number of years. This was based on trends seen in 40 other housing booms in OECD countries since 1970.

In the final years of the Irish housing boom, the housing market was showing signs of a classic bubble. House building was exceeding real requirements and house prices looked unreasonably high and were still rising. This process developed its own momentum as market participants came to expect that there would be continuing growth in demand and continuing increases in prices. Based on such expectations, builders continued to build, banks continued to lend and house purchasers continued to buy—some because they wanted to buy a home as soon as possible before prices rose even higher, while a growing number of other purchasers were buying houses as an investment which they believed would yield a good return.

However, such processes cannot continue indefinitely. House prices and house building peaked in 2007, and both went into prolonged decline. As house prices fell, prospective home buyers had an incentive to wait until prices fell further, which weakened demand and reinforced the downward trend in prices and building. As the market declined, construction employment dropped from over 13% of total employment in 2007 to 6% by 2009 and then continued to fall to less than 5% by 2012 (Whelan 2014). The sudden loss of such a substantial part of economic activity had a depressing effect on other sectors and brought on a recession in the whole economy.

As the housing market collapsed, the banks began to face significant difficulties since they were heavily exposed to that market, through lending to house buyers, builders, and property developers. Foreign banks, whom Irish banks had become reliant on as sources of funding, became increasingly concerned. Consequently, the Irish banks found that they could no longer raise funds on bond markets. In September 2008, the senior management of the major banks had to turn to the government for help.

The government responded by providing a guarantee for the liabilities of the Irish domestic banks for two years. This meant that any default on those bank liabilities would be covered by the Irish government. It has often been argued that the government should not have provided such a broad blanket guarantee as it was unnecessarily risky. But it seems that the government believed at the time that the banks were essentially sound and only had a short-term liquidity problem rather than an insolvency problem, as advised by the Central Bank (Whelan 2014).[2]

Over the following two years, the government became embroiled in an overwhelming financial crisis, for several reasons. In the first place, the government's financial situation was negatively affected by the recession occurring in Ireland, which meant that there was a loss of income-related tax revenue and an increase in social welfare expenditure, as would happen in any recession. This was greatly exacerbated by the fact that property-related taxes (stamp duties, capital gains tax and capital acquisition tax) had become a significant component of total tax revenue during the housing boom. When the housing market collapsed, these taxes declined sharply, from 12.5% of total tax revenue to less than 4% (Whelan 2014).

On top of those difficulties, it emerged that the banks were in a far weaker state than the government had believed, so the government became involved in extremely expensive measures to rescue the banks, to the extent that serious doubts arose about the creditworthiness of the Irish state.

Meanwhile the international context was making the crisis in Ireland even more difficult. An international recession began in 2008 and this included a major financial crisis with bank failures and bank bailouts occurring in a range of countries. This international background added greatly to Ireland's own crisis, which had originated domestically (Honohan 2010).

The combination of these factors undermined the state's creditworthiness so that, by late 2010, the government was forced to seek assistance from the EU and the IMF (Whelan 2014; Kearney 2012).

It is beyond the scope of this book to go any further into the details of the recession and the financial crisis since the focus of this book is on the boom period that ended in 2007. However, it is appropriate to consider here two questions that are relevant to the period before 2007. What measures could have been taken in the years before 2007 to prevent this crisis from arising? Why was action not taken in good time to prevent a crisis?

As regards the measures that could have been taken, it should be recognised that the policy environment was substantially affected by eurozone

[2] Consultants Price Waterhouse Coopers (PWC) were hired to undertake a detailed examination of the banks' loan books, and they reported to the government in the following year, 2009, that the banks did not have insolvency problems.

membership. If Ireland had not been in the eurozone, the Central Bank could have raised interest rates to dampen the housing boom and to reduce inflationary pressures. Also, the commercial banks would not have been able to undertake such heavy foreign borrowing as they did in the last few years of the boom, which would have limited their ability to carry on increasing lending to the property sector (Barry 2016/2017).

However, although Ireland was not free to make its own decisions on interest rates, there were other options that could have been employed instead. Whelan (2014) notes that the authorities had the power to place limits on mortgage lending, such as limiting multiples of income or requiring large down-payments, or they could have restricted the exposure of individual financial institutions to property development. FitzGerald (2012) points out that a general tightening of fiscal policy could have been applied by the government, while a more targeted tax on mortgage interest payments could have had the same effect for households as a rise in interest rates.

Rather than adopting such measures, government policy tended to encourage the property boom. Most of the budgets in the period 2001–2007 increased spending power rather than reducing it, while there was a range of tax-based incentives that encouraged investment in property (FitzGerald 2012; Whelan 2014).

This brings us to the second question—why was effective action not taken to prevent the crisis from emerging? The main reason appears to be simply because it was not sufficiently recognised and accepted that the housing boom was potentially dangerous and could lead to serious consequences. Some people did recognise that there were real dangers of course, and warnings were given, but their view did not become the prevailing view.

To be more specific, it is useful to distinguish between the risk of a recession in the housing market on the one hand and the risk of collapse of the banks on the other hand. There seems to have been very little recognition before 2007 that the banks were at risk of failure, whereas warnings about the housing market were somewhat more common.[3]

For examples on the housing market, Casey (2018) presented a very thorough analysis of a wide range of commentary on the Irish economy

[3] This is partly a matter of degree, since it would have required a major crash in the housing market to bring the banks down, whereas the banks could have survived a less serious downturn in housing.

during the period of the property boom, and he identified a number of economists and journalists who gave warnings about the trends in property and construction. However, warnings about the threat to the banks were scarcer. Lunn (2013) reports that, despite following up on many suggestions, he had not encountered any paper or article prior to Kelly (2007) that contained a warning that came close to reflecting the scale of what was ultimately to occur (i.e., including the banking collapse).[4]

Even on the issue of the housing market, despite the efforts of those who warned about the risks, there was not a general acceptance that the situation was becoming very risky. A wide range of relevant actors showed by their actions or words that they did not believe that the housing boom could have severe consequences. House buyers, builders and property developers presumably did not perceive major risks, while the Irish commercial banks were sufficiently confident to carry on lending. The government and the Central Bank were not sufficiently concerned to intervene significantly. In addition to these Irish-based parties, there were also participants from other countries who failed to recognise the dangers. These included the foreign banks who had enough confidence to lend very large amounts to the Irish banks who were funding the housing boom. There were also foreign investors who willingly held shares in Irish banks as well as building and property companies. In addition, foreign-owned banks were very active directly in expanding their property-related lending in Ireland during the boom, and Honohan (2010) notes that several of them recorded heavy loan losses.[5]

Three international organisations were making regular assessments of the Irish economy, and two of them were at least partial exceptions to the picture of considerable confidence in the Irish housing market. Casey (2014) studied the relevant publications from these organisations in the years before the crash, and he found that the European Commission published little of relevance to the issue, but the International Monetary Fund (IMF) and the Organisation for Economic Cooperation and

[4] As Lunn (2013) notes, the main arguments in Morgan Kelly's (2007) article were included in an *Irish Times* newspaper article by Kelly on 28 December 2006, before the fall in house prices began.

[5] Simon Kelly (2010, pp. 127–129) says that, in his experience as a property developer, Bank of Scotland (Ireland) was still lending very freely late in the boom, offering 100% of the funding required for projects, at a time when Anglo Irish Bank had become noticeably cautious and was reluctant to fund new clients or new deals (Anglo Irish Bank had previously led the charge in property lending).

Development (OECD) advised that trends in the Irish property boom were excessive and presented risks. However, the OECD felt that a soft landing would be the most likely outcome for Ireland. Casey (2014, 2018) considered that the analyses of the housing boom from the IMF and the OECD recognised that there were vulnerabilities, but they failed to predict how severe the consequences would be, including the near-total collapse of construction and the extent of the ramifications for employment, economic output, the banks and the government's finances.

Thus, the warnings from the IMF and the OECD were relatively mild compared to the actual dangers that were present, and they did not have a great impact on opinion in Ireland, which mostly continued to believe that there was no major cause for concern.

So, what can explain the continuing confidence of participants in the housing boom? In the literature on the Irish housing boom and its consequences, one finds words such as "mania", "frenzy" and "collective madness" to describe the behaviour of participants in the boom. Such terms are expressive, but they are not particularly helpful for understanding what happened. This point is underlined by the fact that the Irish housing boom and slump was not a unique occurrence involving uniquely bizarre or aberrant behaviour. Rather, it was one example of many booms and slumps in housing markets that have occurred in many countries. As was mentioned above, Kelly (2007) was able to refer to what happened in 40 other housing booms in OECD countries since 1970 when he was trying to foresee the consequences of the Irish housing boom. Granted, the consequences of the Irish case were exceptionally severe compared with most such booms (Ó Riain 2014). However, this can be explained in terms of the circumstances surrounding the Irish housing boom while the behaviour involved in the boom itself was not very different to other booms. (We will return below to the question of why the consequences of the Irish boom were so severe.)

From the perspective of behavioural economics, Lunn (2013) argues that it is well established that there are some biases that are common when making judgements or decisions and that seven of these biases were instrumental in the development and severity of the crisis in Ireland.[6] As an explanation for the behaviour of those involved, this looks more

[6] The term "bias" here does not imply irrationality or low standards. Rather, it refers to common tendencies or inclinations in the way that people often think when making judgements or decisions.

satisfactory than explanations in terms of a mania or frenzy. The seven biases included:

> Extrapolation bias (placing most weight on the most recent events when predicting future outcomes based on the past).
> Confirmation bias (the tendency to look for and to pay the most attention to information consistent with one's existing beliefs).
> Overconfidence bias (a tendency to be too optimistic regarding one's own abilities and one's own predictions).
> Behavioural convergence (the tendency to copy other people's behaviour and decisions, or to conform to majority views; also known as bandwagon effects, groupthink, information cascades).
> Time inconsistency (inconsistency in individual preferences over time, such that more immediate rewards are felt to be disproportionately attractive).

For example, in the housing market context, extrapolation bias would mean that the expectations of market participants about prices and demand would tend to be heavily influenced by trends in the recent past. Overconfidence bias would mean that market participants tend to have too much confidence in their ability to foresee market trends accurately. Confirmation bias means that market participants would tend to pay attention to evidence that confirms their judgements about the market while ignoring or dismissing evidence that could challenge their views. Behavioural convergence would have the effect of amplifying market trends, in both rising markets and falling markets, as market participants are drawn to join the prevailing trend. And so on. Such biases could affect decision-making by regulators and government as well as the decisions of active housing market participants.

Lunn (2013) argues that there is strong international research evidence showing that these biases are real and can be influential in decision-making situations. He also argues that there is evidence that is consistent with a role for the seven biases in Ireland's crisis.

As regards the question of why the consequences of the Irish housing boom were more severe than in most other housing booms, Lunn suggests that the seven biases may have been enhanced by the sheer length and extent of the boom in Ireland. For example, the length of the boom could have increased the extent of extrapolation bias and overconfidence bias, increased perceived competence in assessing property risk, and increased perceived opportunities for more immediate rewards.

To this we can add that the consequences of the housing boom in Ireland were made more severe by the timing of the end of that boom and the exceptionally unfavourable international context at that time. A major international recession and a financial crisis were the dominant features in the international economy in the years after Ireland's housing and economic booms came to an end. This had negative effects on overseas demand for Ireland's exports, on FDI, on emigration options for Irish jobseekers, and on the ability of Irish banks and ultimately the state to borrow funds abroad. In addition, it has been argued that membership of the eurozone made Ireland's financial crisis more severe and more difficult to resolve.[7]

Before concluding this section, it is worth clarifying what was the relationship between the boom in the Irish economy and the housing boom. The boom in the economy began long before the housing boom and it continued to be independently sustainable until about 2005. The housing boom began about a decade after the boom in the economy began, and it was initially generated by the rising employment and incomes that resulted from the economic boom. Trends in house building, house prices and property-related lending probably started to become excessive and unsustainable at some stage during the period 2001–2004. However, the housing boom was not an important factor driving overall economic growth at that time, because economic growth was still being driven by quite rapid growth in net foreign earnings while the housing boom was still being financed by Ireland's own domestic savings rather than by additional injections of funding sourced from abroad. When the growth of net foreign earnings eventually slowed down, that would probably have brought an end to the boom in the economy in 2005, were it not for the housing boom. By that time, the housing boom was being heavily financed by increasing amounts of funding borrowed by the banks from abroad, and it kept the boom in the economy going for another couple of years until 2007.

[7] Barry (2016/2017) and De Grauwe (2012) include discussions that are relevant to this issue.

The whole Celtic Tiger boom has sometimes been depicted as largely built on a debt-fuelled housing bubble, but such an interpretation is not grounded in reality.

7.2 Conclusion

The boom came to an end in 2007. Although it has often been pointed out that export growth slowed down very markedly as early as 2000, that trend was not particularly serious for the economy because the growth of net foreign earnings did not slow down, due to the changing sectoral composition of exports. Thus, the sustainability of the boom was not undermined by the weakening in export trends until about 2005. The growth of net foreign earnings then slowed down in 2005, which would probably have brought an end to the long boom in the economy at that time were it not for the housing boom. The housing boom and its associated financial inflows kept the boom in the economy going for another couple of years.

For about eighteen of its twenty years, the Celtic Tiger boom in the Irish economy was a sustainable export-led boom, and it was only in its last two years that it came to be largely powered by a debt-financed housing boom.

The housing boom turned into a classic bubble which ended in the collapse of the construction sector and ultimately the banks, with disastrous consequences for the economy. The Irish housing boom and slump was not a unique occurrence involving uniquely aberrant behaviour since it was one example of many booms and slumps in housing markets that have occurred in many countries. However, the Irish case undoubtedly had more severe consequences than most such booms, partly because the Irish housing boom lasted so long and partly because a major recession and financial crisis in the international economy exacerbated the consequences of the conclusion to Ireland's housing boom.

Since housing markets can be prone to damaging booms and slumps, probably because people are naturally prone to the biases and behaviour outlined in this chapter, it is essential to have tight and effective regulation of such markets and banks. It is also not wise to leave the provision of something as essential as housing to be delivered largely by markets.

References

Barry, Frank. 2016/2017. The Irish Single Currency Debate of the 1990s in Retrospect. *Journal of the Statistical and Social Inquiry Society of Ireland* XLVI: 71–96.

Casey, Ciaran Michael. 2014. Averting Crisis? Commentary from the International Institutions on the Irish Property Sector in the Years Before the Crash. *Economic and Social Review* 45 (4): 537–557.

Casey, Ciaran Michael. 2018. *Policy Failures and the Irish Economic Crisis*. Cham: Palgrave Macmillan.

DeGrauwe, Paul. 2012. A Fragile Eurozone in Search of a Better Governance. *The Economic and Social Review* 43 (1): 1–30.

Department of Finance. 2011a, April. Ireland—Stability Programme Update. fin ance.gov.ie.

Department of Finance. 2011b, June. The Irish Economy in Perspective. finance. gov.ie.

FitzGerald, John. 2012. The Irish Economy Today: Albatross or Phoenix? *The World Economy* 35 (10): 1239–1255.

Honohan, Patrick. 2010. The Irish Banking Crisis: Regulatory and Financial Stability Policy 2003–2008. A Report to the Minister for Finance by the Governor of the Central Bank.

Kearney, Ide. 2012. Economic Challenges. In *Does the European Social Model Have a Future?*, ed. Brigid Reynolds and Sean Healy. Dublin: Social Justice Ireland.

Kelly, Morgan. 2007. On the Likely Extent of Falls in Irish House Prices. In *Quarterly Economic Commentary, Summer*, ed. Alan Barrett, Ide Kearney, and Martin O'Brien. Dublin: Economic and Social Research Institute.

Kelly, Simon. 2010. *Breakfast with Anglo*. Dublin: Penguin.

Lunn, Peter D. 2013. The Role of Decision-Making Biases in Ireland's Banking Crisis. *Irish Political Studies* 28 (4): 563–590.

McQuinn, Kieran, and Gerard O'Reilly. 2008. Assessing the Role of Income and Interest Rates in Determining House Prices. *Economic Modelling* 25 (3): 377–390.

National Competitiveness Council. 2011. *Ireland's Competitiveness Scorecard 2011*. Dublin: Forfas.

O'Malley, Eoin. 2004, Winter. Competitive Performance in Irish Industry. In *Quarterly Economic Commentary*, ed. Daniel McCoy, David Duffy, Adele Bergin, Shane Garrett, and Yvonne McCarthy. Dublin: Economic and Social Research Institute.

O'Malley, Eoin. 2013. Ireland's Competitive Performance. In *The Nuts and Bolts of Innovation: New Perspectives on Irish Industrial Policy*, ed. David Jacobson. Dublin: Glasnevin Publishing.

Ó Riain, Seán. 2014. *The Rise and Fall of Ireland's Celtic Tiger: Liberalism, Boom and Bust*. Cambridge: Cambridge University Press.
Whelan, Karl. 2014. Ireland's Economic Crisis: The Good, the Bad and the Ugly. *Journal of Macroeconomics* 39: 424–440.

Open Access This chapter is licensed under the terms of the Creative Commons Attribution 4.0 International License (http://creativecommons.org/licenses/by/4.0/), which permits use, sharing, adaptation, distribution and reproduction in any medium or format, as long as you give appropriate credit to the original author(s) and the source, provide a link to the Creative Commons license and indicate if changes were made.

The images or other third party material in this chapter are included in the chapter's Creative Commons license, unless indicated otherwise in a credit line to the material. If material is not included in the chapter's Creative Commons license and your intended use is not permitted by statutory regulation or exceeds the permitted use, you will need to obtain permission directly from the copyright holder.

CHAPTER 8

Conclusion

The first part of this chapter draws together findings from earlier chapters to explain what caused the boom. The second part of the chapter then discusses some other conclusions from Ireland's experience in the boom.

8.1 Causes of the Boom

Chapter 3 outlined a wide range of possible explanations for the boom that were put forward in previous literature on this subject. In Sect. 3.2, some of those suggested explanations were assessed and it was concluded that they were not convincing or not very important and that it would not be necessary to consider them further. That left eight possible explanations that could have been important—namely, foreign direct investment, the single European market, education for fast-growing industries, the small/regional nature of the economy, Irish indigenous industry, strong demand growth in export markets, EU structural funds, and social partnership/wage moderation. This section presents a brief account of the causes of the boom, referring to each of those eight suggested explanations as well as some other factors that were found to be significant in earlier chapters of this book.

Foreign direct investment was a large part of the explanation for the boom. FDI was by no means new to Ireland since foreign-owned companies had already been prominent in the economy long before the boom, but their contribution to growth had weakened during the 1980s

© The Author(s) 2024

E. O'Malley, *Ireland's Long Economic Boom*, Palgrave Studies in Economic History, https://doi.org/10.1007/978-3-031-53070-8_8

compared to the 1960s and 1970s. Consequently, the strong acceleration in their growth during the boom gave a substantial new impetus to the growth of the economy. The share of foreign-owned companies in Ireland's employment, output and exports all increased during the boom years.

Until about the late 1990s, foreign-owned companies in the manufacturing sector were the main driver of that growth and, within that trend, it was the high-tech and medium–high-tech sectors that were largely responsible for the growth of foreign-owned manufacturing. From about the end of the 1990s, the trends in foreign-owned manufacturing weakened a good deal, but the contribution of foreign-owned services then rapidly became more prominent.

This book has stressed the importance of exports for growth in the small and very open Irish economy. More than that, what matters most is the growth of net foreign earnings, meaning the part of the value of exports that remains in the Irish economy after deducting the outflow of profits that arise from exports and the payments for imported inputs that are used in producing the exports.

Net foreign earnings were generally a much lower proportion of the value of exports in foreign-owned companies than in Irish indigenous companies. Nevertheless, the growth of exports from foreign-owned companies was so strong during much of the boom that the growth of their net foreign earnings made the principal contribution to the growth of the economy. The share of foreign-owned manufacturing and services in total net foreign earnings increased from about 56% in 1985 to 73% in 2000 and then declined a little to 70% in 2007. By that criterion, foreign companies made the major contribution to economic growth over the full period of the boom.

Within the period of the boom, however, the indigenous contribution to growth was relatively important in the late 1980s and again in the 2000s, whereas the foreign-owned contribution was far more important in the 1990s.

The single European market made a significant contribution to causing the boom, primarily because of its effect on FDI. As was discussed in Chapter 6, the motivation for FDI in Ireland had always lain in the areas of tax concessions, government grants, market access and labour. The surge in FDI that occurred during the boom was not mainly caused by new developments in Ireland relating to tax concessions or grants. Rather, the major new developments that initiated the surge occurred outside Ireland, particularly the introduction of the single European market programme and the rise of new fast-growing high-tech industries.

The single European market significantly improved Ireland's ease of access to the EU market because it aimed to remove non-tariff barriers to trade between all EU countries. It was generally expected that one effect of the single European market would be to attract more FDI into the EU from external sources, because of the increased attraction of producing and selling in such a large integrated market. In fact, there was quite a dramatic increase in flows of US FDI into the EU, and it was commonly concluded that improved market access within the single EU market was a major cause of that increase.

In addition, another major new trend in the international economy was increasing the supply of FDI from external sources that was potentially available for the EU and Ireland—namely the emergence and very rapid growth of new industries based on new technologies, particularly in the USA. Such industries included computers, telecommunications equipment and related hardware, as well as software. Later, the development of the internet led to further strong growth. In addition, there was also very rapid growth and development of some longer established high-tech industries, including pharmaceuticals and medical instruments & equipment.

The emergence and rapid growth of such high-tech industries, together with the single European market programme, ensured that there was going to be a substantial increase in the supply of FDI going to the EU. Ireland was already an attractive location for FDI, with a disproportionate share of FDI in the EU relative to its size. Consequently, Ireland was always likely to receive a sizeable share of the new incoming FDI, but in fact, its share of the inflow increased substantially. This increase was not because of significant new policy measures in Ireland, apart from the exceptional case of new tax concessions for financial services. Rather, it was mainly because existing practices in Ireland were very well suited to attracting the type of industries that predominated in the rising wave of FDI.

In particular, Ireland's concessions on corporation profit tax were most attractive for companies that were highly profitable, such as much of the new wave of fast-growing high-tech industries.

Education of technical graduates for such fast-growing industries, and especially the regular interaction between the third-level education system and the industrial policy system, was another aspect of existing practice in Ireland that was well suited to attracting FDI by new fast-growing high-tech companies. This regular interaction had the aim of adjusting the supply of technical graduates from the education system in response to the changing employment opportunities and requirements in growing industries.

This feature meant that, as the opportunities emerged to attract substantially more FDI in the high-tech sectors, the Irish education system was able to respond and adapt to the latest requirements of such industries more rapidly and flexibly than most other EU countries. In this way, the attraction of Ireland's labour supply for FDI could be enhanced relative to some other countries which adapted more slowly. Thus, it became noticeable during the boom that shortages of graduates with the relevant skills became more common in some other countries than in Ireland.

It was possible for FDI to have a major impact on the Irish economy because it is a small and very open economy, and like a regional economy in some respects. The amount of FDI that was available could not have had a comparable effect in a much larger country. In addition, the very open labour market in the small open Irish economy meant that the return of former emigrants and the growth of new immigration facilitated and prolonged the boom by preventing labour shortages from emerging.

There was also a substantial improvement in the growth and development of the Irish indigenous industry in the late 1980s, against a background of prolonged weakness before the boom. Its performance became more uneven later, with some strong points as well as some weak points which grew more evident over time.

More specifically, the trends in indigenous manufacturing looked strong at first in the late 1980s, including exports. Then in the 1990s export trends continued to be good in the high-tech and medium–high-tech sectors, but overall indigenous manufacturing exports looked relatively weak by international comparisons. In the 2000s, export trends also became weaker in the high-tech and medium–high-tech sectors. However, in indigenous services, the trends mostly remained better for longer and exports continued to grow relatively fast by EU standards up to the end of the boom.

Industrial policy was partly responsible for the improvement that occurred, since a series of changes were made in policy for indigenous companies beginning in the mid-1980s and the new policy measures were quite effective in some significant respects. In general, it seems that the industrial policy system had considerable success in promoting the growth of small and medium-sized firms, particularly in the high-tech and medium–high-tech sectors, and in enhancing R&D and innovation. But such success continued only up to a certain point. Few of the companies concerned in the higher-tech sectors became large and the more prominent ones often became takeover targets for foreign MNCs, so that the overall growth momentum tended to weaken over time.

The indigenous contribution to growth over the whole course of the boom was a good deal less than the contribution of foreign-owned companies, when assessed in terms of growth of exports and net foreign earnings. Consequently, indigenous companies' share of exports declined from about 30.0% in 1985 to about 13.4% in 2007, while their share of net foreign earnings declined from about 44.2% in 1985 to about 30.4% in 2007. Thus, the indigenous contribution to net foreign earnings remained much greater than its share of exports, but the indigenous share of net foreign earnings was declining due to faster growth among foreign-owned firms.

The indigenous contribution to the boom was particularly significant at certain times. It was relatively important in the late 1980s and again in the 2000s, whereas the foreign-owned contribution was far more important in the 1990s. This point concerning the late 1980s was seen in Sect. 5.1 where it was shown that Irish indigenous manufacturing exports grew a little faster than exports from foreign-owned manufacturing in 1986–1990, while they also grew significantly faster than manufacturing exports from the EU and the OECD. This was very important at that time since indigenous companies still accounted for almost 40% of manufacturing net foreign earnings. There are no adequate data on services exports by nationality of ownership in the 1980s, but services exports were quite small then.

In 2000–2007, indigenous exports and net foreign earnings grew faster than foreign-owned exports and net foreign earnings, as seen in Table 5.7. Consequently, the indigenous share of total net foreign earnings increased from 27.5% to 30.4%. That was a period when there was a very marked deterioration in trends in foreign-owned manufacturing, particularly in electronics, while the contributions of indigenous companies and foreign-owned services were essential for sustaining a relatively high rate of economic growth.

Thus, the indigenous contribution was influential at the time when the economy was pulling out of the lengthy recession of the 1980s and embarking on a prolonged period of rapid growth, and it was influential again later in maintaining a relatively high rate of growth well into the 2000s.

In fact, the improvement in performance in indigenous industry in the late 1980s was probably the most important change that got the boom started at that time. The value of exports from foreign-owned industries was already growing quite fast before the boom, whereas the trend in indigenous exports was much weaker. Consequently, when indigenous manufacturing export growth then accelerated to more than match the growth of exports from foreign-owned industries, that was a major turnaround which probably changed the trajectory of the economy.

Strong growth in demand in export markets also made a significant contribution to the boom in Ireland, given that the boom was export led. This was shown to be true in the case of strong demand from the UK in the late 1980s (Bradley et al. 1997), while a similar point applied to strong demand from a wider range of countries in 1993–2000.

The rate of growth in Ireland's GNP was at its highest in 1993–2000, at 8.8% per year. Kennedy (2000/2001) pointed out that, in that period, overseas demand for imports was growing rapidly, more rapidly than might have been expected from looking at GDP growth of the countries concerned (see also O'Leary 2015). For example, in the EU GDP grew by 2% per year whereas imports grew at a much higher rate of 8.1% per year, perhaps because of the Single European Market. The volume of Irish exports increased by 16.5% per year in 1993–2000 and this can be broken down into 8.0% per year being attributable to the growth of overseas demand for imports while 7.8% per year was attributable to Ireland's performance in gaining market share (Kennedy 2000/2001; NESC 2003). Thus, fast growth in demand in export markets was clearly important for Ireland at that time, although a good deal remained to be explained by other causes of Ireland's exceptional growth.

Although Ireland's economic growth was particularly fast in absolute terms in 1993–2000, it is worth bearing in mind that its growth was always *relatively* fast compared to the EU or USA throughout the two decades between 1986 and 2007 (see Chapter 1), even in periods when Ireland's growth was considerably slower than in 1993–2000 in a less favourable international environment.

Another potential explanation for the boom that emerged from Chapter 3 was the substantial increase in Ireland's allocation from the EU Structural Funds from 1989 onwards. There has not been much cause to refer explicitly to that issue in this book, but the funds concerned were often at work facilitating measures that were undoubtedly important. Most of the funds were spent on education and training, aids and incentives for investment by private companies, and physical infrastructure. Thus, they helped to encourage and facilitate some of the key trends that have been discussed above, such as increases in FDI and improvements in policy measures for indigenous companies.

Chapter 3 outlined the findings of a range of studies of the structural funds, and it is reasonable to accept their general conclusion that the funds helped to increase Ireland's growth rate, while also noting that this positive effect was probably relatively minor compared to the scale of growth involved in the Celtic Tiger boom.

Finally, another potential explanation for the boom that emerged from Chapter 3 was social partnership, including wage moderation. Again, there has not been much cause to refer explicitly to that issue in this book, although one relevant point was the finding, in Sect. 6.4, that average weekly earnings in the "traditional" (mostly indigenous) manufacturing sector increased more slowly than the value of its net output per head in 1986–1992. Consequently, the profitability of traditional manufacturing was protected and enhanced. This was consistent with the wage moderation aspect of social partnership, which sought to underpin economic growth by delivering competitive national wage agreements.

This point supports other evidence, already cited in Chapter 3, which showed that there was wage moderation during the boom. However, it does not shed any light on the question, discussed in Chapter 3, whether wage moderation was caused by social partnership or by market conditions such as high unemployment and the influence of the UK labour market. Although we cannot resolve that issue, we can at least observe that social partnership was the main way of doing wage bargaining during the boom, that wage moderation did occur, and that economic growth was very successful at that time. These facts were at least consistent with the idea that social partnership facilitated wage moderation and helped to provide suitable conditions for strong economic growth. Even if labour market conditions were initially responsible for wage moderation, one might have expected rapid employment growth during the 1990s to have caused wages to rise faster than they did if social partnership was not having a significant moderating influence. There were also other aspects of social partnership, apart from wage formation, which are widely agreed to have been helpful, such as the scarcity of major industrial disputes, as well as the achievement of widespread agreement on a range of public policy issues.

8.2 Other Conclusions

It was sometimes claimed that the Celtic Tiger boom was bogus or phoney. One version of this is that it was an accounting mirage, created by the practices of MNCs seeking to maximise tax advantages. Another version is that it was merely an unsustainable effect of a debt-financed property boom. It has been shown here that this type of view is far from the truth. Granted, the practices of MNCs and the property boom both tended to exaggerate or magnify the reality of the boom in the economy, but the economic boom was nevertheless real and substantial.

Compared to the state of the economy in 1986 before the boom began, the period from that time until about 2005 amounted to a significant economic success. This is certainly not to say that all problems were resolved, or that there was progress in every respect, but the contrast between the mid-1980s and 2005 is clear and undeniable.

In the mid-1980s, just before the Celtic Tiger period began, the long-standing failure to generate sufficient employment was very much in evidence as there was an unprecedented level of unemployment together with a substantial rate of emigration. The proportion of the population that was in employment was very low at just 31%. Average incomes (GNP per head of population) were low at little more than 60% of the UK or EU levels, and there had been little sign of convergence towards EU levels for decades. In addition, the national debt as a percentage of GNP was very high and rising.

Starting from this bleak situation, the Irish economy began two decades of exceptional growth. By the mid-2000s, the employment situation was transformed, attracting a continuous flow of net immigration, while average income levels were above the average UK and EU levels, and problems with the national debt were a distant memory.

However, despite this undoubted success, some significant problems remained. Most obviously, it quickly became clear that the housing boom was unsustainable and it turned out to have disastrous financial consequences, as discussed in Chapter 7. For some years after the boom, the severe problems resulting from this issue dominated the economic and political agenda in Ireland.

Apart from the housing boom, there were also more long-term issues concerning the type of economic growth that had been occurring since the late 1980s. In Chapter 1 (and again in Chapter 2) we discussed barriers or difficulties confronting relatively late developers such as Ireland. We also noted that important questions to be considered in this book are whether, and how Irish indigenous companies made progress when faced with such barriers, and whether the alternative strategy of attracting foreign direct investment proved to be an adequate substitute.

As regards indigenous companies, the conclusions are that they did make some progress and that industrial policy measures were important in explaining how this happened. However, despite the progress that was made, the overall results remained unsatisfactory, mainly because of the scarcity of larger companies emerging in the high-tech and medium–high-tech sectors and because of the common tendency for the more promising companies to be taken over by overseas companies.

As regards the role of FDI in Ireland, foreign-owned companies contributed very substantially to growth, especially through the growth of their net foreign earnings. They also increased their skill levels as more advanced activities were introduced. This made them more integrated into the Irish economy and more capable of sustaining higher pay levels. However, with their low purchasing linkages and relatively low R&D intensity compared to the same industries in advanced economies, they did not become as deeply rooted in Ireland as they would be in their home countries, and most of them probably did not develop the sort of capability base that could continuously generate higher standards of living over the long term.

Of course, it would be reasonable to ask whether such shortcomings really mattered. It was seen during the boom that outstanding results for the economy were achieved by a policy of relying heavily on such FDI and accepting a more limited role for indigenous companies. Would it not be logical to continue indefinitely with such a policy?

There are two main reasons why these issues matter. First, the type of FDI that grew in Ireland might sometimes prove to be unstable, which could mean declining or closing down rather abruptly for reasons that could be mostly external to Ireland. An example of this was seen in the case of the electronics manufacturing sector at the end of the 1990s, but it was fortunate that a rise in services FDI was on hand to soften the potential adverse impact at that time. Later, in 2005–2007, the growth of net foreign earnings in foreign-owned companies ceased, while continuing growth of net foreign earnings in indigenous companies showed that general conditions were not unfavourable for growth. However, these trends were overshadowed by the housing boom that was occurring at the same time.

It is also worth remembering that, although Ireland's policies for FDI were much the same before the boom as they were during the boom, they were much less successful in the earlier period before external events caused a surge in FDI in Ireland. This shows again that the results of a policy of heavy reliance on FDI can vary greatly for reasons that can be external to the Irish economy.

The second main reason for concern about heavy reliance on FDI is that the corporation tax concession regime in Ireland, which has been the most important attraction for FDI, has periodically caused resentment in other countries with whom Ireland needs to maintain good relations. This policy has commonly been seen by others as damaging to their interests, and Ireland has repeatedly come under pressure to change it. Although Ireland has mostly succeeded in resisting the pressure to make fundamental changes, this must come at the cost of some loss of goodwill and a weakening of the country's negotiating position on other important matters.

The implication of these issues for present-day policy is that heavy reliance on FDI may be a strategy that could work out well for Ireland in some periods, but it is a strategy with risks so it is also possible that it might have quite poor results at other times.

In order to achieve more lasting and sustainable success in economic development, Ireland needs to put greater emphasis on the development of indigenous companies. For that purpose, it would be necessary for industrial development agencies to invest more substantially in developing the scale and capabilities of selected promising companies, going beyond the scale of investment in companies that was normal for the agencies during the boom. Crucially, too, there needs to be a way of deterring or preventing foreign takeovers of the more promising indigenous companies. Such a policy of focusing greater resources on selectively building stronger companies would not be a completely new departure for Ireland, since it would amount to a significant enhancement of the policy that was implemented during the boom. Since the policy applied during the boom had proven although ultimately limited success, and was clearly a substantial improvement over the 1980s, it should be possible to learn from and build further on that experience to develop a more effective approach.

References

Bradley, John, John Fitz Gerald, Patrick Honohan, and Ide Kearney. 1997. Interpreting the Recent Irish Growth Experience. In *Medium-Term Review: 1997–2003*, ed. David Duffy, John Fitz Gerald, Ide Kearney and Fergal Shortall. Dublin: Economic and Social Research Institute.

Kennedy, Kieran. 2000/2001. Reflections on the Process of Irish Economic Growth. Symposium on Economic Growth in Ireland. *Journal of the Statistical and Social Inquiry Society of Ireland* 30: 123–139.

National Economic and Social Council. 2003. An Investment in Quality: Services, Inclusion and Enterprise. Report No. 111, NESC, Dublin.

O'Leary, Eoin. 2015. *Irish Economic Development: High-Performing EU State or Serial Under-Achiever?* Abingdon and New York: Routledge.

Open Access This chapter is licensed under the terms of the Creative Commons Attribution 4.0 International License (http://creativecommons.org/licenses/by/4.0/), which permits use, sharing, adaptation, distribution and reproduction in any medium or format, as long as you give appropriate credit to the original author(s) and the source, provide a link to the Creative Commons license and indicate if changes were made.

The images or other third party material in this chapter are included in the chapter's Creative Commons license, unless indicated otherwise in a credit line to the material. If material is not included in the chapter's Creative Commons license and your intended use is not permitted by statutory regulation or exceeds the permitted use, you will need to obtain permission directly from the copyright holder.

Index

A
accounting activities, 159
Aer Lingus, 158
Aer Rianta, 158
agriculture, 19, 20, 40, 53, 84, 94, 96, 115, 123, 139, 142, 156
aircraft leasing, 5, 98, 211
Anglo Irish Bank, 239
Apple, 212
architectural activities, 159

B
B&I line, 158
balance of payments, 9, 11, 13, 23, 25, 38, 40, 92, 98, 112, 115, 116, 213, 214, 223, 225, 230
Bank of Scotland (Ireland), 239
banks, 10, 11, 234–240, 242, 243
barriers to entry, 11, 28
Barry, Frank, 18, 19, 30, 53, 55–58, 60–63, 65, 67, 94, 198, 201, 202, 205, 208, 210–212, 215, 216, 238, 242
behavioural convergence, 241
behavioural economics, 240
Best, Michael H., 202, 203
bias, 240–243
Blanchard, Olivier, 53, 59, 62
borrowing, 38–40, 42
Bradley, John, 50, 54–57, 60, 205, 208, 210, 252
Breathnach, Proinnsias, 55, 61
budget deficit, 9, 39, 44, 50
business expenditure on research & development (BERD), 143, 144, 146, 161, 197

C
Casey, Ciaran Michael, 238–240
Celtic Tiger, 1, 2, 10
Central Bank, 232, 237–239
chemicals, 96, 97, 99, 103, 105–107, 110, 113, 114, 119, 120, 126, 132, 133, 137, 139, 146, 166, 168, 190, 192, 202, 221
Clancy, Paula, 221, 222
clusters, 12, 202, 213, 220–222
competitiveness, 232, 233
computers, 190, 193, 196, 201, 203, 207, 208, 211, 220, 221, 249

© The Editor(s) (if applicable) and The Author(s) 2024

E. O'Malley, *Ireland's Long Economic Boom*, Palgrave Studies in Economic History, https://doi.org/10.1007/978-3-031-53070-8

construction, 1, 10, 11, 83, 85, 89, 91, 99, 100, 102, 103, 107, 112–115, 123, 154, 234, 236, 239, 240, 243
convergence, 52, 53, 67–71, 75
corporation tax, 204–206
Crone, Mike, 163, 164, 166, 168
Culliton report, 195, 220

D
dairy, 96, 166, 168, 180, 181, 220–222
deadweight, 175, 176
deregulation, 65, 74, 75
devaluation, 64, 74, 75
displacement, 175
Doyle, Eleanor, 50, 54, 64
Duffy, David, 50, 55, 60

E
economies of scale, 27, 28
education, 53–55, 61, 64, 66, 75, 195, 203, 208, 210, 215, 232, 247, 249, 250, 253
EEC, 25, 32, 39, 40, 194, 195, 206
electronics, 31, 32, 96, 99, 100, 103–106, 110, 113, 145, 148, 171, 192–198, 211, 251, 255
emigration, 1, 7, 8, 12, 17, 18, 20, 23, 37, 38, 40–44, 54, 66, 93, 254
employment, 1, 5–8, 10, 17–23, 25–28, 31–34, 37–44, 51, 54, 58, 60, 63, 66, 69, 70, 72, 83, 89–91, 93, 95, 102, 113, 124, 125, 127–134, 137, 138, 148, 150–152, 154–156, 162–164, 166, 167, 172–176, 179, 183, 189, 190, 192, 199, 202, 204, 205, 207, 208, 212, 213, 215, 217, 218, 223, 229, 234–236, 240, 242, 248, 250, 253, 254
engineering, 87, 99, 103, 105–107, 110, 113, 114, 125, 139, 159, 163, 167
Enterprise Ireland, 161, 175, 183
entry barriers, 12
EU, 1–3, 6, 7, 9, 51, 54–58, 60, 62–64, 66, 68–71, 75, 124, 125, 129–138, 143, 144, 171, 177, 195, 205–209, 233, 235, 237, 247, 249–252, 254
Europe, 18, 25, 33, 39
European Community (EC), 28, 32, 33, 38, 195, 204, 239
European Monetary Union (EMU), 64, 234
eurozone, 234, 235, 237, 238, 242
external economies, 12, 29

F
financial crisis, 237, 242, 243
financial services, 84, 85, 87–89, 91, 97, 98, 102, 113, 116, 121, 155, 156, 159, 161, 162, 166, 168, 183, 184, 193, 207, 209, 212, 221, 249
fiscal policy, 39, 42, 43, 52, 53, 69, 71
FitzGerald, John, 5, 43, 50, 51, 54–57, 59, 61, 71, 234, 238
food, 22, 27, 96, 97, 105–107, 110, 113, 114, 119, 120, 127, 130, 133, 136, 137, 139, 146, 180, 181, 191
food services, 159, 160
foreign direct investment (FDI), 12, 14, 24, 31–34, 36, 39, 40, 45, 51, 52, 55, 56, 60–65, 67, 88, 121, 170, 189, 193–195, 201, 203, 205–216, 223–225, 247–250, 253, 255, 256

foreign-owned companies, 4, 13, 26, 30, 37, 86, 87, 114, 116, 117, 119, 120, 139–142, 149, 157, 158, 164, 166, 168, 170, 171, 177–179, 182–184, 189, 190, 192, 200, 201, 204, 212–215, 222–225, 247, 248, 251, 255, 256
foreign-owned firms, 230
foreign-owned manufacturing, 190, 192, 193, 197, 200, 205, 213, 216–218, 223, 224
free trade, 21–23, 25–28, 38, 45

G
Gallagher, Liam, 50, 54, 64
GDP, 2–6, 37, 38, 41, 51–54, 60, 68–73, 83, 84, 87–89, 118, 235, 252
GNP, 2–6, 9, 11, 37–41, 44, 50, 52, 57, 58, 70–73, 75, 83, 87–89, 111, 112, 118, 229, 230, 234, 252, 254
grants, 24, 25, 31, 32, 35–37, 60, 67, 134, 150, 151, 169, 173, 174, 194, 203–205, 212, 224, 248
Great Britain, 17, 21
Great Famine, 17
Guinness Peat Aviation (GPA), 211

H
hardware, 168, 196, 201, 208, 211, 212, 221, 249
Hewitt-Dundas, Nola, 56, 61, 64, 148–151, 199, 219, 220
high-tech, 145, 163, 169, 170, 176–178, 190, 192, 202, 208–210, 213, 220, 222–224, 248–251, 255
high-technology, 125, 127–131, 133, 134, 137, 138, 145, 148, 163, 164, 190, 194
Honohan, Patrick, 41, 42, 50–55, 57, 59, 63–65, 69, 70, 207, 234, 235, 237, 239
hotel & restaurant, 160, 161
house prices, 234–236, 239, 242
housing, 14, 229–232, 234–243, 254–256
HP, 212

I
IBM, 212
immigration, 1, 7, 8, 93, 250, 254
import-substitution, 23
industrial development, 21
Industrial Development Authority (IDA), 32, 37, 195, 201, 209, 210
industrialisation, 21, 23
industrial policy, 24, 25, 34, 36, 45, 64, 150, 151, 168, 173–178, 194, 195, 208, 216, 220, 249–251, 255
Industrial Policy Review Group, 195, 220
Industry Evaluation Unit, 175
inequality, 9, 10
inflation, 9
information technology, 168
innovation, 13, 143, 148–151, 198, 199, 222, 232, 251
input-output, 99, 116, 117, 119, 140, 142, 159, 160, 182–184
instruments, 190, 194, 198, 203, 209, 249
interest rates, 234, 235, 238
International Monetary Fund (IMF), 237, 239, 240
Irish indigenous, 190, 192, 193, 197, 198, 200, 201, 220, 221

Irish indigenous companies, 12, 13, 26, 114, 139, 145, 151, 153, 158, 162, 165, 170, 172, 174, 182, 183, 230, 231
Irish indigenous industry, 63, 64, 75, 247, 250
Irish MNCs, 153, 154
Irish-owned companies, 158, 164, 183, 215

J
Jacobson, David, 127, 196, 201, 219
Jordan, Declan, 222

K
Kearney, Ide, 235, 237
Kearns, Allan, 150, 198
Kelly, Morgan, 236, 239, 240
Kennedy, Kieran A., 18, 35, 54, 55, 59, 63, 64, 173, 174, 252
Kirby, Peadar, 61
Krugman, Paul R., 60, 62, 93

L
labour costs, 43, 44, 58–60, 72
labour supply, 54, 63
latecomer(s), 11, 29
late developers, 255
late-developing, 22, 23, 28
late-developing country, 11
late-industrialising, 29, 154
Lawless, Martina, 159, 160
Leddin, Anthony, 50–52, 58, 59, 63–65
legal activities, 159
linkages, 13, 32, 37, 194–196, 203, 213, 216–219, 223–225, 255
Lotus, 165
Love, James H., 150
Lunn, Peter D., 239–241

M
machinery, 87, 97, 99, 100, 103, 104, 125, 126, 129, 132, 133, 137, 140, 145, 190, 193, 199
Mac Sharry, Ray, 27, 50, 54–56, 58, 61, 63, 209
management, 29, 34, 36, 154, 168, 169, 195, 199, 202, 219, 223, 225
management consultancy, 159
manufacturing, 22, 23, 25, 28, 31–33, 39, 44, 83–91, 96, 99, 106, 107, 110, 113–116, 120, 123–135, 137–142, 144, 145, 148–156, 161–164, 169–172, 176–184, 189, 190, 192, 194, 196–198, 200–204, 206, 210–214, 216, 217, 219, 220, 222, 223, 230, 231, 248, 250–253, 255
marketing, 29, 32, 34–37, 151, 165, 168, 169, 195, 198, 199, 201, 203, 232
Matthews, Alan, 57
meat, 96
medium-high-tech, 248, 250, 251, 255
medium-high-technology, 126–131, 133, 134, 137, 138, 190, 194
Microsoft, 165, 212
modern sectors, 131
multinational companies (MNCs), 4, 13, 26, 29–32, 35, 56, 60, 61, 64, 83, 86, 87, 89, 110, 114, 115, 118, 123, 129, 145, 149, 162, 165–168, 170, 177, 195–203, 210, 213, 216, 219–223, 231, 251, 254
music industry, 220

N
National Competitiveness Council, 233

national debt, 9, 38, 40, 43, 44, 254
National Economic and Social Council (NESC), 27, 34, 38–40, 44, 50, 53–56, 58, 59, 62–64, 220, 221
National Software Directorate, 163, 164
net exports, 102–104
net foreign earnings, 13, 14, 84, 98, 102–114, 116–118, 121, 123, 138–142, 155–157, 170, 171, 178, 182, 192, 193, 195, 213, 214, 223, 224, 230, 231, 234, 242, 243, 248, 251, 255, 256
Nolan, Brian, 9, 10

O

O'Connell, Philip J., 57–59, 64
O'Donnell, Rory, 35, 56–59, 63, 64, 173, 174
OECD, 50, 52–58, 60, 63, 68, 126, 132, 135, 143–147, 151, 167, 171, 181, 197, 251
O'Gorman, Colm, 163, 166–168, 215, 221
Ó Gráda, Cormac, 18, 20, 51–53, 55–58, 67–69
O'Hearn, Denis, 60, 61, 64
O'Leary, Eoin, 50, 54, 62, 64, 222
Oracle, 165
Organisation for Economic Cooperation and Development (OECD), 236, 240
Ó Riain, Seán, 57, 58, 63, 64, 165, 169, 240
O'Rourke, Kevin, 18, 20, 52, 55, 56, 58, 67–69
O'Sullivan, Mary, 61, 64, 196, 225
outward-looking, 24, 25

P

pharmaceuticals, 5, 31, 32, 87, 96, 125–127, 129, 146, 163, 168, 190, 194, 195, 198, 201–203, 209, 220, 221, 249
Porter, Michael E., 220–222
privatisation, 65
productivity, 6, 7, 22, 30, 44, 215, 219, 220
profit outflow(s), 13, 83, 84, 86–91, 99, 102–105, 107–109, 113–121, 138, 140, 142, 182, 231
property, 1, 9–11, 112, 114, 234–240, 242, 254
protection, 22–25, 27, 28

R

research & development (R&D), 13, 25, 35, 37, 143–145, 148–151, 162, 166, 169, 170, 175, 177, 178, 195, 197–199, 201–203, 207, 212, 224, 225, 251, 255
Riordan, Brendan, 115, 116
Roper, Stephen, 56, 61, 64, 148–151, 175, 219
Ruane, Frances, 150, 198, 219, 220
Ryanair, 159

S

scientific research, 159
services, 25, 29, 31, 33, 35, 37, 39, 40, 83–89, 91–95, 97–100, 102, 105–107, 110, 113–116, 120, 121, 123, 139–142, 154–162, 164–166, 169, 171, 173, 176, 177, 183, 192, 193, 199–201, 206, 207, 210–214, 217–219, 222, 224, 230–233, 248, 250, 251, 255

Single European Market, 54, 56, 57, 61, 63, 75, 207–209, 212, 224, 247–249, 252
size class, 152, 153
social partnership, 58, 59, 64, 75, 247, 253
software, 32, 99, 100, 113, 159, 161–170, 177, 190, 192, 195, 201, 207, 208, 212, 215, 219–222, 249
start-ups, 29, 34, 35
structural funds, 57, 58, 64, 75, 247, 252, 253
Studnicka, Zuzanna, 159, 160
Sun Microsystems, 212
Sweeney, Paul, 51, 54, 56, 58, 63, 64

T
tax, 24, 25, 29, 31–33, 40, 42, 51, 58, 60, 62, 71–73, 75, 194, 203–207, 209, 211, 212, 217, 224, 237, 238, 248, 249, 254, 256
technology, 29, 34, 36, 126, 127, 129, 132, 134, 137, 138, 143, 145, 150, 151, 165, 175, 202, 213, 220–223, 225, 232
Telesis, 200, 209
tourism, 97, 98
traditional sectors, 131
transport, 97, 98, 102, 126, 129, 132, 154, 158–161, 190

U
unemployment, 1, 7, 8, 10, 12, 51, 54, 59, 66, 72, 253, 254
United Kingdom (UK), 3, 10, 18, 19, 21, 22, 25, 28, 31, 32, 38, 42–44, 53, 54, 59, 62, 69, 70, 194, 204, 252–254
USA, 2, 3, 6, 7, 32, 33, 39, 60, 68, 69, 93, 124–126, 135, 158, 165, 167, 181, 194, 195, 205, 208, 249, 252

V
Van Egeraat, Chris, 196, 198, 201, 202, 211, 212, 221

W
Walsh, Brendan, 41, 42, 50–53, 55, 57, 59, 63–65, 69, 70
Whelan, Karl, 50, 234–238
White, Padraic, 27, 50, 54–56, 58, 61, 63, 209
World Economic Forum, 233

FSC
www.fsc.org
MIX
Papier | Fördert
gute Waldnutzung
FSC® C083411

Kolibri 360 GmbH
Ferdinand-Jühlke-Straße 7
99095 Erfurt, Deutschland
produktsicherheit@kolibri360.de